The
EVERYTHING
Kabbalah Book

Dear Reader,

It was the summer of 1967. I was fifteen years old, listening to the radio in the kitchen. A news item about the Beatles going to India to study meditation came on. My mother, who, unlike me, was not a huge Beatles fan, said in her thick Eastern European accent, "What do they have to meditate about? Kabbalah, that's something to meditate about!"

Though I had been very interested in Judaism, I had never heard of Kabbalah before that. And though I felt my mother was far too parochial in her perspective, my curiosity was really piqued.

That began a journey that continues to this day. Kabbalah spoke to me immediately. It continues to inspire me daily, and I hope that a glimpse of its depth and insights will come through in these pages.

My goal in writing this book is to offer you a doorway into this spiritual universe, some tools, and direction for delving into it further if it calls to you. I hope this will be an exciting adventure for you and one that may offer you continuing paths for growth.

Mark Elber

The EVERYTHING® Series

Editorial

Publishing Director	Gary M. Krebs
Associate Managing Editor	Laura M. Daly
Associate Copy Chief	Brett Palana-Shanahan
Acquisitions Editor	Gina Chaimanis
Development Editor	Rachel Engelson
Associate Production Editor	Casey Ebert

Production

Director of Manufacturing	Susan Beale
Associate Director of Production	Michelle Roy Kelly
Cover Design	Paul Beatrice
	Matt LeBlanc
	Erick DaCosta
Design and Layout	Colleen Cunningham
	Holly Curtis
	Sorae Lee
Series Cover Artist	Barry Littmann

Visit the entire Everything® Series at *www.everything.com*

THE
EVERYTHING
KABBALAH
BOOK

Explore this mystical tradition—from
ancient rituals to modern day practices

Mark Elber

Technical Review by Rabbi Max Weiman

Adams Media
Avon, Massachusetts

This book is dedicated to my best friend and partner in life, Shoshana.

An Everything® Series Book.
Everything® and everything.com® are registered trademarks of F+W Publications, Inc.

Published by Adams Media, an F+W Publications Company
57 Littlefield Street, Avon, MA 02322 U.S.A.
www.adamsmedia.com

ISBN: 1-59337-546-8
Printed in the United States of America.

J   I   H   G   F   E   D   C   B   A

Library of Congress Cataloging-in-Publication Data
Elber, Mark.
The everything Kabbalah book : explore this mystical tradition :
from ancient rituals to modern day practices / Mark Elber.
          p.   cm. -- (An everything series book)
Includes index.
ISBN 1-59337-546-8
1. Kabbalah--History. I. Title. II. Series: Everything series.

BM526.E43 2006
296.1'6--dc22

2005034692

This publication is designed to provide accurate and authoritative information with regard to the subject matter covered. It is sold with the understanding that the publisher is not engaged in rendering legal, accounting, or other professional advice. If legal advice or other expert assistance is required, the services of a competent professional person should be sought.
—From a *Declaration of Principles* jointly adopted by a Committee of the American Bar Association and a Committee of Publishers and Associations

Many of the designations used by manufacturers and sellers to distinguish their products are claimed as trademarks. Where those designations appear in this book and Adams Media was aware of a trademark claim, the designations have been printed with initial capital letters.

This book is available at quantity discounts for bulk purchases.
For information, please call 1-800-872-5627.

Contents

Acknowledgments

This book would not have been written without the incalculable support and understanding of my wife, Shoshana Brown, and the patience of my stepdaughter, Mira, and my son, Lev.

I would also like to thank the following people for their support and encouragement: Rabbi Mark Greenspan, Daniel Matt, Rabbi Alvin Wainhaus, my agent, Grace Freedson, and my editors, Gina Chaimanis and Rachel Engelson.

Top Ten Kabbalistic Insights

1. There is no place where God is not. God fills and transcends all universes.

2. Everything in this world has its parallel in the realm of the Sefirot and therefore everything we do can have cosmic significance.

3. The highest state and ultimate goal of existence is union with the Divine (*devekut*) and perfecting the world in which we live (*tikkun*).

4. Every person has her own letter in the Torah; meaning, you have a unique insight that only you can teach.

5. The inner meaning of *mitzvah* ("commandment"; "good deed") is an act that unifies us with God.

6. All souls stood at Mount Sinai and heard the first letter of the first of the Ten Commandments—the silent *aleph* of the word *anokhi* (I am).

7. Where your consciousness is, there you are. Your consciousness (*kavana*) makes all the difference.

8. All knowledge has its own melody (*niggun*). The niggun that contains the knowledge behind the greatest paradox is silence.

9. God is only found in joy (*simkha*).

10. Reb Zusya said that he wasn't worried that at the end of his life God would ask him, "Why weren't you Moses?" but, rather that God would ask him, "Why weren't you Zusya?"

Introduction

▶ There is no one correct way to study Kabbalah. Kabbalah itself, in fact, has many different voices (some more prominent and influential than others). Though these voices don't always agree, they speak a common language and share a passion and devotion to the realm of life visible to the inner eye.

Kabbalah has a long history that began in the mystical elements that are already found in the Bible and which began to flower in the early rabbinic period around the time of the destruction of the Second Temple in Jerusalem in 70 C.E. and the following centuries. What can properly be called Kabbalah emerged in the twelfth century and drew from all the previous forms of Jewish mysticism, centering on a specific language of divine emanations and powers called Sefirot, and a transcendent, infinite, ultimately Unknowable Divinity called Ein Sof.

Kabbalah represents a lifestyle, practice, and mystical philosophy that aim to connect with God to transmute daily existence into a holy and spiritual one. Kabbalah is not meant to be an abstract body of thought. It is intended by its practitioners to inform and transform the way you perceive and experience the world around you and the divinity that surrounds and fills you.

Kabbalah, like any religious phenomenon, exists in a particular environment and grows out of the spiritual experiences of the people in that environment. It therefore has a specific cultural language, in this case primarily Hebrew and Aramaic. At the same time, it has universal elements that are shared with other forms of mysticism.

Over the last forty years, people of varied backgrounds and orientations have become increasingly interested in the study of Kabbalah as they search for spiritual fulfillment. There was a period of time in Jewish history, particularly during the nineteenth and early twentieth centuries, during which people relied on a belief in rationalism and were distrustful of the perspectives of Kabbalah. Even science became a sort of religion. Now we are beginning to see an approach in which science and mysticism are understood as supplementing and complementing each other, rather than being in conflict. Some scientists are even reaching conclusions that Kabbalists expressed almost 1,000 years ago.

Kabbalah is no longer a secret study reserved for an initiated few. There are an increasing number of Kabbalistic texts and books about Kabbalah available to anyone interested. As a student of Kabbalah, you have the choice and freedom to approach it in many different ways. You can sample it as an interesting spiritual phenomenon, reading about it as a historian might, you can apply it to your own life and experience, or you can even attempt to live according to it. Perhaps you will become part of the next phase in the future of Kabbalah.

This book will give you an overview of Kabbalah, including its history, concepts, techniques, and symbolic language. It also makes available translations of Kabbalistic texts in order to provide a more immediate taste of original Kabbalistic material rather than merely being a book about Kabbalah. Kabbalah may become a lifelong pursuit and practice or an interesting detour in any person's life journey. This book is intended to help the interested reader follow either of those directions or any in between.

Foreword

For those curious about the mystical side of life, Kabbalah can give answers to many of life's most difficult questions, and bring meaning to life's most challenging dilemmas. All of us have the ability to deal with our challenges. Inside we all have a storehouse of wisdom. But how do we access that storehouse? That's the trick. Kabbalah articulates paths to our eternal wisdom. It opens up channels of communication between our mind and our soul.

Kabbalah is "wider than the sea," and it's often difficult to wade into that water without quickly getting in over your head. The sages have had an unbroken tradition from teacher to student that helps guide the way. This tradition is now becoming more accessible to the masses.

The time is ripe for new avenues of spirituality. Many people are disenchanted with the religion of their youth, or merely sense that something is missing. Others don't subscribe to any particular religion and want some spiritual principles to live by. These two events, the search for meaning and the increased accessibility of Kabbalah, are coinciding in history.

The Everything® Kabbalah Book is a welcome addition to the modern library of this ancient study. It is a part of the "opening of the storehouses" of this once secret wisdom. The author has provided a detailed yet easy to read account of some of the major trends in Kabbalah. The author has done the work for you by sifting through the mountain of information to put some gems on a platter. Without becoming too esoteric for the layman to grasp, he has given a glimpse into the upper realms of thought.

May this book add meaning to your life and lead you down the path of wisdom.

Rabbi Max Weiman
Author of *A Map of the Universe*
Editor of ✒*www.kabbalahmadeeasy.com*

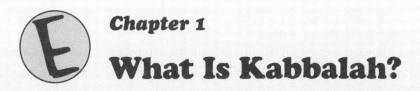

Chapter 1

What Is Kabbalah?

In order to facilitate the study of Kabbalah, it is essential to understand a few basics about the field. In this first chapter, you will discover the answers to questions such as: What is Kabbalah? Where does it come from? What are different approaches to it? And, even, Why study it? This fundamental information provides a framework for you to build on when constructing a comprehensive understanding of Kabbalah in subsequent chapters.

Why Study Kabbalah?

Kabbalah is a treasure house of spiritual insights and a source of enormous inspiration. It has the ability to help one open up to the wonders of life and God. Through its study, one's spiritual senses can be sharpened. It can serve as a catalyst to seeing the world from a new perspective or provide a vocabulary and framework to express timeless truths that the student may have already experienced or sensed.

Kabbalah has much to offer a person, whether your own orientation is traditionally or nontraditionally religious or even secular. If the student is approaching it from a Jewish perspective, it has the ability to teach a whole new level of Judaism that too few people are familiar with. It provides an incomparable spiritual depth to one's Jewish life regardless of which branch of Judaism you might identify with. As many of Kabbalah's insights are universal, it can serve as an inspiration regardless of a person's religious affiliation or lack thereof.

What Does Kabbalah Mean?

The term "Kabbalah" comes from the Hebrew root *l'kabel*, which means "to receive," so Kabbalah means "received teachings." Kabbalah also denotes "tradition," meaning a body of knowledge and customs passed down from one generation to another.

FACT

Hebrew words are generally constructed upon a "root" of three consonants. Understanding the root of a word gives you a deeper insight into its true meaning. Sometimes Kabbalists might reinterpret the meaning of a word by suggesting that it derives from a different root than the conventionally accepted one.

Kabbalah also has the connotation of the *oral* transmission of tradition and knowledge containing the inner and secret mystical teachings of the

Torah. A good example of this understanding is already found in the Mishnah (part of the oral Torah, the Talmud, written down circa 200 C.E.), which opens with the statement, "Moses received Torah from Sinai and transmitted it to Joshua."

The word *Kabbalah* itself, though used in the Talmud over 1,500 years ago, did not originally have a mystical connotation. It acquired this specific meaning in the early 1200s in the Kabbalistic circles surrounding Isaac the Blind (c. 1160–1235) in southern France.

Origins of Kabbalah

While it is difficult to know the historical origins of Kabbalah with absolute certainty, discovered texts indicate that it surfaced in the late 1100s in southern France in the area of Provence, and soon spread to northern Spain. The first unequivocal Kabbalistic text, Sefer HaBahir, is written as though it has a readership that is familiar with its Kabbalistic terminology, even though such terms had never appeared in writing before. How was this possible?

Oral Communication

The earliest Kabbalists speak of the oral transmission of secret knowledge from master to disciple throughout the generations. In earlier forms of Jewish mysticism, such as those referred to in the Talmud, certain types of esoteric knowledge are only taught to one or two people at a time. In order to restrict the spread of the secret knowledge detailed in Kabbalah, masters likely taught disciples their mystical teachings primarily through oral communication.

Keeping the Esoteric Secret

The reasons for not printing mystical texts are twofold. Firstly, Kabbalists avoided printing these texts to protect them from the public's likely misunderstanding of Jewish mysticism. Secondly, it was (and remains) a challenge to express divine experiences through language. One of the early major figures in the history of Kabbalah, Nachmanides (1194–1270), said that although Kabbalistic texts exist, one could only truly understand them when apprenticed to a teacher who would teach "mouth to mouth," meaning orally and in person.

In addition to the hesitation to print mystical texts, there were other factors that contributed to shrouding the origins of Kabbalah in mystery, including Kabbalists' self-censorship about speaking autobiographically regarding mystical experiences. Also, because oral transmission was a significant factor in the communication of mystical knowledge and methods, and travel in ancient and medieval times was very difficult, it is not easy to trace the spread of mystical teachings from the Land of Israel to Europe.

FACT

Kabbalah was not the only term used to refer to this mystical body of knowledge. Among the numerous other expressions were: Chokhmah Penimit (inner wisdom), Torat HaSod (secret teachings), Sitrei Torah or Razei Torah (secrets of the Torah), Chokhmah Nistarah (hidden wisdom), and Derekh HaEmet (the way of truth).

The Languages of Kabbalah

Despite the fact that Hebrew had ceased to be the spoken language of the Jews even before the destruction of the Second Temple in Jerusalem by the Romans in 70 C.E., the vast majority of Kabbalistic texts are written in Hebrew. A particularly striking exception for the history of Jewish mysticism is that the most influential Kabbalistic text of all, the Zohar, is mostly written in Aramaic. Since the Zohar is so heavily quoted in later sources, it is very common to find Hebrew Kabbalistic texts from the end of the 1200s and after sprinkled with Aramaic phrases.

Over the centuries some Kabbalistic texts were translated into other languages such as Latin beginning in the late fifteenth century. In our own day some Kabbalistic texts are finding their way into English translations of varying quality. Even though the authors of Kabbalistic texts did not use Hebrew as a spoken language, it was generally the language of much, if not most, of their study.

Aramaic is a sister language of Hebrew, as is Arabic. Aramaic became the spoken language of the Jewish masses centuries before the destruction of the Second Temple in 70 C.E. Hebrew thus went from being the vernacular to becoming the holy language used in Scripture and prayer.

The Hebrew of the Middle Ages was different in certain ways from the Hebrew of the Mishnah, which, in turn, was different from the Hebrew of the Bible. There were words that entered the language from other sources, such as philosophical terms and words borrowed from other languages, that may not have existed before the Middle Ages. In addition, even terms that existed in the Bible and the Mishnah may have acquired somewhat different meanings during the Middle Ages. These nuances of the Hebrew language have helped modern scholars date the composition of certain Kabbalistic writings.

ALERT!

The Gemara, the major component of the Talmud, was written in Aramaic and not in Hebrew because unlike the Bible, which was written when Hebrew was the spoken language in the land of Israel, the Gemara was written when Aramaic was the language of the masses. The Gemara is written in the vernacular because it records the discussions of rabbis.

Approaches to Kabbalah

There are a number of different ways of studying and understanding Kabbalah. Adherents to the traditional orthodox approach believe that Kabbalah is divinely inspired and written under the influence of Ruakh HaKodesh, literally "the Holy Spirit." People who maintain this orientation believe that Kabbalah, even though it is an oral tradition, has the authority of Scripture and that its insights are part of the oral Torah that Moses received at Mount Sinai. Orthodox Kabbalists tend to read texts literally, even elements that seem fantastical, because they do not believe that God is limited by the laws of nature.

Another major orientation that has proliferated particularly in the last eighty years or so is the academic approach. Though an academic study of Kabbalah has existed for many years, because of increased interest in the subject of Kabbalah, it has grown enormously both in the breadth and depth of its research and in the number of scholarly studies of Kabbalah available. The academic study of Kabbalah now exists in a number of universities in the United States and Europe and in every university in Israel. This orientation is primarily historical, philological (uncovering some of the history of the texts based on the language of the texts themselves), and phenomenological (studying the phenomenon of Kabbalism). Academic researchers studying Kabbalah aim for objectivity and attempt to keep their own religious and spiritual beliefs separate from their analyses of the subject of Jewish mysticism.

The differences between these two approaches to the study of Kabbalah are especially evident when examining religious texts. Someone with a traditional, pious, orthodox orientation toward Kabbalah may find it irreverent to look critically at a text. An individual with a less traditional reverence may draw much inspiration from a spiritual text while interpreting it more metaphorically or poetically than more literal readers.

FACT

Halakhah is the word for Jewish Law, though it literally means "the way." Many laws are mentioned in the Torah and debated in the Talmud. There are also various codifications of Jewish Law, the best known of which, the *Shulkhan Arukh* (The Set Table), was written by Yosef Karo (1488–1575), a Kabbalist in Tzfat, Israel.

In addition to the previously mentioned two schools of approaching Kabbalah, there are still others who have appropriated and incorporated elements of Kabbalah into their study of spiritualism, tarot, and various New Age interests. There are individuals who use Kabbalah as a source of inspiration for their art or take the fundamentals of Kabbalah's perspective on life and the universe and attempt to leave behind the specifically Jewish content in which it is steeped.

Mysticism and Esotericism

Two terms that are essential to comprehending Kabbalah are mysticism and esotericism. For the purpose of learning about Kabbalah, you should understand mysticism as the conviction that personal communication with or experience of God, or the Divine, is possible through intuition or sudden insight rather than through rational thought. You must also keep in mind that esotericism, or esoteric knowledge, is wisdom that is communicated only to a select group of people.

Though the Kabbalists largely refrained from speaking or writing about their personal experiences, they invested a lot of energy in using symbolic and metaphorical language to communicate their understanding of God and the universe. In other words, instead of attempting to describe an intimate spiritual encounter with the Divine, a Kabbalist might articulate this experience by using imagery, such as that of bright light. Kabbalists most commonly used the symbolism of the Sefirot (which you will learn about in detail in Chapter 6) to talk about their religious experiences with God.

Although Kabbalists attempt to convey the power of their divine experiences, mystical experience by its very nature is incommunicable. At the same time there is a paradoxical desire to express what is inexpressible. In this sense Kabbalah is both mysticism and esotericism, in that the mystical experience is understood only by others who have undergone similar experiences.

The word *mitzvah* means "commandment" and has the connotation of "good deed." The Jewish tradition comprises 613 mitzvot (the plural of mitzvah): 248 positive (for example, love your neighbor as yourself) and 365 negative (for example, don't steal). Kabbalists reinterpreted mitzvah as deriving from the word *tzavta*, meaning "together," so mitzvot were understood as acts unifying the divine realms.

For most of its history, Kabbalah was esoteric in that its communication was limited to select individuals. Even though a book might appear in print, one who didn't share the spiritual experiences would understand the words differently from one who did. An early nineteenth-century mystical text, *Yosher Divrei Emet* ("Straightforward Words of Truth"), likened it to trying to communicate an exquisite taste to someone who had never experienced the food.

Traditional Restrictions on the Study of Kabbalah

Not only was the exploration of Kabbalah (by the complexity of its nature as a mystical, intangible experience) limited to a select group of individuals, but it was also restricted by teachers who would only instruct students who the teachers felt were morally and spiritually prepared to engage in it. It is a common misconception that the study of Kabbalah was restricted to married males over the age of forty. One possible source for this supposed restriction is contained in an ancient rabbinic text, Pirkei Avot, which lists the following ages for various religious endeavors: "five years old for the study of Bible, ten years old for the study of Mishnah . . . fifteen for the study of Talmud . . . forty for understanding"(5:24).

FACT

Hebrew had no symbols for vowels until circa 800 c.e., so all Scripture originally was written without vowels. The vowel symbols were created to provide a definitive reading of the biblical text. Most Hebrew works continue to be written without vowels, with the exception of prayer books, poetry, and volumes of the Bible (to reduce ambiguous meanings in these works).

Other possible reasons for the emergence of this tradition are that, according to legend, Rabbi Akiva (c. 40–135 c.e.), who was the dominant rabbi of his time and a renowned mystic, did not begin his study of Torah until the age of forty, and that a common belief was that a person should have "a belly full of Talmud" before beginning the study of Kabbalah. Despite this popular belief, while some Kabbalists, such as Nachmanides (who you will learn about in Chapter 4), were extremely well versed in Talmud, many others don't appear to have been (but they generally were very well educated in the Jewish tradition).

Though the age minimum of forty for the study of Kabbalah may have been taken seriously for a certain historical period, it was generally not adhered to—most of the major figures in the field became involved in Kabbalah study long before this age. It's interesting to note that two of the most influential Jewish mystics, Isaac Luria and Rebbe Nachman of Bratzlav, both died before they were forty years old, and another giant in the history of Kabbalah, Moshe Cordovero (who is discussed in more detail in Chapter 13), was a teacher of Isaac Luria before Cordovero himself died in 1570 at the age of forty-eight. Cordovero, who finished his first comprehensive systematic exposition of Kabbalah, *Pardes Rimonim* (The Pomegranate Orchard), when he was twenty-seven, thought it reasonable to begin the study of Kabbalah by the age of twenty.

ALERT!

Knowledge or *knowing* were understood mystically as implying "union with," as in the expression "Adam knew Eve" (Genesis 4:1). Union also, therefore, takes on a sexual, erotic connotation. The mystic's union or communion with the Divine is often described using erotic imagery.

Is Studying Kabbalah "Dangerous"?

All of this concern about who should study Kabbalah and who should not arose because people feared that mystical studies could pose a danger to a person, emotionally, psychologically, and even physically. Since the study of Talmud is a rigorous mental activity, the restrictions mentioned here were essentially ways of ensuring that those engaged in Kabbalistic studies came to them with a lot of stability in their life (and being married and forty years of age might ensure a certain emotional groundedness in the student).

Already in Talmudic times, many judged the pursuit of mystical knowledge as not being suitable for everyone (as we shall see when we examine the story of the four who entered Pardes in Chapter 3). Even the great Kabbalist Abraham Abulafia (1240–c. 1292) recognized the danger and cautioned against using his meditative methods without preparing for their spiritual demands because of the potential for psychological damage.

Women and Kabbalah

Before the twentieth century, Kabbalah was generally a male dominion, with some notable exceptions in the Hasidic world such as Hannah Rachel of Ludomir and Malkah of Belz, both of whom were spiritual leaders in their communities. The twentieth century began to see an increasing number of women engaged in these studies, particularly outside the orthodox world.

With greater access to works about Kabbalah and increased freedom in Western societies, there are now no real external restrictions to the study of Kabbalah, for women or anyone else who may be exploring spirituality. Of course, there remain the inherent difficulties of reading and deciphering the original sources, and of understanding their symbolism.

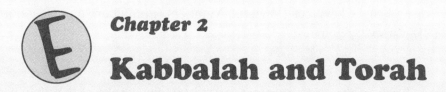

Chapter 2

Kabbalah and Torah

The Torah is the foundational document of the Jewish tradition. All subsequent spiritual movements within Judaism look back to it for inspiration and validation. Like these other developments within Judaism, Kabbalah is interactive with the Torah. Kabbalists communicate their teachings and insights often through commentaries on the Torah, finding startling new ways to read the words of the Torah, and in doing so, they uncover the nature of Torah itself.

Different Meanings of Torah

The word Torah comes from the Hebrew root meaning "to teach," so Torah is literally "Teaching," with a capital T (in other words, the great teaching). The word Torah has many different connotations. The word's first basic meaning refers to the initial five books of the Bible: Genesis (Bereshit), Exodus (Sh'mot), Leviticus (Vayikra), Numbers (Bemidbar), and Deuteronomy (Devarim).

FACT

None of the Hebrew names for the first five books of the Bible has the same meaning as the English name. In Hebrew what determines the book's name is the first significant word in the book itself. *Bereshit* means "in the beginning," *sh'mot* means "the names of," *vayikra* means "and (God) called," *bemidbar* means "in the wilderness," and *devarim* means "words."

The next traditional understanding of the word *Torah* is that it refers to both the oral and written Torah. Finally, the term can also refer to any valid spiritual teaching. Therefore, all Midrashic literature, Kabbalah, Hasidic texts, and Torah commentaries are called "Torah" because they are valid spiritual teachings.

Metaphysical Torah

Torah also acquired other meanings over the course of the centuries. When the ancient Midrash Bereshit Rabbah speaks of God looking into the Torah to create the universe, this use of Torah clearly doesn't fit any of the previously mentioned definitions of the term. Now we're talking about a metaphysical Torah of sorts, a Torah that not only predates history, but even predates the creation of the universe.

This metaphysical Torah can also be synonymous with the word *wisdom* (Chokhmah), as in the biblical book Proverbs. Proverbs, referring to wisdom, says: "YHVH [God] created me at the beginning of his way" (8:22).

The word light (*or* in Hebrew) appears five times in the description of the first day of Creation in the Book of Genesis. This is interpreted as representing the five books of the Torah, which are a great source of spiritual light. This light is also understood as being embedded in the core of the letters of the Torah.

Primordial Torah

The "primordial Torah" (*Torah K'dumah*) is another term for the Torah that preceded all creation. The Torah K'dumah is often seen by Kabbalists as part of the manifestation and revelation of God's essence, and it is therefore not separate from God. The well-known kabbalistic phrase for this perception is that "the Blessed Holy One and the Torah are One" (*Kudshah Brikh Hu V'Oraita Khad Hu*).

Oral and Written Torah

The Five Books of Moses, also called the *Chumash* in Hebrew (which comes from the Hebrew root that connotes the number "five"), are the first level of meaning of the written Torah. The rest of the twenty-four books of the Bible comprising the section called the Prophets (Nevi'im) and the third section called the Holy Writings (Ketuvim) are likewise considered part of the written Torah. The oral Torah in this basic division is made up of the two parts of the Talmud. The earlier Hebrew part is called the Mishnah and the much more extensive later portion, written in Aramaic, is called the Gemara.

The idea of the oral Torah is broader than the traditional guidelines mentioned here. Kabbalists see the Talmud as authoritative, but they also believe that all of the nonbiblical parts of the spiritual tradition such as Midrash and Kabbalah itself make up the oral tradition.

The Kabbalistic tradition, in accordance with the rabbinic tradition out of which it grew, sees these two components, the oral and written Torah, as inherently intertwined. One cannot be understood without the other. Many things in the Torah scroll (that is, the Five Books of Moses) would not make sense or would be impossible to implement without the explanations, adaptations, and embellishment contained in the oral tradition.

Kabbalists derive the belief that Moses received both the oral and written Torah during his forty days on Mount Sinai from Exodus: "YHVH said to Moses, come up to me to the mountain. . . . I will give you the Tablets of stone and the Torah and the Mitzvah" (24:12). Kabbalists interpret the word *mitzvah* as the oral tradition that clarifies the mitzvot.

Four Levels of Torah

Everything in the Jewish tradition, including all of the commentaries and explanations, refers back to the written Torah. Therefore as Judaism inevitably evolved, interpreting the Torah became increasingly important. Regardless of how radical certain aspects of the Kabbalistic viewpoint was in comparison to the literal reading of the Torah, Kabbalah always looked back to the Bible to explain, justify, and lend authority to its insights.

Pardes

By the thirteenth century, Spanish Kabbalists began to speak of the Torah as existing on four different levels. Three particular Kabbalists who knew each other were the first to use this framework in their writings. They were Moshe de Leon, Yosef Gikatilla, and Bakhya ben Asher. Moshe de Leon coined the term *Pardes* to refer to these four levels.

Pardes, which literally means "orchard" but also has the connotation of Paradise, refers to mystical knowledge. The famous story of the "four who entered Pardes" (which you will read about in Chapter 3) has been a staple of mystical lore for close to 2,000 years.

Pshat, Remez, D'rash, and Sod

Moshe de Leon treated the term Pardes as an acronym for the four levels of reading Torah. Each of the consonants in the word Pardes stands for one of the levels of meaning in the Torah. The *p* stands for *pshat* or the simple, literal meaning of the words. The *r* stands for *remez*, which means "hint," but in medieval Hebrew came to stand for the allegorical reading of the text that was the mainstay of Jewish philosophy. The *d* stands for *d'rash*, which essentially means "to investigate, to seek out, to expound" and here refers to Aggadic and Talmudic interpretations. The *s* stands for *sod*, the secret meaning of the text. Kabbalah itself is understood as constituting this secret meaning of the Torah.

FACT

Though the body of the Zohar speaks about the four levels of Torah interpretation, the term *Pardes* is not used in the text. Instead of using the term *sod* to describe Kabbalistic interpretation, in the Zohar it is replaced with the phrase "secret (or mystery) of faith" (*raza d'mehemanuta*).

In Bakhya ben Asher's Torah commentary, written in 1291, he uses all four levels of Torah interpretation to discuss many portions and particular verses of the Torah. He refers to remez as "the way of the intellect" (*Derekh HaSekhel*), d'rash as "the way of the Midrash," and sod as "the way of the Kabbalah." In his sod commentaries he sometimes quotes from the Zohar. Bakhya's commentary, in fact, is one of the first texts to quote from the Zohar.

Kabbalah as "Secret" Torah

All the levels of the Torah complement each other. Kabbalists often use the analogy of a nut to visually communicate the relationship between these levels. The outer shell conceals the soft, deep core that is the most nourishing part of the nut. All the levels need one another to exist. One does not negate another, but merely exposes a deeper level.

The Kabbalists for the most part, historically, were very traditional in their adherence to the precepts of Judaism. Their thoughts at times may have been very radical compared to mainstream believers, but in practice they were at least as traditional as (and at times were even more extreme than) mainstream believers in their ritual observance.

Yosef Gikatilla's first book is called *Ginat Egoz* (The Nut Garden). The term *ginat* (the garden of) in the title is an acronym for *gematria, notarikon,* and *temurah,* techniques that Ecstatic Kabbalists used to delve into the mystical depths of the Torah, whose levels are symbolized by the "nut" (egoz).

Another way of communicating the interrelationship of all of the levels of the Torah is to understand it as an organic whole. Azriel of Gerona (who lived in the early thirteenth century), in his commentary on the Aggadot (rabbinic legends), explains that the Torah has different limbs and should be thought of as a complete structure:

> "Just as a person has different parts of the arms and legs and joints . . . nothing is superfluous and there is no deficiency in the creation of the body. Thus, there are portions of the Torah and Bible that will appear to someone who doesn't know the deeper insights of their meanings as deserving to be burnt, but someone who attains knowledge of their meaning will see that they are essential parts of the Torah. A Torah that lacks one letter or point is as one lacking a complete body. There is no difference here between Esau's genealogy and the Ten Commandments; they are all part of one body and one structure."

Very often Kabbalists find particularly deep insights in the very sections of the Torah that on the literal level seem dull or superfluous.

Kabbalah and Jewish Law (Halakhah)

The Torah itself has quite a number of laws in it and the Talmud spends a considerable amount of time discussing the particulars of these laws. Without the Talmud, many of these laws would be problematical to follow.

Talmud and Codifiers

The Torah describes certain foods that are forbidden to eat, such as any animal that is not vegetarian, or a fish that does not have fins and scales. There are also three verses that specify, "You shall not boil a kid in its mother's milk" (Exodus 23:19, 34:26, and Deuteronomy 14:21). The dietary restriction that forbids eating meat with dairy products comes from this verse. The Talmud draws out the implications of verses such as these and presents guidelines usually through the discussions of different rabbinic authorities. All of the customs and practices that constitute "observing the Sabbath day and keeping it holy" are determined by the Talmud and later commentators and codifiers of Jewish Law.

FACT

The Rabad (Rabbi Abraham ben David) of Posquières lived from 1125 to 1198 in Provence in southern France and was an early Kabbalist. His knowledge of Talmud and halakhah lent great credibility to Kabbalah. He was famous for his learned criticisms of Maimonides' codification of Jewish Law, *The Mishnah Torah*. His son, Isaac the Blind, was a major Kabbalistic figure.

Kabbalists as Interpreters of Jewish Law

Kabbalah was very respectful and supportive of halakhah. A number of well-known Kabbalists were giants in the field of Jewish Law, such as Yosef Karo in the 1500s in Tzfat, Nachmanides in the 1200s in Spain, and Rabbi Abraham ben David (the Rabad) of Posquières, France, in the 1100s. These people gave mainstream legitimacy to Kabbalah. People could not doubt these scholars' loyalty to Torah and traditional Judaism. The Kabbalistic ideas they espoused, therefore, were not subjected to suspicions of heresy.

Though it was traditionally believed to be written by Shimon bar Yokhai, an important figure in the Talmud, the Zohar was rarely looked to for halakhic decisions. This was even truer of other Kabbalistic books. The main contribution that Kabbalistic literature made to halakhah was supporting its centrality in Jewish life by providing deeply spiritual explanations for the mitzvot. A sizable portion of Kabbalistic works is devoted to such explanations. An exception to the general lack of halakhic influence on the part of Kabbalah is the work of the sixteenth-century Kabbalist, Isaac Luria. Though his teachings are primarily known through the work of his disciples, he exercised a great influence on ritual and custom in Jewish life even among non-Kabbalists.

ALERT!

Medieval Jewish philosophers tended to find allegorical meanings to explain the purpose of mitzvot that threatened to make their observance superfluous. Kabbalists found ways of spiritualizing ritual practice. Azriel of Gerona in his commentary on the Aggadot critically noted this phenomenon of not observing Jewish customs and thinking the underlying goals could be achieved without the practice.

God and Torah Are One

It is a common assertion among Kabbalists that God and Torah are one. In other words, Torah at its deepest level contains the essence of divinity. What exactly does this mean?

Power of Language in the Torah

By equating the Torah with God's essence, Kabbalists emphasize the primacy and strength of language in Judaism. The power of language is evident in the Creation story in Genesis, where it says, "Let there be . . . and there was." The part of Genesis where Adam names the animals illustrates this relationship between language and essence as, according to traditional understanding, Adam chose the names based on the essence of the animals.

The power of language is particularly stressed in Kabbalistic literature. Words are seen as forces of creation and as containing great energy. If this is true of words in general, it is particularly true of the words of the Torah and even more so of God's names, of which YHVH is the most important.

A legend about the power of language is that of the Golem, a clay figure created by Kabbalist Yehuda Loew of Prague. The word for "truth," *emet* (spelled *aleph, mem, tav*), on his forehead gives him life. A servant to the rabbi, the Golem becomes uncontrollable. The rabbi erases the aleph on his forehead, leaving letters that spell "dead," and the Golem collapses.

The Torah as God's Name

In the Ramban's (Nachmanides') introduction to his commentary on the Torah, he says, "There is still in our hands a true Kabbalah that all of the Torah is entirely names of the Blessed Holy One. . . . Because of this a Torah scroll that has one letter incorrect . . . is forbidden to be used [in a service]." This sense of the Torah being entirely composed of divine names is a standard Kabbalistic interpretation. It doesn't negate the conventional reading of the Torah; it merely adds a vitally new dimension to our understanding of Torah. In fact, the Zohar suggests an even slightly more radical reading than Nachmanides', which is that the Torah comprises one long holy name of God.

The concept that the Torah and God are one includes the idea that the language of the Torah is a garment for its soul. Just like a human soul requires its garment (the body) in order to exist and through which to express itself, the letters and words of the Torah are garments for manifesting divinity in the world.

The perception that God and Torah are one lends a completely new meaning to the study of Torah. Recognizing the spiritual power of the letters of the Torah makes meditating on a passage of Torah particularly potent. It becomes as important as any other way of learning Torah, though it is not meant as a substitute for other ways, but rather as a supplement to them. When you engage in Torah study, you are learning ethical lessons to help improve your life as a human being and refining your spirit by attending to the deeper meanings of the text itself. The sense of attempting to live a life that is holy embraces all of these elements.

Torah of Black Letters, Torah of White Letters

There is a Talmudic teaching attributed to a third-century Amora (a rabbinic authority from the era of the Gemara) in the land of Israel, Shimon ben Lakish (also known as Resh Lakish), that the Torah is written with "black fire on white fire." Nachmanides quotes this in his introduction to his commentary on the Chumash (the Five Books of Moses). He goes on to say that "the writing was continuous without a break between words and a reading was possible according to the 'way of the Names' [of God, meaning that the entire Torah comprises Names of God] and you could read it according to our [conventional] reading concerning the Torah and the Mitzvah (Exodus 24:12). The Torah was given to Moses according to the division of the reading of 'the Mitzvah,' and transmitted orally to him according to the reading of the Names."

The late-twelfth-century Kabbalist Yitzkhak Sagi Nahor (Isaac the Blind) of Provence elaborates upon this theme. According to him the white fire is the written Torah and the black fire is the oral Torah. The image of black fire over white fire conveys the interrelation of the oral and written Torahs. What we have today that we think of as the written Torah is not exactly the same as the written Torah of white fire. The Torah we read, of black ink handwritten on parchment, is perceived through the prism of the oral Torah of black fire. Only someone who has attained the level of prophecy can still perceive the written Torah of white fire.

Torah of Emanation and Torah of Creation

The Torah that we have today contains many mitzvot that say what you should do and what you should not do. The Kabbalists saw this Torah—the Torah that comes from the second set of tablets of the Covenant that Moses brought—as deriving from the Tree of Knowledge of good and evil. The first set of tablets, however, derived from the Tree of Life and had a very different content. This was the Torah as it was originally intended and this will be the Torah that we will read in the messianic era. Those who attain the level of insight that the Kabbalists strive for can glimpse this Torah from the Tree of Life. It is as though the Torah from the Tree of Life is visible underneath the Torah that derives from the Tree of Knowledge.

Moses ascended Mount Sinai twice to receive the Ten Commandments and the Torah. The question of whether what was inscribed on the first set of tablets was the same as what was inscribed on the second set is an important one. Mystical teachings often distinguish between the two.

There are two additional important distinctions in the origins of Torah. These are discussed, for example, in the last stratum of the Zoharic literature in two texts called *Tikkunei Zohar* (Embellishments on the Zohar) and *Raya Mehemna* (The Faithful Shepherd), which were written by an anonymous author after the main body of the Zohar was finished. One type of Torah is called the Torah of Emanation (*Torah d'Atzilut*) and the other is called the Torah of Creation (*Torah d'Beriyah*).

As in the descriptions of the upper worlds, the world of emanation is usually synonymous with God's essence, whereas the world of Creation is not quite at that undiluted level of divinity. According to the mystical Midrashim concerning Adam and Eve before their transgression, they were clothed in spiritual light originally, but later had to put on a different type of garment. Similarly, the Torah we have in our possession wears the garment of the words read in accordance with the knowledge of good and evil. In the messianic era the Torah will shed that garment and be read at its higher level, the level of the Torah of Emanation.

 Uncovering Early Jewish Mysticism

There were elements of mysticism throughout the major bodies of Jewish literature long before the emergence of Kabbalah in the late 1100s. Authors of Kabbalistic literature saw components of Kabbalah in these earlier works and referred back to them regularly, developing the themes of these earlier texts and incorporating them into Kabbalistic writings.

Biblical Sources of Mysticism

One of the sources of the Bible's power is its ability to accommodate various interpretations. As a result of this flexibility, the Bible has often been understood from a mystical perspective. The two main areas of the Bible that particularly attracted mystical speculation are the story of Creation in the beginning of Genesis and Ezekiel's vision of the divine chariot, or *Merkavah* as it's called in Hebrew.

In Genesis it says, "*Elohim* [God] created the Human Being [*Adam*] in His image . . . male and female [God] created them" (1:27). Over the ages there was much commentary on the meaning of this verse. In Kabbalah this "primordial human," Adam Kadmon (male and female together), becomes an image of the world of the *Sefirot* (divine emanations).

The Creation story's poetic and grand nature makes it apt for mystical contemplation. The emphasis on the "Oneness of God" (Deuteronomy 6:4), the central belief of Judaism, is generally a major component of mystical experience. Some of the biblical Hebrew words themselves are ripe with mystical overtones. The name *Adam*, which means "human being" in Hebrew, shares a root with the words *earth* (*adamah*) and *blood* (*dam*). The root of *Eve* in Hebrew (*chava*) means "life." *Avraham* (Abraham in English), whose original name was *Avram* (Abram in English), means "high (or exalted) father." He was the first Jew according to the biblical narrative. The Torah states that God changed the names of both Abram and his wife Sarai, adding the letter *hey*. After the change, their names together contain two *hey*s, mirroring the divine name YHVH.

The Ineffable Name

The unpronounceable four-letter name of God, YHVH (mistransliterated as Jehovah or Yahweh), contains the root that means "being," with elements of this root in the past, present, and future tenses. In Deuteronomy there is a passage saying that this Torah (which literally means "teaching") "is in your heart" (30:10–14). Though these words could be understood in more than one way, it's easy to read them in a mystical manner as implying that God is everpresent (in the past and future) and is within an individual at all times. Another key biblical passage that resonates with mystical consciousness is found in Isaiah: "Holy, Holy, Holy is YHVH of Hosts: the whole earth is full of His Glory" (6:3). This sense of divinity filling all of Creation is an important Kabbalistic theme.

ALERT!

Instead of pronouncing the name YHVH in prayer, the custom is to say "Adonai" (literally meaning "my Lord"). In Hebrew Bibles and in many prayer books the vowels of the name Adonai were put under the letters YHVH to indicate the use of this substitute name. Pronouncing YHVH with these vowels led people to think the name was Yehovah (Jehovah in English).

Elijah the Prophet and Kabbalah

Another figure and biblical passage that exude a mystical feel and became important in later mystical imagery is Elijah the prophet and the story of his escape to the desert after defeating the prophets of the false god, Ba'al. Elijah travels for forty days and nights back to the "mountain of God, Horeb." (Horeb was another name for Sinai.)

In this passage from I Kings, Elijah stands in the presence of YHVH and "YHVH passes and a great and powerful wind shatters mountains and breaks rocks before YHVH, but YHVH is not in the wind. And after the wind an earthquake and YHVH was not in the earthquake. After the earthquake, fire, and YHVH was not in the fire; and after the fire, the subtle sound of silence" (19:11–12). The "subtle sound of silence" (often translated as "a still, small voice") is that full silence that those practicing meditation seek.

Elijah remains an important presence throughout Jewish history, literature, and ritual, and plays a unique role in Kabbalistic and Hasidic works. A seat is set aside for Elijah at a *brit milah*, the ritual circumcision that marks a boy's entrance into the covenant with God. In addition to the four cups of wine that Jewish people drink at the Passover Seder representing four expressions of redemption used in the biblical story of the Exodus, they set aside a fifth cup of wine for Elijah, symbolizing the future redemption of the messianic era. At the ceremony that marks the end of Shabbat (the Sabbath), a day that is understood as a taste of the world to come, a traditional song about Elijah is sung. Elijah is supposed to reappear to herald the dawning of the messianic era. There is a complex relationship in Judaism between messianism and mysticism, which we will explore later.

FACT

Forty days is the amount of time Moses was atop Mount Sinai receiving Torah and the number of years the Jews wandered in the desert on their way from Egypt to the Promised Land. The number is especially significant because forty is also the number of weeks of human gestation, implying that after each of these periods is a spiritual rebirth.

Mysticism in the Talmud

The Talmud is an encyclopedic body of texts consisting of sixty-three volumes, or tractates. The Jewish tradition considers it the oral Torah, which God revealed to Moses on Mount Sinai and was eventually written down in two stages. The first stage, called the Mishnah, was completed circa 200 C.E. The second stage, called the Gemara, was completed around 450 C.E. To orthodox Jews, the Talmud is essentially of equal validity to the Torah and the Torah can only be understood properly when read in light of the Talmud.

Within the vast "sea of the Talmud," as it is often referred to, there are sections that speak of mystical matters. The classic story of the four who entered Pardes appears in *Tractate Chagigah* (which generally speaks about the three holidays, or *Chagim*, on which a pilgrimage was made to the Temple in Jerusalem during the time of the First and Second Temple). The word *Pardes*, which appears only three times in the entire Bible and literally means "orchard," came to imply mystical experience and knowledge.

The Orchard of Mystical Knowledge

In the Garden of Eden story, two trees are specifically mentioned that remain prominent symbols throughout Jewish literature: the Tree of Life and the Tree of Knowledge. Mystical experience, like the Tree of Knowledge, promises an uncommon wisdom, and this special knowledge adds another dimension to understanding life.

Each of the consonants in the word Pardes stands for one of the levels of meaning in the Torah. *P* stands for "pshat," the literal level; *r* stands for "remez," which is the allegorical meaning; *d* for "d'rash," the Midrashic interpretation; and *s* stands for "sod," which is the mystical level of meaning.

The story of the four who entered *Pardes* is as follows: "[F]our entered the Pardes and they were Ben Azzai, Ben Zoma, Aher [meaning "the other"], and Rabbi Akiva. Ben Azzai looked and died, Ben Zoma looked and was hurt [probably meaning he was overwhelmed and went a little crazy], Aher cut the young plants [an image that implies that he became a heretic], and Rabbi Akiva left in peace." The word for "peace," *shalom*, has the same root as the word for wholeness and perfection, *shalem*.

This story warns of the potential hazards of seeking mystical knowledge for those not ready to glimpse the light. At the same time, the story illustrates the sublime state one can attain through mystical study, as Rabbi Akiva did, leaving the orchard of mystical experience with a sense of "wholeness and perfection."

Keeping the Secrets Secret

Also in Tractate Chagigah we find the statement that one doesn't expound about the secrets of Creation to even two people at a time and one doesn't explain about the Merkavah·(the divine chariot) to even one person unless that person is "wise" and already has understanding about the matter. The combination of these restrictions and the warnings implicit in the Pardes story tell us a lot about the secretive manner in which this special knowledge was held. To protect the secretive nature of mystical experiences, explicit descriptions of mystical knowledge is scarce.

FACT

Gematria is a form of biblical interpretation in which each Hebrew letter has a numerical value. The gematria of a Hebrew word is used to show its connection to another word of the same numerical value. This method of interpretation dates as far back as the Talmud. Numbers of great significance are 26 (YHVH), 18 (life), and 32 (heart).

The Talmud is generally made up of discussions between various rabbis known as *Tannaim* (from the era of the Mishnah) or *Amoraim* (from the era of the Gemara). There are often differing opinions among the rabbis, and occasionally no conclusion is reached. Because of this, sometimes passages end with the word *Teku,* an acronym (which stands for *Tishbi Y'taretz Kushiot U'V'ayot*) that means that "Tishbi" (Elijah the prophet) will someday "answer these questions and problems." On other occasions a discussion with two differing conclusions might end with the expression that both positions "are the words of the Living God."

Divine "Speech"

Unique among the sixty-three tractates of the Talmud is "The Chapters of the Ancestors" (Pirkei Avot; often called "Ethics of the Fathers" in English). This Mishnah is devoted to primarily (but not exclusively) ethical statements. One saying, in Chapter 5, Mishnah 1, that resonates throughout the history of Kabbalah is the statement that speaks of the power of language and specifically of divine speech: "[W]ith ten [divine] utterances the universe was created." This statement refers back to the beginning of Genesis, in which God creates the world by speaking. In Genesis, "God said: Let there be light and there was light" (1:3). The sense of the divine word and the power of language is a crucial Kabbalistic tenet.

Words themselves are forces of creation, capturing, in a sense, the essence or soul of things. When translating from Hebrew, though, words no longer capture the spirit of what they were intended to describe. Hebrew, according to the biblical myth, was the language of all of humanity before God created different languages (as explained through the story of the Tower of Babel in Genesis, Chapter 11).

The first letter in the Torah is *bet* in the word *bereshit* ("in the beginning") and the last letter is *lamed* in the word *Yisrael* (Israel; i.e., the Jewish people). Together those are the letters of the word *lev*, which means "heart." Kabbalists note that the entire Torah was embraced by the word *heart*.

An important corollary of this is that the Hebrew letters in the Bible also have numerical values, musical notation, and even various crownlike additions to certain letters in the Torah scroll. All of these have significance and no translation of these extra components is possible. Each element can become part of an interpretation of a word or phrase, and the potential for varied interpretations is huge.

Also in Pirkei Avot (Chapter 6, Mishnah 2) is the statement that "[e]very day a Divine Voice emanates from Horeb." In other words, revelation is always possible. The Kabbalist's mystical experience is a form of revelation; it is an individual version of standing at Mount Sinai and receiving Torah.

Merkavah Mysticism

Near the end of the period of the Second Temple (which was destroyed by the Romans in 70 C.E.) the dominant form of Jewish mysticism was Merkavah mysticism. It revolved around the mystic's attempt to experience the vision, described in the beginning of the Book of Ezekiel, of the divine chariot (Merkavah). Ezekiel writes, "It came to pass . . . as I was in the midst of exile by the river K'var, the Heavens opened and I saw visions of God" (1:1).

This form of Jewish mysticism was prominent for about 1,000 years. Probably because of the secretive, exclusive nature of this mystical movement, there are relatively few surviving documents from it. Most of what modern Kabbalists do have exists in fragments of texts. The most significant of these texts are the *Hekhalot Zutarti* (the Lesser Hekhalot), the *Hekhalot Rabbati* (the Greater Hekhalot), *Ma'aseh Merkavah* (the Mysteries [or Works] of the Divine Chariot), and *Shiur Komah* (the Measure of [God's] Stature).

The main focus of these texts is the ascent through the seven celestial palaces called Hekhalot. There are descriptions of the difficulties and dangers of this journey, angels that are encountered along the way (protecting and restricting the passage from palace to palace), and sacred names of God learned during the journey that protect the Merkavah mystic.

FACT

During the time of the destruction of the Second Temple (70 C.E.), there were three major Jewish sects: the Pharisees, the Sadducees, and the Essenes. The Pharisees, whom most contemporary Jews descend from, were the vast majority. They alone accepted the authority of the Bible and the oral tradition (Talmud)—the Sadducees only accepted the Bible, and the Essenes were an ascetic sect.

Rabbi Akiva, Rabbi Ishmael, and Ezekiel

Rabbi Akiva, the central figure in the story of the four who entered Pardes, is the main figure in Hekhalot Zutarti, which despite its fragmentary nature possibly contains the oldest existing texts. Segments of it may date as far back as the second century. Rabbi Ishmael, a contemporary of Rabbi Akiva, is the dominant figure in Hekhalot Rabbati. Though scholars agree that neither wrote the tracts that they dominate, they were both well known as mystics in the Merkavah tradition (a fact that is attested to in the Talmud and other rabbinic works of that era).

Hekhalot Literature

In the Hekhalot literature, there are seven Heavens to pass through and the seventh Heaven has seven Hekhalot (palaces) within it. In the seventh and last Hekhal (singular of "palace"), the divine throne sits upon the *Merkavah*. Upon the divine throne is the *Kavod*, the divine glory. The terms *Kavod* along with *Shekhinah*, another term for the Divine Presence, are the main words the Merkavah mystics used in reference to God. Both of these terms figure prominently in Kabbalistic literature of 1,000 years later.

Even though the Hekhalot are not mentioned in the Book of Ezekiel itself, in biblical passages there exist many parallels with the visions of the Merkavah mystics. Ezekiel speaks of *K'vod* YHVH (the Glory of YHVH) and of a "stormy wind coming from the north." However, this seemingly straight-forward detail can easily be read as having a deeper meaning. The word for "wind," *ruakh*, also means "spirit" or "soul," so there is a stormy soul or spirit coming from the "north." But the word for "north," *tzafon,* can also be read as *tzafun*, meaning "from a hidden, secret place." The river K'var (which means "already"), where Ezekiel sits in exile, has the same three-letter root as the word *Merkavah*, but in a mixed up order. This reflects his sense of exile before his awakening to the divinity that was already there.

The Gate to Heaven

Another relevant biblical passage is found in chapter 28 of Genesis, in which Jacob, Abraham's grandson, has a dream. In it there is a ladder that reaches up to the Heavens, and angels of God are ascending and descending it. When he awakens from his dream, Jacob declares, "Indeed YHVH is in this place and I didn't know . . . How awesome is this place! It is none other than the house of God and this is the gate of Heaven." The image of the gate of Heaven, the angels, and the theme of ascending and descending to the Heavens are all highly developed in Merkavah texts.

Though the Merkavah doesn't have palaces or chambers in the Book of Ezekiel, there is a rabbinic tale from the fourth century that tells the story of Isaac, when he is about to be sacrificed on Mount Moriah by his father, Abraham (Genesis 22:2), and he has a vision of the Blessed Holy One and the "chambers of the Merkavah." According to the Jewish tradition, Mount

Moriah became the site upon which the First and Second Temples were built in Jerusalem (II Chronicles 3:1). The name *Moriah* means "God is my teacher."

The tabernacle was created by the children of Israel in the wilderness on the way to the land of Israel after the Exodus from Egypt. Called the *Mishkan* in Hebrew, it housed the Ark of the Covenant that held the Ten Commandments. The root of the word *Mishkan* (Sh, K, N) means "to dwell" and implied that God's presence (Shekhinah) was most intensely sensed here.

The word *hekhal* also means "temple." The very spot where Abraham bound Isaac in order to sacrifice him was traditionally believed to be the location of "the Holy of Holies," the tabernacle for the Ark of the Covenant in the Temple of Jerusalem. The Ark of the Covenant was where the Glory of God, the *Kavod* or *Shekhinah*, was believed to be most strongly present.

Pilgrims to the Inner World

The entire process of the ascent of the Merkavah mystic can be understood as an internal spiritual pilgrimage comparable in many ways to the pilgrimage to the Temple in Jerusalem during the three pilgrimage holidays of Passover, Shavuot, and Sukkot (which is the focus of the Talmudic tractate that contains the story of the four who entered Pardes). The pilgrim, like the Merkavah mystic, makes various preparations to ensure his ritual purity. For the mystic this includes ritual baths, possibly fasting, and sexual abstinence. In Jerusalem in the vicinity of the Temple, Levites (who, of the twelve Jewish tribes, were the one that officiated in the Temple) were there to make sure that pilgrims were ritually fit to enter the Temple grounds. Undergoing a ritual bath before entering the Temple was part of the preparation.

Parallel to the role of the Levites is the role of the angels guarding the gates from one Hekhal to the next. Music and song were an important part of the pilgrimage process. The Levites were the musicians in the Temple. In the mystic's ascent, chants and hymns play an important role in the passage from one Hekhal to the next and in inducing the ecstatic state of the mystic during his journey.

The word for pilgrimage in Hebrew is *aliyah*, which literally means "ascent." The pilgrim made his ascent to the Hekhal (Temple) in Jerusalem where the Divine Presence was most strongly felt. On the Ark of the Covenant in the Holy of Holies, there were the images of two *keruvim* (cherubim). Similarly, the Merkavah mystic attempted his aliyah to the inner Holy of Holies, to the Throne of the Glory.

One of the three pilgrimage holidays was Shavuot, which means "weeks." Though originally an agricultural holiday, by Talmudic times (which was also the time for Merkavah mysticism) it came to be associated with the receiving of Torah on Mount Sinai. It occurred at the end of seven weeks from the beginning of Passover (that is, seven cycles of seven). After the seven cycles of seven, Torah, the divine word, is received. There is a pattern of "seven" imagery with the inner journey of the Merkavah mystic who traverses seven Heavens and then finally seven Hekhalot in the seventh Heaven to approach the Divine Glory on the throne.

In Hekhalot Zutarti the following passage appears: "Rabbi Akiva said that at the moment that I ascended to the Merkavah, a *Bat Kol* (a divine voice) emanated from beneath the Throne of Glory." The divine voice emanating from beneath the Throne of Glory reminds us of the Talmudic phrase in Pirkei Avot: "Every day a Divine Voice emanates from Horeb." The experience of the Merkavah mystic echoes the experience of Moses at Mount Sinai on the holiday of Shavuot receiving Torah, hearing the divine voice.

Descending to Spiritual Heights

Even though the Hekhalot texts themselves clearly talk about "ascending" to the Throne, the phrase that refers to the Merkavah mystics is *Yordei Merkavah*, which literally means "descenders to the divine chariot." One conjecture as to why this term may be used returns to the image of the Ark in a Talmudic phrase that speaks of "descending before the ark." It could also refer to the traditional posture of the Merkavah mystic during his ecstatic/trancelike journey. Elijah the prophet assumed this posture—

sitting with his head between his knees—in prayer on Mount Carmel before his confrontation with the prophets of the false god Ba'al, which preceded his own encounter at Horeb with the Divine Presence and the "subtle sound of silence."

What does *anthropomorphism* mean?
The term *anthropomorphism* means to give something a human form. *Anthro* means "human," and *morph* means "shape." This term when used in reference to God means to speak of God in human terms. Since Judaism insisted on God's lack of physical characteristics, anthropomorphisms were either strongly disapproved of or interpreted as metaphors.

Divine "Dimensions": Shiur Komah

Most extreme in certain senses among the Merkavah texts is the Shiur Komah, literally "the measure of the stature" (of God). This text describes the dimensions of God's Glory as perceived by the mystic. It attributes astronomical proportions to God's hands, legs, and other parts, describing distances between them that at times amount to a million miles or more. In a way, they use anthropomorphic imagery to point out its own absurdity. Yet, again, we can see biblical imagery that may have inspired this kind of speculation. Two quotations from the Book of Isaiah echo the Merkavah texts' descriptions of God's scale: "I saw my Lord sitting on a high and sublime throne and the edge of His garment filled the Temple" (Isaiah 6:1); and "Thus said YHVH: the heavens are my throne and the earth is my footstool—what house can you build me?" (Isaiah 66:1). Through the astronomical metaphors, the grandeur of the Divine Presence is communicated in language that is visceral, rather than abstract and unemotional.

A third-century Talmudic authority, Shimon ben Lakish (commonly known as Resh Lakish), authored a statement that would become very important in later forms of Jewish mysticism such as Kabbalah and Hasidism. He said that "the Patriarchs [Abraham, Isaac, and Jacob] were the Merkavah." This statement totally changed the perspective on the subject. Now human beings were seen as acting as the divine chariot, bringing the Divine Presence into the world through the spiritual quality of their lives.

Oral Esoteric Traditions

As we saw in the Talmud in Tractate Chagigah, there was great reservation toward teaching the subjects of mystical investigations. When mystical experiences actually were shared, they were done so face to face to one or two students at the most. Throughout the history of Jewish mysticism there was significant hesitation to commit esoteric teachings to writing, and the more the text pertained to actual experiences or techniques of meditation and ecstasy, the greater the hesitation. Most of these works, if they were ever written down, remained in manuscript form despite the advent of the printing press.

There's a legend that the patriarchs Abraham, Isaac, and Jacob observed all of the 613 mitzvot of the Jewish tradition hundreds of years before Moses received the Torah. Kabbalists revered the patriarchs as spiritual giants whose intimacy with God was only surpassed by Moses.

Some of the greatest Jewish mystics barely wrote down any of their teachings, and what has been recorded of their thoughts was written by their disciples and students. Two striking examples of famed Jewish mystics who did not write down their own works are Isaac Luria (1534–1572) and the founder of Hasidism, the Ba'al Shem Tov (1700–1760). There's a well-known quotation by the Ba'al Shem Tov in response to what a Hasid (devotee) of his wrote: "I said one thing, you heard another, and you wrote a third." Isaac Luria is quoted as saying that whenever he tries to write down his teachings, so many interrelated things come to him simultaneously that it is impossible for him to do them justice.

Practice over Study

The master/disciple relationship is very much an interpersonal experience. Even learning to read a text is much more than a matter of picking it up and assuming you can understand it. Though Hasidism is chronologically the last major phase in the history of Jewish mysticism, its insights about master/disciple relationships are relevant to any period. There's a well-known Hasidic anecdote in which the Hasid says he's going to the rebbe (the spiritual master) to watch him tie his shoes. In other words, the disciple is going to be with the rebbe because the rebbe is a living model of how to sanctify every part of one's life, even such a seemingly mundane act as tying one's shoes.

"A person whose wisdom is greater than his actions, to what is he comparable? To a tree whose branches are numerous and whose roots are few: a wind comes and uproots it and topples it" (Pirkei Avot 3:22).

Shimon the son of Gamliel is quoted in Pirkei Avot as saying, "it's not the study that is the main thing, but rather the practice" (1:17). As much as study of Torah was paramount in traditional Jewish life, the practice that emanates from it was still more important. The lifestyle of Kabbalah and earlier forms of Jewish mysticism included much study, but the study was not theoretical. It was meant to sanctify your actual life, not merely to stimulate you intellectually.

We know from Talmudic and other rabbinic sources that Rabbi Akiva, for example, was deeply involved in the Merkavah mysticism of his time, but despite all of the quotations from him, we don't really know what he taught his disciples in the hidden (*Nistar*) tradition. We possess books in which he is the main teacher, but they are written long after his death. We know that members of the desert community of the Essenes, in the days of the Second Temple, also engaged in esoteric studies, but we lack information about their explorations into spirituality and therefore don't know how it came to influence other Jewish mystics through the ages. We don't know how much of the mystical traditions, even those that we have remnants of in writing, were primarily communicated orally, master to disciple.

It seems that ideas that first appeared in ancient times in the land of Israel or in the diaspora in Babylonia (where Jews were taken after the destruction of the First Temple by the Babylonians in Jerusalem in 586 B.C.E.) later emerged in Europe, but how they made the journey is still a mystery. Even today certain Kabbalistic yeshivot (advanced Torah academies) in Jerusalem will not share their more esoteric teachings with the uninitiated. The same is true of the inner core of the Bratzlaver Hasidim. (We will discuss Bratzlaver Hasidism in detail in Chapter 16.)

FACT

"Someone whose actions are greater than his wisdom, to what is he comparable? To a tree whose branches are few and whose roots are many and even if all the winds in the world came and blew upon it, there's no moving it from its place" (Pirkei Avot 3:22).

Hidden in Plain Sight

Even the manuscripts that survived to this day (certain passages of Hekhalot texts, for example) are difficult to understand without a mentor. Partially it could be because of errors in the manuscripts, but it also could be because the explanations were given orally and the texts were not meant to be understood completely independent of a mentor or master.

An early Hasidic text (*Yosher Divrei Emet*, "Straightforward Words of Truth") encapsulates this sense of teaching the hidden (Nistar) tradition:

"I heard from the mouth of my holy teacher, Rabbi Menachem Men-

del, that what is called *Nistar* is something a person can't communi-

cate to another . . . it's impossible to explain to him in speech how and

what. . . . This is the case with the love and awe of the Creator, may His

Name be blessed. It's impossible to explain to another how this love is in the heart, which is why it's called 'hidden.' But people refer to the wisdoms of Kabbalah as Nistar. How is that hidden? Look, anyone who wants to study, the book is in front of him. If a person doesn't understand, he's ignorant, and for that person Gemara and Tosephta [other rabbinic teachings from the period of the Mishnah] are also hidden. But the true secrets of the entire Zohar and the writings of the Ari [Isaac Luria], of blessed memory, are that they're founded upon union with the Creator. [They are] for someone who merits union and gazing upon the sublime Merkavah like the Ari for whom the celestial paths were illuminated and he traversed them continually in his mind's eye like the four who entered Pardes."

Midrash and Mysticism

Midrash is both a body of rabbinic literature and a type of literature. Midrash literally means "to seek out, expound, and to interpret." Midrash provided a method of incorporating new insights into a tradition based upon canonized texts. Since the entire Bible was believed to be the word of God or divinely inspired, the words themselves were considered holy. Therefore the words could not be altered.

In Kabbalistic literature there is no sense that only one commentary contains the entire truth. There is a famous rabbinic expression from the Midrash, Numbers (Bemidbar) Rabbah that states that there are "70 faces to the Torah"; that is, there are many valid ways of reading and interpreting the Torah.

Having canonical texts also meant that it was rare for a writer to express ideas without referring back to biblical or Talmudic passages to illustrate their point by showing how the writer's ideas are already found in the earlier literature. Sometimes this would induce a rereading of the quoted passages, occasionally in brilliant, startling ways.

The Purpose of Midrash

The fact that biblical narratives were often written very sparsely left a lot of room for Midrash. Midrash would often fill in the many gaps in a biblical narrative, giving a behind-the-scenes explanation. Chapter 22 of Genesis, for example, contains the story of "the binding of Isaac" by his father Abraham. Chapter 23 begins shortly after this highly dramatic thirteen-verse episode by relating the length of the years of Sarah's life. Sarah, Isaac's mother and Abraham's wife, had just died.

FACT

"The person of understanding will understand" is an expression (in Hebrew: *HaMayvin Yavin*) often used when the author doesn't want to go into greater detail, often because of the esoteric nature of the material. This expression is frequently found in Kabbalistic and Hasidic texts.

A Midrash explains that these two events are related, insinuating that when Sarah heard the news of her husband attempting to sacrifice their son, she died of shock and heartache. Reading the narrative in this way also means that Isaac was thirty-six years of age when the incident took place. This provides a very different understanding of what transpired from the more conventional interpretation, which is that Isaac was a boy when his father tried to sacrifice him. The 36-year-old Isaac is much stronger physically than his 136-year-old father, so Isaac's role suddenly becomes much more active both in his willing self-sacrifice and in his respect toward his father.

Midrash and Kabbalistic Texts

Another avenue for rereading the Bible lies in the fact that all the original biblical texts are written without vowels. Therefore you can suggest another way of vocalizing the same consonants in order to find a new meaning in the same letters. Masters of Kabbalistic and Hasidic literature used this method to find new meanings in the Torah.

Midrashim (the plural of Midrash) are found in the Talmud itself and in numerous collections of Midrashim. A volume of Midrash might be organized according to the order of the portions of the Torah, but the individual Midrashim for any particular portion might be strikingly unrelated to each other and may come from many different sages. Two short sayings, both from the Talmud, illustrate the openness to interpretation that Midrash and Kabbalah embody: "Turn [the Torah] over and turn it over [i.e., keep examining it] for everything is in it" (Pirkei Avot 5:28); "Torah spoke in the language of human beings" (Tractate Brakhot 31a). The verses of Torah can be read metaphorically or symbolically because they were not meant to be taken strictly literally.

Kabbalah arose within a traditional, scripturally based Judaism. The dominance of canonized texts such as the Bible and Talmud made it nearly impossible not to refer all spiritual insights back to these earlier sources. Consequently many Kabbalistic texts provide mystical commentaries on parts of the Bible or prove their points by referring back to it, sometimes even radically reinterpreting it.

The earliest volumes of Midrash that we have are from circa 400 C.E. In Bereshit Rabbah, a collection of Midrashim on Genesis from the fifth century, we find the statement that "[t]he Blessed Holy One looked into the Torah and created the universe." This idea that Torah preceded the creation of the universe is a step toward the later Kabbalistic perspective expressed in the classic work the Zohar, which says that God and Torah are one. Midrash, though most of it is not mystical in content, provided a method of relating to

Scripture that has been incorporated by much of Kabbalistic literature. Kabbalah became at times a mystical Midrash. One of the sections of the Zohar, in fact, is called Midrash HaNe'elam, "the Hidden Midrash."

Kabbalistic circles employed many Midrashic methods of interpreting Scripture. Since every aspect of the Torah was considered holy, even the shapes of the letters could provide insight. One could read the first or last letters of consecutive words to obtain an additional teaching beyond the one conveyed in the straight text. In Kabbalistic literature it was common to see the first letter of the first four words of a passage spell out YHVH. We find this in the Shabbat evening ceremonial blessing over wine (Kiddush) that begins the meal. The first four words said out loud, which quote Genesis (1:31 and 2:1), are "The sixth day. And the Heavens were completed . . ." (*Yom Hashishi Vayikhulu Hashamayim . . .*).

The Book of Creation: Sefer Yetzirah

Sefer Yetzirah is a unique creation in the body of Jewish literature. It's a small book in terms of its actual number of words. (It was printed in two versions, but even the longer version has no more than 2,000 words.) Its influence, however, was immense. It inspired an abundance of commentaries from Kabbalists and philosophers, both of whom found in it inspiration and corroboration for their views.

Sefer Yetzirah is written in a very cryptic style, and for that reason is difficult to understand. It's composed in the form of the Mishnah, but is a mystical Mishnah. It coins terms that never appeared before in Hebrew literature. A key term in Kabbalistic literature, *Sefirot*, occurs for the first time in Sefer Yetzirah.

ALERT!

It was not uncommon for religious texts to be attributed to earlier well-known spiritual leaders who were not the actual historical authors. These works are called *pseudepigrapha*. Modern scholars attempt to discover the true identities of the authors by comparing the language and concepts in numerous texts.

The time of the book's composition is a matter of controversy. Until recently, scholars believed it was written in the third century C.E., but the latest research indicates it was probably created before the destruction of the Second Temple. Its author is anonymous, though it was ascribed to the patriarch Abraham. Others in the Middle Ages thought its author was Rabbi Akiva.

The book opens with the following passage: "With 32 wondrous paths of Wisdom *Yah* [a name of God], YHVH of Hosts, the God of Israel, the Living God and Eternal Ruler, God Almighty, Compassionate, Merciful, Sublime, Elevated, Dwelling in Eternity on High whose name is Holy engraved and created his universe. . . ." (Though the translation keeps repeating the word "God" in English, each Hebrew name of God is slightly different.)

The next passage elaborates on the thirty-two wondrous paths: "Ten *Sefirot Bli Mah* [of Nothing-ness] and twenty two letters of Foundation." Contained in this passage are the two fundamental orientations of Kabbalah. One school focuses on the Ten Sefirot (divine emanations) primarily and the other on the Hebrew alphabet (which has twenty-two letters). We should not forget that thirty-two is also the gematria (the numerical equivalent) for *lev*, the Hebrew word for *heart*.

Chapter 4

Acquiring Mystical Knowledge

Various paths lead to the acquisition of mystical knowledge. Traditionally you would study with a master whose mentoring of you would be very individually tailored. Ultimately, the only real knowledge can come through your own experiences. However, studying with a master will help you understand and assimilate your own experiences and guide you toward having them in the first place.

Oral Transmission

Despite the fact that hundreds of Kabbalistic books have been printed and thousands of manuscripts exist, much of Kabbalah has traditionally been taught orally. There are a number of reasons why some Kabbalists would only teach orally and not commit their words to writing.

Writing about the Ineffable

Some Kabbalists felt that it was not possible to write down their ideas and do them justice. Writing on Kabbalah tends to be more "about" and around the subject rather than conveying actual "Kabbalah" itself. This is unavoidable. True understanding comes only from the direct experience of God. This experience suddenly makes the teachings appear in a different light.

Much of Theosophical Kabbalah (which is one of the two major schools of Kabbalah and makes up the overwhelming majority of the Kabbalistic texts that exist) speaks about God but cannot provide an experience of God. (We will explore Theosophical Kabbalah and other forms of Kabbalah in depth in Chapter 11.) It can, however, acquaint you with a community of like-minded seekers. It can offer the knowledge that others have had these experiences and that they are, therefore, attainable. It can provide a framework and vocabulary through which you can both think about your own experiences and bring increased meaning and insight to life in general.

"I have learned much from my teachers; and from my friends I have learned even more than from my teachers—but from my students I have learned more than from all of them" (Babylonian Talmud, Tractate Ta'anit 7b).

There are other aspects of the oral transmission of Kabbalistic teachings that are important. Kabbalah at its highest is a lived experience, not a cerebral exercise. There is always the danger that it can lose its experiential core if so much focus is put on study to the exclusion of practice. As it says in Pirkei Avot, "It is not the theory [or study] that matters most, but the practice" (1:17). Oral transmission from a teacher who lives Kabbalah is greater insurance that Kabbalah will be a living practice and not a mere theory.

Learning How to Learn

Many Kabbalistic texts are heavily encoded with symbolic language. They are also often written with a lot of the thoughts unfinished and fragments of quotations given in the briefest number of words, just enough to make them recognizable to those familiar with the traditional sources. Usually a few words of a classic phrase will be mentioned followed with "etc.," assuming that the reader will be familiar enough to grasp the point.

Oral transmission embellishes the written word, which becomes the starting point for the fuller teaching that is "given over" (a traditional phrase used in reference to teachings) in person. The ease with which a lot of Kabbalistic material can be misunderstood also made oral transmission an important method of acquiring knowledge.

ALERT!

"If you have read, you haven't repeated, if you have repeated, you haven't gone over it a third time" (Babylonian Talmud, Tractate Brakhot 5a). Texts open themselves up to you the more you open yourself up to them.

Learning how to read a text is something you assimilate from studying with someone who has far more experience. In traditional yeshivot (academies of higher Torah study), the major method of study is *khevruta* meaning in partnership with another person with whom you read the text out loud and work together on trying to decipher it. This is usually done after the teacher has gone over the section of the text with the entire group first.

Often oral teachings were given on Shabbat and holidays when it is considered a desecration of the holiness of the day to write but a great mitzvah to study. Traditionally there were students trained to memorize a long teaching that might last an hour so that they could repeat it to others and discuss it together.

Spiritual Guidance of a Mentor

In some circumstances there are teachings that are only passed on to people deemed ready to understand them. The mentor can only determine this, of course, by knowing the student well and acquiring a good sense of the student's grasp of the teachings. In serious Hasidic yeshivot, students had their "spiritual guide" (*mashpiah rukhani*) who would help the student grow spiritually through their studies and practice, helping them integrate the two. This degree of individualized guidance can only be done face to face. There is so much communicated by the presence of another person in addition to the words they use. All of this facilitates learning as a living experience and not a merely academic one.

The Ba'al Shem Tov (the founder of Hasidism) is quoted as saying that "the essence of involvement with Torah and prayer is uniting yourself with the innermost spiritual Light of Ein Sof that is the core of the letters of the Torah and prayer. This is what is called 'study for its own sake.'"

Master and Disciple

The master and disciple relationship is a direct outgrowth of the process of oral transmission of secret teachings. Learning Kabbalah is different from conventional learning in that the study is for the cultivation of your soul, not for the acquisition of information. (Of course, Kabbalah is not the only study whose true purpose is the cultivation of your soul.) The actual study is a means rather than an end. It is a means of opening yourself up to the Divine Presence.

In order for disciples to grow to the best of their potential they require the individual attention that a master can give them. The master is someone who has traversed this terrain before, who will therefore be able to understand what the student/disciple is experiencing along the way. The master can also discern, through the close relationship between the two, the strengths and weaknesses of the disciple and therefore individualize the teaching to the maximum benefit of the student.

With few exceptions, the master/disciple relationship was the major path through which a person became initiated into Kabbalah. Of course, your own experiences and understanding will generally lead you to seek out a teacher. Occasionally the disciple may even surpass the understanding and insight of the master, but even in those circumstances, the mentorship of the master helped the disciple attain his or her insights.

FACT

A traditional description of the master/disciple relationship is offered in Pirkei Avot: "Let your house be a gathering place of the wise, sit at the dust of their feet [i.e., study humbly under them], drink their words with thirst" (1:4).

One element of the traditional master/disciple relationship is that of living in a community of practitioners. Unfortunately, this practice has been lost to a large degree in modern society. In orthodox circles the loss is less prevalent, but in nonorthodox circles the cohesion of community has been greatly diluted. Kabbalistic practice is a lifestyle, not a set of beliefs. Deepening your spiritual life is greatly aided by living around other people who are models of this lifestyle. A significant element of mentoring is being taught by example. This point is poignantly captured, as mentioned in Chapter 3, by the tale of the Hasid going to the rebbe to watch him tie his shoes.

The "Opening" of the Text

The study of Kabbalistic texts can be a spiritual practice. There is an element of study that can be very contemplative, even meditative. Studying a spiritual text is not like reading a novel or a history book. There is a layering of words, a trait of Kabbalistic literature that becomes more apparent the more times you go over the same passages. Re-examining a certain passage and using it as a focus of meditation can suddenly reveal its many meanings to you.

Many passages in the Zohar begin with the phrase "Rabbi so and so opened. . . ." Such passages proceed with quoted Torah or biblical passages and over time offer a deeper and deeper understanding of the text. The literal meaning may then appear as a veneer for the symbolic Kabbalistic insight that lies beneath its surface. You can open Scripture to reveal many secret levels that exist simultaneously. They complement rather than contradict each other, even when they reveal very different teachings. This is part of the apparent paradox inherent in trying to communicate mystical insights.

ALERT!

"It's impossible to attain . . . 'truth' unless someone possesses Wisdom . . . and the opposite: one who unifies himself with the quality of truth and distances himself completely from falsehood can come to Wisdom. But if he's sunk in falsehood it's impossible to arrive at true wisdom" (from *Degel Machaneh Ephraim*, by Moshe Chaim Ephraim of Sudylkov). Falsehood is believing the surface image is reality.

The following Hasidic passage, which builds around a verse from Psalms ("The Mitzvah of YHVH is pure, enlightening the eyes" [19:9]), gives some insight into the "opening of the text": "Torah and the Blessed Holy One are entirely One. Therefore, when a person binds himself to the letters of the Torah he is able to know that which exists . . . for he himself becomes beyond time. This is what it means to say 'the Mitzvah of YHVH is *Bara*' [which in the Psalm means 'pure,' but can also mean 'outside' or 'beyond']. Mitzvah comes from Tzavta [which means 'together']." Therefore, when you become joined together with YHVH through doing a mitzvah, you move beyond time and space, because God is beyond these limits. This truly "enlightens the eyes," allowing you to see in a completely new way. The state of being "beyond," as implied in the word *Bara*, is the true "purity" (which is the other meaning of the word in the verse).

ESSENTIAL

"[W]hen a person learns to unite the Torah to its root, he unifies himself with the Blessed One through the Torah that he studies. The joy of Torah then flows into him . . . and his consciousness is opened like a spring of wisdom. All this comes from studying Torah for its own sake" *L'Shon Hasidim* (in English, *The Language of Hasidim*) 255.

Altering Consciousness

There are various techniques that people use when seeking to break out of their conventional ways of seeing the world. Our standard way of perceiving the world is by seeing with "our physical eyes" instead of seeing with our "spiritual eyes." Viewing the world using your "spiritual eyes" is an important goal for Kabbalists.

Meditation, prayer, contemplative study, fasting, chanting, and other techniques or combinations of techniques can help a person see the world differently. Sometimes you see the world in a new light while in the midst of using these methods, and sometimes you may achieve this goal after you have stopped using these methods as a result of their impact.

FACT

On the Day of Atonement, Yom Kippur, at one of the many peaks during the service, the congregation chants that *teshuvah* (returning to God), *tefillah* (prayer), and *tzedakah* (charity) can change your life. These are daily practices, each of which we can perform more deeply to our own benefit and the benefit of society.

Yom Kippur, the Day of Atonement, which is considered the holiest day in the Jewish calendar, is a day in which a number of these techniques are used. It is a day of fasting from food and drink, a full day of prayer, self-examination, song, and study that culminates with the blowing of the *shofar* (the ram's horn), which is intended to awaken your soul.

Altering your consciousness is referred to in various manners. It might be called *Gilui HaShekhinah* (Revelation of the Shekhinah), it might be called having *Ruakh HaKodesh* (the Holy Spirit), or it might be called "prophecy." A revelation may be offered to you in a dream. The question is bound to arise whether this is a true revelation or a false one. One traditional way of deciding this is to determine if it illuminates canonized teachings or deviates from them.

The Divine Voice from Horeb

At any moment, anywhere you can suddenly have a revelation of God's presence. This is an implication of the verse in Genesis, in which Jacob wakes up from his "sleep" and realizes that "[i]ndeed YHVH is in this place and I didn't know" (28:16). This is true of every place and every time in which we don't have an awareness of God's presence.

When that awareness comes it is like the revelation at Mount Sinai. It is a teaching of "the inner depth of Torah (*P'nimiyut HaTorah*)." It is hearing the "subtle sound of Silence" (*kol d'mamah dakah*; I Kings 19:12). It is the "divine voice that emanates daily from Horeb [Mount Sinai]" (Pirkei Avot 6:2).

Revelations of Elijah the Prophet

There have been Kabbalists who claimed that the Torah they teach does not come from their own understanding or imagination or from the master under whom they studied, but that it is a revelation from the Prophet Elijah (the Hebrew term for "revelations of Elijah the prophet" is *Gilui Eliahu*).

Because the tradition is so grounded in canonized Scripture, it is difficult to offer new revelations. They generally have to be presented through new insights into authoritative Scripture.

"Joshua the child of Perakhyah said: Provide yourself a teacher, acquire for yourself a companion, and judge everyone favorably" (Pirkei Avot 1:6). "Shammai said: Make your Torah study a steady habit, say little and do much, receive everyone cheerfully" (Pirkei Avot 1:15). "Hillel said: Be among the students of Aaron [Moses' brother]: Love peace and pursue peace, love all people" (Pirkei Avot 1:12).

The revelation of Elijah the prophet opens up the tradition to novel insights. Elijah is one character in the Bible who doesn't die, but rather ascends. According to the tradition, he is supposed to return to announce the imminent arrival of the Messiah and the reign of the messianic era. Elijah is also supposed to resolve all unresolved issues of Torah, and answer all unanswered questions. Elijah is the most common disembodied teacher in the tradition.

Heavenly Messengers: Maggidim

One more avenue of attaining secrets of Torah is through the phenomenon of *maggidim*. The term *maggid* has numerous meanings, the most common of which is the "traveling preacher." However, in this case a maggid is a disembodied heavenly messenger that visits someone to reveal secrets of Torah and often appears as a voice emerging from the person visited by the maggid. Probably the most famous maggid is the one that appeared with regularity to Rabbi Yosef Karo.

Historically, this phenomenon began to be spoken of during the sixteenth century. A number of well-known Kabbalists were visited by maggidim. In addition to Yosef Karo, Rabbi Moshe Chaim Luzzato and the Vilna Gaon also claimed to have been visited by maggidim.

It would be easy to attribute psychological explanations to the phenomenon of maggidim, but the Kabbalists did not see the voice that they believed to be a maggid as emanating from within them in any way. Usually the phenomenon was accompanied by enormous awe and fear on the part of the Kabbalist undergoing the experience, and in those rare instances when there were witnesses to it—as in the case of Yosef Karo's maggid—on the part of the witnesses, too. Generally, however, despite the awe and fear evoked by the phenomenon of the maggid, those who were visited considered it a great gift of knowledge.

Kabbalistic and Mystical Communities

Kabbalistic communities usually formed around a great teacher or two. In the earliest days of Kabbalah, some of these teachers didn't write themselves, apparently feeling that mystical ideas shouldn't be disseminated too widely, just as the Talmud had advised in Tractate Chagigah. However, often their disciples or their disciples' students later committed the original teacher's words to paper.

The Rabad

The first Kabbalistic community that we know of was very small and consisted of the students of the Rabad (Rabbi Abraham ben David), who lived from approximately 1120 to 1198.

FACT

Often a famous Rabbi will be known by an acronym rather than by his full name. Rashi, which stands for *Rabbi Shlomo Yitzkhaki* (the *Y* acts as a vowel here), the most influential and popular commentator on the Bible and Talmud (1040–1105), and Rambam (*Rabbi Moshe ben Maimon*; also known as Maimonides) are two common examples.

The Rabad was not only a Kabbalist, but he was also primarily known as the authoritative Talmudist in Provence. His son Isaac the Blind (Yitzkhak Sagi Nahor, literally "Isaac full of light" in Aramaic), however, wrote exclusively about Kabbalah and cited his father's teachings. Isaac the Blind reached a larger group of Kabbalists and he was the teacher of the main leaders of the Kabbalistic community in Gerona, Spain, not far from Barcelona. Rabbi Isaac the Blind wrote a Kabbalistic commentary on Sefer Yetzirah and other texts dealing with the Creation story in Genesis, which as you'll recall was one of the two mystical areas of inquiry mentioned in the Talmud. Both Isaac the Blind and his father testify to a chain of oral transmission of Kabbalistic teachings of which they were recipients. Though they mention this essential oral component of Kabbalah, they don't divulge details beyond that.

Kabbalistic Center of Gerona

Gerona was by far the largest Kabbalistic community of its era. Its members also began to circulate their manuscripts to a wider readership. The two main writers in this group were Rabbi Ezra and Rabbi Azriel of Gerona.

Isaac the Blind became concerned about the wide dissemination of Kabbalistic thought because of the activities of his disciples Rabbi Ezra and Rabbi Azriel, and he sent a representative to strongly convey his discouragement. This attempt to restrain the spread of Kabbalistic ideas may have been successful to a certain degree in that most of the writings that have survived from Ezra and Azriel predate this effort by Isaac the Blind.

The Kabbalistic communities functioned in the context of the larger Jewish community and certainly were faithful to Jewish practice and law (halakhah). In fact, despite the radical ideas of the Kabbalists, in terms of Jewish practice they were very conservative traditionalists. They differed from most conservative traditionalists, however, because Kabbalists understand the reasons for the observance of the Mitzvot as primarily cosmic. In other words, Kabbalists believe that their proper observance affects the very state of Creation, bringing harmony to the world of the Sefirot.

QUESTION?

Is *halakhah* the name for all Jewish Law?
No. There are many words for Jewish "laws." One particular type, *khok*, refers generally to laws that have no rational explanation. These were difficult for the philosophers to justify. The Kabbalists, however, treated these as the most profound laws because they transcended rational thought.

The Kabbalistic community in Gerona that functioned most intensively from 1230 to 1260 C.E. crystallized much of the Kabbalistic thought that preceded it. From it we have teachings about the Sefirot, commentaries on the Torah and rabbinic literature, and commentaries on Sefer Yetzirah. Another area of study in this community focused on providing mystical explanations of the mitzvot. The Kabbalists of Gerona also presented many ideas in their writings that are later echoed in the most influential of all Kabbalistic works, the Zohar. Some of these ideas are modified in the Zohar and are presented in a more literary and less directly explanatory way.

Nachmanides: The Ramban

Among the great Kabbalists of Gerona was the Ramban (Rabbi Moshe ben Nachman) who lived from 1194 to 1270. Nachmanides was one of the great Talmudists of his era. He is well known for his commentary on the Torah, one of the most influential such commentaries. Nachmanides wrote very little that was explicitly Kabbalistic. However, his Torah commentary included within it quite a number of Kabbalistic teachings generally introduced with the phrase "according to the true path" (*Al Derekh HaEmet*).

A New Reading of Torah

Nachmanides wrote an introduction to his Torah commentary in which he says that the Torah contains within it the written Torah as we have it from Moses and an oral tradition given to Moses also. The primordial Torah is written in black fire on white fire. This idea of a primordial Torah goes back to the early Midrash in Bereshit Rabbah, which said that the Torah preceded Creation, that it was the blueprint of Creation.

The Hebrew term *panim* has a number of meanings. In addition to meaning "face" or "presence," it can also mean "depth" or "surface." When the term speaks of God's Presence it combines the two meanings, expressing a great depth, yet at the same time only the relative surface compared to that which is ultimately unknowable.

Nachmanides continues by explaining that the Torah can be read in a totally different manner from the way in which it is traditionally read. The original Torah, he explains, is not divided into words, but is an unbroken chain of letters. Nachmanides gives an example of an alternate reading, using the opening line of the Torah. Keeping the order of the letters the same, he divides the letters of the first three words into three different words so that the end result is "At first Elohim [God] was created." Nachmanides writes that the Torah consists entirely of names of God. He calls this reading of the Torah as the reading "according to the Names," in contrast to our conventional reading. Both of them are equally valid for him.

Nachmanides' inclusion of Kabbalistic comments in his Torah commentary helped legitimize Kabbalah to the larger Jewish community. Kabbalah was slowly becoming more acceptable and would continue to become so over the next few hundred years. Nachmanides included quotations from Sefer HaBahir in his Torah commentary, too, referring to it as the Midrash of Nekhunia ben HaKanah.

Though Nachmanides himself mentioned Kabbalistic teachings in his Torah commentary, he did so sparsely and without great detail. He felt that the true Kabbalah could only be communicated from master to disciple, face to face. He forbade his disciples to write down his teachings, but by a couple of generations manuscripts were emerging that began to divulge his Kabbalistic teachings.

Understanding with Your Heart

An important thing to understand when speaking about things such as the Torah being all names of God and other striking statements is that these are not intended as intellectual concepts. This is part of the esoteric nature of Kabbalah. When these statements remain "ideas" or "concepts," they are truly hidden. It's only when one begins to experience what is implied by these words that Kabbalah ceases to be a cerebral activity and becomes a much more spiritual one. The process is achieved, if ever, by entering the lifestyle of contemplative study, meditation, kavana, and so on. As Pirkei Avot says, "it's not the study that is most important, but the practice" (1:17).

Chapter 5

The Mysterious Book of Illumination: Sefer HaBahir

 abbalists view their mystical knowledge as originating with the revelation at Mount Sinai and thereafter being communicated orally from master to disciple. Eventually Kabbalistic teachings were written down. Kabbalists incorporate their own worldview and symbols into their readings of the Bible and earlier works of Jewish mysticism. Eventually, Kabbalists gave expression to their traditions and practices through books. The first book of this kind to emerge was Sefer HaBahir, the Book of Illumination.

An Unsolved Mystery

Some of the most basic questions about Sefer HaBahir remain unanswered. The Bahir is acknowledged by all modern scholars as the first true work of Kabbalah because it contains the major elements that distinguish Kabbalah from other, earlier forms of Jewish mysticism. While traces of the earlier mystical traditions are evident in the Bahir, a new literature had clearly emerged.

Although it is unclear where the book first appeared, it may have been in Germany in the area where another very important mystical school flourished. This other school was called *Hasidei Ashkenaz*, which means the German Pietists (that is, very pious people), and is also known as the Hasidim of medieval Germany. The other possible location of the Bahir's origin is Provence in southern France. The latest research points toward a German origin with a later editing stage in Provence.

FACT

There are two basic pronunciations of the Hebrew language. One is called *Ashkenazi,* the other *Sephardi.* These terms come from the Hebrew words for the locations of the two largest Jewish communities in medieval times. *Ashkenaz* in Medieval Hebrew means "Germany," and *Sepharad* means "Spain." So, Ashkenazi means "German" and Sephardi means "Spanish."

Many manuscripts of Sefer HaBahir exist, the earliest of which comes from about 1297. However, other Kabbalistic texts written at an earlier date quote the Bahir frequently. The Bahir was probably written in the latter half of the 1100s, but it may not have taken on its final form until around the year 1200.

One of the most striking and puzzling components of the Bahir's emergence is that it employed certain symbols and vocabulary without explanation, as though it had a readership that would understand them (yet we have no earlier written evidence of the existence of some of these terms). The possibility does exist that earlier texts were lost or that there was an oral tradition that used these terms prior to the emergence of the Bahir.

An important fact to remember in terms of the existence of Jewish manuscripts is that there was so much persecution of the Jewish communities, particularly in Europe, from the Middle Ages on that many manuscripts were burned and destroyed.

ALERT!

Some discrepancies between different manuscript editions of Kabbalistic texts can be attributed to "scribal error." Most Kabbalistic manuscripts predate the printing press, so all versions that exist were handwritten copies of other texts. Sometimes the scribe may have misread a word or not understood it and wrote in its place similar letters that made more sense according to the scribe's understanding.

Sefer HaBahir is written in a very Midrashic style. The author of the Bahir brings in many Scriptural quotations to prove a certain perspective, but reinterprets those passages in radically new ways that characterize much of Kabbalistic literature afterward. The Bahir is primarily written in Hebrew with an occasional Aramaic phrase incorporated (as is common in Midrashic literature).

Who Wrote the Bahir?

The Bahir is essentially an anonymous text, though it has been attributed to Rabbi Nekhunia ben HaKanah, who was a *tanna* (a sage of the Mishnah) who lived during the second half of the first century. He figures prominently in Hekhalot Rabbati (the Greater Hekhalot) as the teacher of both Rabbi Akiva and Rabbi Ishmael, the two main figures of Hekhalot literature.

The Bahir is attributed to Nekhunia ben HaKanah because the opening sentence of the book is a statement made in his name. The Bahir was often referred to as the Midrash of Nekhunia ben HaKanah. The more common title, Sefer HaBahir (meaning the Book of Illumination), comes from the use of the word *bahir* in the first sentence of the book in the same quotation attributed to Rabbi Nekhunia ben HaKanah.

About a century later, the Zohar—whose name is reminiscent of the Bahir, because both names are references to bright light—is attributed to another tanna, Rabbi Shimon bar Yokhai. He was a prominent student of Rabbi Akiva, the most influential Rabbi and mystic of his time.

FACT

Jewish Law forbids destroying anything that has God's name in it. Such writing must be buried if no longer usable. Every traditional Jewish community had a *genizah* (storage place) for these objects. The most famous is the Cairo Genizah in Egypt.

The Structure of the Bahir

The Bahir has a very loose structure. There aren't many long, sustained passages that deal with a particular issue in great detail. Rather there are a lot of reflections that are not structured along an obvious line of thought, such as a commentary on the Torah portion by portion (a format that characterizes many later Kabbalistic texts). The lack of a consistent structure makes it conceivable that the book is not the work of one author, but rather the work of a number of authors. It could even possibly be a collection of Kabbalistic teachings edited into its present form sometime during the course of its evolution. The book itself quotes numerous rabbis in addition to Nekhunia ben HaKanah, some of whom appear in no other work.

What Characterizes Kabbalistic Literature?

Most Kabbalistic literature is characterized by the system of ten Sefirot, or divine emanations, which mark the transition from Ein Sof, the absolute transcendent God or the Infinite, to the physical universe we inhabit. Each of the ten Sefirot has names, qualities, characteristics, and a host of symbols representing it. Though the term Sefirot first appears in Sefer Yetzirah, it doesn't acquire the meaning of "divine emanations" until Sefer HaBahir.

Though there are ten standard names for the Sefirot there are some alternative names found throughout Kabbalistic literature. The first, *Keter* (crown), and the last, *Shekhinah* ("indwelling," or Divine Presence), are both used in Sefer HaBahir. Though the term *Shekhinah* has a long history in both a verb form in the Bible and in this noun form already in the Talmud, it doesn't carry its Kabbalistic sense before the Bahir. Here Shekhinah becomes a distinctly feminine aspect of God, an idea that begins in the Bahir and becomes a prominent component of later Kabbalistic literature.

There are many names of God in the Bible. For most contemporary biblical scholars these indicate different authors and strata of the Bible. However, the rabbis in Talmudic times interpreted them as referring to different qualities of the One God, and they explained verses according to this understanding. In Kabbalistic literature these names are understood as referring to different Sefirot.

God as Male and Female

The idea of masculine and feminine aspects of the Divine did not exist in previous Jewish mysticism. This was a revolutionary change and one that received little opposition. Another name for Shekhinah is Kavod (the divine glory), the vision of which was the ultimate goal of the Merkavah mystics. In this way the *M'kubalim* (the Hebrew word for Kabbalists, meaning "those who received") maintained a direct connection to their mystical predecessors and saw their own visions reflected in the mystical experiences of those that came before them.

Symbols and Parables

The abundance of symbols for the Ten Sefirot began in the Bahir. Kabbalists often interpret passages in the Torah as indicating what was simultaneously happening in the divine realms while concrete events occurred in the Torah. Various prominent biblical figures became standard symbols for particular Sefirot. Each of the patriarchs (Abraham, Isaac, and Jacob), for example, symbolizes a different Sefirah. The Bahir features this particular symbolism and is filled with parables employing these symbols.

Beginning in the Bahir, the Ten Sefirot came to be associated with earlier fundamental images of "ten." The "Ten Divine Utterances," by means of which the universe was created as mentioned in Pirkei Avot (5:1), became identified with the Ten Sefirot, as did the Ten Commandments. One of the passages of the Bahir also refers to the ten fingers of the priest's hands as they are held up over the people when bestowing the priestly blessing.

Another term used for the Ten Sefirot was the word *middot.* In Kabbalistic usage, the word *middah* (the singular of middot) refers to a divine emanation (or "divine attribute" as used in Medieval philosophical literature). Middot are also ethical qualities, so the world of the Sefirot becomes implicitly connected not only with mystical knowledge, but also with high ethical standards. Though Kabbalah is a departure from the past, it succeeds in incorporating earlier Jewish mysticism within its scope.

The sense of the divine realm of the Sefirot as in a constant state of flux that is affected by human activity is an important Kabbalistic perspective. The Bahir introduces this worldview, which becomes a crucial part of much, if not most, Kabbalistic literature.

QUESTION?

What is theurgy?
According to *Merriam-Webster's English Dictionary, theurgy* is the term that refers to the influence that humans have on God. The most significant way in which a person affects God is through the performance of the mitzvot, particularly when done with proper kavana (focus of your consciousness).

The Cosmic Tree and Primordial Human

The major symbols that represent the entire world of the Ten Sefirot appear in Sefer HaBahir. One is the symbol of the inverted tree with its roots above, its body growing downward from the roots. This cosmic vision echoes the image of the Tree of Life in the Garden of Eden, and like the story of Genesis, marks the beginning of the human world that God created from nothingness.

Sefer HaBahir also introduces the image of the primordial human, male and female united, which is the other major symbol of the world of the Sefirot. Sefer HaBahir expresses a belief in reincarnation, which was a belief held by many Kabbalists, some more strongly than others. There is no attempt on the part of the book to explain this beyond pointing to a verse found in Ecclesiastes as support: "A generation passes and a generation comes . . ." (1:4). The Bahir explains that the implication is that this generation had already come. Jewish philosophers of the Middle Ages had emphatically denied belief in reincarnation by the time the Bahir appeared. The author of the Bahir ignores this fact and writes as though the philosophical arguments didn't exist and required no response.

Influence of the Bahir

Sefer HaBahir has exerted an enormous influence over Kabbalistic literature. Hardly a single Kabbalist can be said to be free of its impact. It introduced many of the terms, concepts, symbols, and vocabulary of Kabbalah that became standard from its first appearance onward. Many of the earliest Kabbalists refer back to it and quotations of it appear regularly throughout Kabbalistic literature.

Certain Hebrew terms occur in plural forms though the words themselves refer to a singular entity. *Mayim* means "water." *Shamayim* means "Heaven." A name of God, Elohim, is plural, though it's conjugated in the singular. *Panim*, which usually means "face" or "presence," is also constructed in the plural.

The mystical Midrashic way of looking at Torah begins with Sefer HaBahir. Similar to how the Bahir looks back to earlier mystical works such as Sefer Yetzirah and Hekhalot literature in supporting its own teachings, later

Kabbalistic works looked to Sefer HaBahir as a proof text. The Bahir's impact was most noticeable in the century or two after its appearance, while during that period much Kabbalistic literature was written.

Since the Bahir is not a book with a crystal clear agenda written in a systematic fashion, it enabled it to be adapted by people with different orientations. The most influential Kabbalistic text of all, the Zohar, was clearly itself influenced by Sefer HaBahir in its Midrashic style, its ancient setting, its extensive use of homilies and parables, and its symbolism. In this way the indirect impact of the Bahir was enormous. After the general acceptance of the Zohar among Kabbalists, it dwarfed all other previous texts as the authoritative reference work.

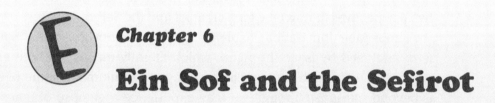

Chapter 6

Ein Sof and the Sefirot

W hat distinguishes Kabbalah from all previous forms of Jewish mysticism is the doctrine of Ein Sof (the Infinite, unknowable divinity) and the Sefirot (the divine emanations). Though Kabbalah is nurtured by earlier forms of Jewish mysticism, the consciousness that characterizes Kabbalah is expressed and mapped through the unique concepts of Ein Sof and the Sefirot.

The Infinite One

Kabbalah embodies two major experiences of Divinity. One is that God is transcendent, eternal, and unchangeable. The other is that God is also deeply personal, in other words, the very same Transcendent One is also dynamic and immanent throughout Creation. Kabbalah depicts these two perspectives through the terms Ein Sof and the Sefirot.

Rabbi Meir Ibn Gabbai explains that we cannot grasp Ein Sof—a term first used by Isaac the Blind, which literally means "without end," or "infinite"—through contemplation or logic. The ultimate nature of God is beyond our grasp, though we may experience a glimpse of that reality and recognize the existence of that which is so far beyond our comprehension. Ein Sof itself is a negative formulation, meaning that there is no end. This is similar to Maimonides' explanation that we can only say what God is not, because God transcends our human ability to define. To define is to limit, whereas God is limitless. The Kabbalists understood that Ein Sof is beyond language and thought, so nothing could actually be said about it.

Sefer Yetzirah, Chapter 1, Mishnah 4, opens with the following: "Ten Sefirot of Nothingness. Ten and not nine, ten and not eleven. Understand with Wisdom [Chokhmah] and be wise with Understanding [Binah]." Rabbi Azriel of Gerona comments on this passage, saying that Ein Sof is not to be counted among the Sefirot (ten and not eleven).

Before the Beginning

Ein Sof precedes all emanation and Creation. Emanation proceeds from Ein Sof and brings forth the world of the Sefirot [*Olam HaSefirot*]. The classic poem and prayer from the eleventh century, "Adon Olam" [meaning simultaneously both "Eternal Lord" and "Lord of the Universe"] attributed to Solomon Ibn Gabirol, contains a number of phrases that capture the sense of Ein Sof: "Adon Olam who ruled before anything was created and after all creation ceases [Adon Olam] alone will rule awesomely . . . without beginning and without end."

Ein Sof is understood as that state of undifferentiated divinity out of which everything emanated. There is no duality in Ein Sof. There is no "personality" in Ein Sof. Ein Sof is absolute being. Since there is no duality and no differentiation, no adjectives can be used to describe Ein Sof. Ultimately everything exists within Ein Sof in some sense.

Divine Will, Creation, and Ein Sof

Many Kabbalists approach the Sefirot, their map of reality, philosophically. A number of questions arose for them in regard to Ein Sof, emanation, and the world of the Sefirot. Why did Ein Sof create the universe? If emanation led to Creation, did this diminish the perfection of Ein Sof?

There is no definitive answer for the question of why Ein Sof created the universe. There were some Kabbalists who saw Creation arising out of God's will, often identifying this will with Keter, generally considered the first Sefira. Will was not attributed to Ein Sof, for no characteristics can be attributed to It. There were different perspectives on this question of "will" and which Sefira was its source.

It is important to remember that Kabbalah has a history, as does Judaism itself. Different Kabbalists have varied perspectives, philosophical orientations, and mystical experiences. Some Kabbalists are more "orthodox" than others, meaning they are more hesitant to introduce a new perspective or one that might appear to conflict with traditional Jewish beliefs and practices.

There Is Only Ein Sof

Ein Sof is not at all diminished by emanation. An analogy to describe the relationship between Ein Sof and emanation likens the relationship to that of a flame that is used to light candles. Though the candles derive their flame from a greater fire, their flame doesn't in any way diminish that original fire. Similarly, Ein Sof is not in any way diminished through the emanation of the Sefirot.

Moshe Cordovero (1522–1570) explained that though the imagery of light was used in regard to Ein Sof, it is important to remember that Ein Sof is not "light," however sublime the light may be, for even light is a physical entity of sorts and Ein Sof is not.

In his book *Elimah Rabbati*, Cordovero gives a classic explanation of Ein Sof in the following passage: "Before all emanation there was only Ein Sof which is all reality. Even after Ein Sof emanated all that exists, there still is only Ein Sof and nothing outside of It. There is no entity without the power of God within it. If that were not the case, you would be setting limits to God and attributing duality, God forbid. God is everything, but not everything is God."

The mystical experience of the oneness of God and of all existence is beyond the ability of language to express. The more philosophically minded Kabbalists attempted to explain their understanding of God and existence with a coherent system of symbols, which is the Sefirot.

The World of the Sefirot

The emanation of the world of the Sefirot provided a framework for explaining how God could be both transcendent and simultaneously immanent in all of Creation. Emanation explained the Kabbalist's experience of existence as overflowing with divinity. This perspective is expressed in the Bible by the prophet Isaiah, who states that "the whole world is filled with God's Glory" (Isaiah 6:3). The Kabbalists interpreted the word glory (Kavod) as another term referring to the tenth Sefira, the Divine Presence (Shekhinah).

The Sefirot provide an explanation of the progression from Absolute, Infinite Divinity (Ein Sof), which transcends this world, to the creation and existence of the physical universe that we inhabit. The Sefirot are the manifestation of the Divine emanated from Ein Sof, which itself is divinity undifferentiated. Their emanation is the beginning of a process that ends in the creation of the physical universe.

Deciphering the Term Sefirot

Kabbalists tried to explain the core meaning of the word Sefira and thereby convey its nature. Sefer HaBahir, the first Kabbalistic text, explains the term by referring to a verse from Psalms: "The Heavens declare [*M'saprim*] the Glory of God" (19:2). The word *M'saprim* has the same root as Sefira. In other words, the Sefirot are the means by which the hidden essence of God, which is concealed in Ein Sof, is manifested. The Sefirot, in this sense, declare the "glory" of God.

Another word sharing the same root as Sefira, *sappir,* is also used to illuminate the term Sefirot. Sappir is a sapphire. The explanation is offered that just as the sappir glows from multiple facets though it is one stone, so the Sefirot, which glow with divine "light" in numerous facets, are also one. The sappir was one of the twelve stones in the breastplate of the high priest.

QUESTION?

Is *Sefira* a Hebrew word or a Greek word?
The word Sefira does not derive from a similar-sounding Greek word, *sphaira,* that means "sphere." Its construction is a Hebrew one. On the other hand the word *gematria*, which refers to the numerical value of letters, is a word directly borrowed from Greek.

From Ein Sof to the Physical Universe

Within the world of the Sefirot itself, there are various patterns and distinctions that are important. Each Sefira, as it "descends" from Ein Sof, contains less divine energy. The *Or Ein Sof,* the infinite divine "light," is increasingly diminished. In other words, each upper Sefira contains all the lower ones within it and each successive Sefira contains all the upper ones within it, but in a diluted form.

Symbols of the Sefirot

Those Kabbalists who focused on the world of the Sefirot developed a vast and elaborate symbolic system. This system is found throughout the Theosophical Kabbalah with some variation, but mostly with great consistency (see Chapter 11 for more information on Theosophical Kabbalah). While things changed dramatically with the emergence of Isaac Luria's Kabbalistic system, until then the way in which the Sefirot were discussed was quite uniform for hundreds of years.

The Ten Sefirot in descending order in their emanation from Ein Sof are as follows:

- *Keter* (crown)
- *Chokhmah* (wisdom)
- *Binah* (understanding)
- *Hesed* (loving kindness) or *Gedulah* (greatness)
- *Gevurah* (power) or *Din* (judgment)
- *Tiferet* (beauty) or *Rakhamim* (compassion/mercy)
- *Netzakh* (eternity and/or victory)
- *Hod* (splendor)
- *Yesod* (foundation)
- *Malkhut* (Kingdom) or *Shekhinah* (Divine Presence)

Differing Configurations of the Sefirot

The dynamics of the Sefirot are divided and explained in a number of different ways. One way is to organize them into three columns: right, left, and center. The right has the essence of Hesed and is seen as overflowing with love. The left has the essence of power (Gevurah) and judgment (Din). These two parts require each other. Without boundaries, loving kindness is overwhelming and knows no limits. On the other hand, nothing can withstand pure judgment. Existence requires both, one tempering the other. The middle column is the synthesis of these two forces. The synthesis of Hesed and Gevurah is Tiferet (beauty), which is also known as *Rakhamim* (compassion/mercy). There is a Midrash that says that many universes were created before the one in which we exist. The previous ones could not survive because the perfect balance between Din and Hesed had not yet been reached.

The Ten Sefirot

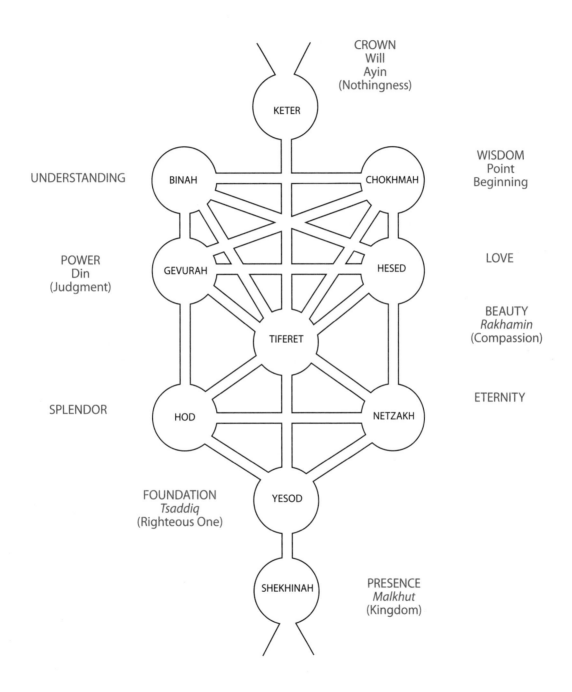

CROWN
Will
Ayin
(Nothingness)

KETER

WISDOM
Point
Beginning

UNDERSTANDING

BINAH

CHOKHMAH

POWER
Din
(Judgment)

GEVURAH

HESED

LOVE

BEAUTY
Rakhamin
(Compassion)

TIFERET

SPLENDOR

HOD

NETZAKH

ETERNITY

FOUNDATION
Tsaddiq
(Righteous One)

YESOD

SHEKHINAH

PRESENCE
Malkhut
(Kingdom)

Another way of dividing the Sefirot is into three sets of three triangles. The first set is Keter, Chokhmah, and Binah, which are the beginnings of emanation. The next three are Hesed, Gevurah, and Tiferet. The last three are Netzakh, Hod, and Yesod, with all of them culminating in Shekhinah, which is the gate through which Shefa (divine energy) emanates into the physical universe.

The lower seven Sefirot are often separated from the upper three. The lower seven are sometimes referred to as "the Building" (*Binyan* in Hebrew). These seven also represent the primordial days of Creation as described in Genesis. Each Sefira represents another day of Creation. The seventh day, Shabbat, the holiest day of the week, coincides with Shekhinah, the feminine Divine Presence, the Sefira closest and most accessible to the physical universe.

Through the observance of Shabbat, which is a day devoted more to "being" than to "doing," we may draw closer to the Divine Presence, the Shekhinah. Shabbat was also called *Shabbat HaMalka,* the Sabbath Queen, or the "Bride" which were direct references to its connection with the Shekhinah.

YHVH and the World of the Sefirot

The entire world of the Sefirot was seen as symbolized in God's explicit name, YHVH. The *yud,* which begins the name, is the smallest letter in the alphabet and represents Chokhmah (wisdom), the flash of insight. Chokhmah is nourished in the "womb" of Binah, which is a growth of comprehension that represents the nurtured flash of insight. Binah, the supernal Mother, is symbolized by the first *hey* in YHVH. Hey is the letter that ends most feminine singular words in Hebrew. The *vav,* which is next in the Name, represents the next six Sefirot. Vav has the gematria of six. Finally, the last *hey* in YHVH symbolizes Shekhinah, the other Mother/Bride/Queen that gives birth to the created universe by bringing forth Shefa.

In two Biblical passages (Psalm 111:10 and Proverbs 4:7) the phrase "*reshit chokhmah*" is found. Literally, it means "the beginning of wisdom," however the Kabbalists interpreted it as reshit *is* chokhmah. This is a viable reading because the word "is" essentially doesn't exist in Hebrew but is understood from the context of a phrase. Therefore both readings of reshit chokhmah are possible.

Since Chokhmah is called *reshit* (beginning), it is appropriate that YHVH begins with the *yud* that symbolizes Chokhmah, but what happened to Keter (crown) in this depiction? The *yud* is usually printed with a tiny tip at its top pointing upward. This tip, which "crowns" the *yud*, symbolizes, or points toward, Keter.

QUESTION?

Where do the names for the Sefirot come from?
A number of the names of the Sefirot come from a verse in the Bible, in Chronicles I: "Yours, YHVH, is the Greatness [Gedulah] and the Power [Gevurah] and the Beauty [Tiferet] and the Victory/Eternity [Netzakh] and the Splendor [Hod] for all that is in Heaven and on the earth, Yours is the Kingdom" (29:11).

The Cosmic Tree

The entire world of the Sefirot is often configured in two ways: the tree and Adam Kadmon, the primordial human. The symbol of the tree, which appears in Sefer HaBahir, is inverted (its roots are above and its branches are at the bottom). The "roots" of the tree, of course, are the highest Sefirot, which ultimately emanate from Ein Sof.

Pardes and the Garden of Eden

The symbol of the tree carries with it an association with Pardes, the orchard, which is an image used to convey mystical experience and knowledge. We also make the connection with the two trees specified in the Genesis story of the Garden of Eden, the Tree of Life and the Tree of Knowledge of good and evil. The Tree of Life itself is associated with the Sefirot of

Tiferet (beauty) or Yesod (foundation), and the Tree of Knowledge is connected to Shekhinah (the Divine Presence).

FACT

There are four New Years in the Jewish calendar. The most familiar is Rosh Hashanah, occurring in September or October, which commemorates Creation. The fifteenth day of the Hebrew month of *Sh'vat* (called *Tu B'Sh'vat*) is the New Year for trees, which became an important holiday for Kabbalists because of the tree symbol in the Sefirot.

Kelipot: Blocking Divine Energy

The bark of the tree is its *kelipah*, meaning the outer covering that blocks the divine "light" from coming through. The idea of kelipot (plural of kelipah) interfering with the flow of divine energy is crucial in the Kabbalistic worldview. There were divergent views concerning the kelipot. Some Kabbalists spoke of ten kelipot, while others believed there were four, which they derived from the opening passage of Ezekiel's vision (1:4). Three of the four kelipot are essentially evil, but the fourth has the potential to become good or evil depending on our behavior. This is comparable to the coexistence of good and evil in the Tree of Knowledge.

The Primordial Human: Adam Kadmon

The other dominant symbol for the world of the Sefirot is that of the primordial human, Adam Kadmon, which is male and female together in one being. In this symbolic map of the Sefirot, each Sefira represents a different part of the body. The first three Sefirot are the head, Hesed is the right arm, and Gevurah is the left. Tiferet is the torso, Netzakh the right leg, and Hod is the left leg. Yesod is the male sexual organ, Malkhut, the female.

Genesis (1:27) describes human beings as being created in the image of God. It is not characteristic of the Bible to make a statement and then elaborate upon it, and because of this lack of explanation, commentaries on the meaning of this phrase are numerous. For the Kabbalists, the Adam Kadmon image of the world of the Sefirot is the true explanation.

Anthropomorphism and Metaphors for God

Though the Bible is full of humanlike depictions such as the "hand" or "voice" of God, Judaism generally insists that God is a purely "spiritual" being and has no physical characteristics. This is emphasized by Maimonides in his Thirteen Principles of Faith, in which he insists that all such physical descriptions are metaphorical. The Talmud says that "[t]he Torah spoke in the language of humans" (Tractate Brakhot 31a), meaning in a manner that people could understand. A line from Isaiah, "To whom can you compare God?" (40:25), is often used as proof that God is a being of a totally different nature than anything else in existence.

Different names of God are associated with different Sefirot. The name *Ehyeh* is associated with Keter; the name *Adonai* (as it is actually spelled *aleph, dalet, nun, yud*), which literally means "my Lord," with Shekhinah; and the name YHVH with all of the Sefirot together.

The Kabbalists are quick to emphasize and re-emphasize that though they use very visual, physical language to refer to God, they are speaking symbolically and God is incorporeal, meaning that God has no physical form. At the same time this visual language enables the Kabbalists to write in a way that is much less abstract than it might otherwise be. This is also true of the Bible. The Bible retains a powerful emotional impact partially because it communicates its lessons through stories and it uses very human language that can touch the reader in a way that abstract thought is incapable of.

Created in God's "Image"

The image of Adam Kadmon makes every human being a symbol of Divinity. All of our actions suddenly can be seen as reflecting God's Presence in the world. Every other person that we look at becomes not only a human being, but simultaneously a symbol of the world of the Sefirot, and the phrase "in my flesh I will see God" (Job 19:26) takes on a new relevance.

The concept of kelipot acquires psychological and emotional ramifications. We can understand our own internal blocks as kelipot, impediments to our drawing close to God and to our own divine nature. Though the Kabbalists are very careful to stress that God is utterly spiritual, the image of Adam Kadmon brings new meaning to the phrase that humans are created in God's image.

Shiur Komah

Shiur Komah, a text detailing the measurement of God's stature, was one of the earliest forms of Jewish mysticism. The descriptions it presented of the Divine body were so vast in their dimensions that they seem to emphasize the absurdity of physical descriptions of God. Those who opposed mysticism in the Jewish tradition were often extremely critical of this work. On the other hand, Kabbalists considered it one of the deepest secrets of mystical thought and experience. Even though the term *Shiur Komah* continues to be used, its meaning evolved over the centuries. The image of Adam Kadmon as a symbol of the world of the Sefirot fits the evolved meaning of Shiur Komah.

So Above, So Below

Kabbalists read the Torah on many levels. The events described on the literal level of the text are understood as also referring to what was occurring in the divine realms and between humans and the Divine. Kabbalists interpret the people in the biblical narratives as symbols of other realms of reality. Abraham, for example, is not solely the human being depicted in Genesis, but is also representative of the Sefira of Hesed. Events like the battle with Amalek, a tribe that attacked the Jewish women and children from behind immediately upon the Exodus from Egypt, are symbolic of the cosmic struggle between good and evil.

ALERT!

For a Kabbalist, verses in the Torah can have many meanings simultaneously. In the *sod* ("Secret," mystical) level of the text, for example, one interpretation does not exclude others, even if they appear to be quite different. The literal reading of Scripture, though never negated, often takes a back seat to the mystical understanding, which is seen as "the way of truth."

Kabbalists also view Creation from a symbolic perspective, understanding the seven days of Creation as the emanation of the last seven Sefirot, which are called *Binyan* (the building). Shabbat, the seventh day of the week, is the day associated with Shekhinah. Kabbalists see Shabbat as the day when the Divine Presence is most accessible and the day humans exist on a higher spiritual level. All human activity, however mundane it may appear on the surface, becomes cosmically significant in the Kabbalistic worldview, as the divine energy (Shefa) is affected by our every action. This injected enormous vitality into traditional Jewish life.

Chapter 7

The Book of Enlightenment: Zohar

In the 1280s in Castile, Spain, the most influential Kabbalistic text of all was written. This is the Book of Enlightenment, Sefer HaZohar. At first it was circulated among Kabbalists in short fragments, having a great impact but only among a very limited group of mystics. It took about two centuries for it to achieve the status that it eventually attained. The Zohar is the only text besides the Bible and the Talmud ever to be considered a canonical book in the Jewish tradition.

Who Wrote the Zohar?

This question has been an issue since the first fragments of the Zohar began to circulate among Kabbalists. There are a few complicating factors in identifying the authentic authorship of the book. First of all, the Zohar has a number of different components. Most of the Zohar is written in Aramaic, but what is believed to be the earliest part, the Midrash HaNe'elam (the Hidden Midrash), is written largely in Hebrew. The Aramaic that is used in the bulk of the Zohar is an Aramaic likely learned from reading other texts, as it does not appear to be the author's spoken language. From its earliest stages people questioned the presumed authorship of Shimon bar Yokhai, though most Kabbalists who accepted the work over the centuries did not. The Zohar was circulated by Rabbi Moshe de Leon, a Kabbalist who lived in Spain from about 1240 to 1305. He claimed that this ancient manuscript had come into his hands having found its way to Spain from the Holy Land.

FACT

Shimon bar Yokhai was a tanna (a Rabbi of the Mishnah) who lived during the second century c.e. He was a disciple of Rabbi Akiva. Bar Yokhai strongly opposed the Roman occupation, and as a result he was sentenced to death. He survived by living in a cave for twelve years, the time during which legend says he composed the Zohar.

Shimon bar Yokhai

Many believe that the Zohar is an ancient text written by Shimon bar Yokhai, whose spoken language was Aramaic. The Aramaic of the Zohar, however, contains numerous grammatical mistakes, terms that are clearly translations from Medieval Hebrew, philosophical terms that were coined in the Middle Ages, and other elements that would never characterize something written by an authentic Aramaic speaker such as Shimon bar Yokhai.

The Land of Israel, where Shimon bar Yokhai lived and which is the landscape regularly depicted in the pages of the Zohar, is described with geographical errors that a native inhabitant would not make. However, all of these characteristics make sense if this was the imaginative setting of a work written in late-thirteenth-century Spain. All modern nonorthodox scholars believe this to be the case. Orthodox believers, however, maintain that Shimon bar Yokhai is the author of the Zohar.

Isaac of Acco and the Zohar

In 1291 the Mamluks, a military class of Muslims that held much power in the Middle East, massacred most of the Jews and Christians living in Acco (or Acre), Israel. Among the few who escaped was a Kabbalist who came to be known as Isaac of Acco. He was one of the more influential Kabbalists of the fourteenth century.

From Acco, Isaac fled to Italy and eventually went to Spain, having heard of this ancient Kabbalistic text from the Land of Israel. He met Moshe de Leon, who promised to show him the original manuscript when Isaac came to visit him, but Moshe died on his way home. When Isaac arrived in Spain, Moshe's widow told him that there was no ancient manuscript, but that Moshe wrote the work himself. These details are from parts of Isaac's diary that have survived.

Many modern scholars believe that Moshe de Leon was the actual author of the Zohar, but the most recent research has veered toward the conclusion that Moshe was not the sole author. Much of the Zohar revolves around a group of ten Kabbalists, with Shimon bar Yokhai at the center. The latest theory is that a number of Kabbalists who studied together, much like the Kabbalists depicted in the book itself, all contributed to the composition of the Zohar, with Moshe de Leon as the main author.

The term *Zohar* appears in a passage in the biblical Book of Daniel: "The enlightened will shine like the illumination [Zohar] of the firmament" (12:3). This passage is quoted in the introduction to the first volume of the Zohar. *Zohar* appears one more time in the Bible in Ezekiel (8:2), in the description of one of Ezekiel's visions of God.

Pseudepigraphy (writing under a false name or ascribing authorship falsely) is not unprecedented in spiritual writings and could possibly be attributed to a number of different factors. The author may not want to draw attention to himself both out of humility and a sense of being a mere vessel receiving these insights from another source. The author might even believe himself to be the reincarnation of the rabbi in whose name he is writing. Remember that in Sefer HaBahir, which greatly influenced the Zohar, reincarnation was an accepted belief.

The Structure of the Zohar

The Zohar is largely written as a mystical Midrash. As the *Khevraya* (the Kabbalistic companions) wander the countryside of the Land of Israel, they discuss secrets of the Torah. The Midrashic style consists of opening the discussion by taking a verse of Scripture and essentially finding new insight in it. Usually this process occurs, as in the case of traditional Midrashim, by adding other verses that elucidate the original verse. The author or authors of the Zohar exhibit a remarkable ability to find profundity in even seemingly mundane sections of Scripture.

The Zohar itself has quite a number of sections. There is the main body of the Zohar, which is organized around the weekly Torah portions. Traditionally the Zohar is published in three large volumes comprising approximately 2,000 folio pages. The first volume covers Genesis; the second volume is devoted to Exodus; and the third deals with Leviticus, Numbers, and Deuteronomy. Interspersed within these three volumes, however, are smaller sections. Among these we find:

- **Sifra D'Tzeniuta** (The Book of Concealment)
- **Idra Rabba** and **Idra Zuta**
  (The Great Chamber and the Small Chamber)
- **Raza D'Razin** (The Secret of Secrets)
- **Midrash HaNe'elam** (The Hidden Midrash)
- **Raya Mehemna** (The Faithful Shepherd)
- **Sitre Otiyot** (The Secrets of the Letters)

In addition to these sections are a number of others that are significantly smaller and less well known.

The *Sifra D'Tzeniuta* is a short section that provides Kabbalistic commentary on the first weekly Torah portion, Bereshit (which is essentially the first six chapters of Genesis). In the sections *Idra Rabba* and *Idra Zuta*, Shimon bar Yokhai assembles his disciples for the purpose of revealing mystical secrets to them. There is a climax in each section, as the overwhelming ecstasy of consciousness leads to the death of three disciples in Idra Rabba, and Rabbi Shimon himself dies in *Idra Zuta*.

FACT

The biblical book the Song of Songs, on the surface a collection of love poems, was in ancient times interpreted as a metaphor for the relationship between God and the people of Israel. Despite the fact that parts of the book are quite erotic, Rabbi Akiva said that while all the books of the Bible are holy, the Song of Songs is the Holy of Holies.

The segment of the Zohar entitled *Raza D'Razin* contains sections on physiognomy (discerning someone's character through the study of their face) and chiromancy (analyzing someone on the basis of their palm). Midrash *HaNe'elam* largely focuses on Creation, the soul, emanation, and the nature of God. Raya Mehemna concentrates on the purpose of the mitzvot. Sitre Otiyot speaks about the secrets of the letters that comprise God's name.

There are two other volumes of Zoharic literature in addition to the traditional three bound volumes. One is called *Zohar Chadash,* literally "the New Zohar," which is a collection of Zohar writings from manuscripts assembled after the printing of the original volumes, but written at the same time as the teachings in the standard three volumes. The other is *Tikkunei Zohar,* which scholars believe was written in the early 1300s in imitation of the style of the Zohar. The contents consist of basically seventy explanations of the first word of the Torah, *bereshit* (in the Beginning). This is a Kabbalistic offshoot of the rabbinic statement (in the Midrash *Bemidbar Rabba* 13) that there are seventy faces to the Torah.

Symbolism of the Zohar

There are a number of factors that contribute to the difficulty of reading the Zohar, but the greatest is the abundance of symbolism. Once you have a handle on the symbolic vocabulary, the Zohar becomes considerably more accessible. The difficulties in comprehending the text led to a significant number of commentaries trying to explain and decode it. The two most important are *Ketem Paz* (Fine Gold) by Shimon Lavi of Tripoli from circa 1570, and *Or HaKhammah* (The Light of the Sun), edited by Abraham Azulai from 1619. Or HaKhammah combines commentaries from Moshe Cordovero; Chaim Vital, from before he studied with Isaac Luria; and Abraham Galante, who studied with Cordovero. Many Zohar commentaries superimpose the perspective of Isaac Luria's teachings, which therefore do not give an accurate sense of what the Zohar itself said. (Issac Luria is discussed in detail in Chapter 13.)

There are three key expressions from Zoharic literature that characterize its understanding and experience of God and which were regularly quoted in later Kabbalistic and Hasidic texts: *"leit atar panui minay"* (there is no place absent of God); God is *"sovev kol almin"* (encompassing all universes); and *"m'malei kol almin"* (filling all universes).

Though the Zohar repeatedly addresses the inner workings of God, it hardly uses the word Sefirot. The Sefirot are generally referred to symbolically. Each Sefira has a number of different terms that are used to refer to it, some Sefirot having more symbols than others. Keter (crown), the first Sefira, is referred to as *Ayin* (nothingness) and *will*. Keter is not spoken of often. Chokhmah (wisdom), the second Sefira, is spoken of considerably more. Chokhmah is also referred to as *reshit* (beginning) and as *the primordial point*. It is also the Supernal Father. Binah (understanding) is the Supernal Mother, womb, and Hekhal (palace). In the image of the primordial human (Adam Kadmon), the first three Sefirot are the head, with Keter as the top of the head or above it as, literally, a crown.

Pronouns for the Sefirot

Another term used to refer to Binah, the Supernal Mother, is *mi* (spelled in Hebrew *mem, yud*), which means "who"—implying a level beyond our ability to truly know. Shekhinah, the tenth Sefira, the closest to Creation, is called Queen and Mother among other feminine images. Shekhinah is also referred to as *yam*, which means "sea"—the great sea into which all of the divine energy flows. There is an intimate connection between Binah and Shekhinah, which is embedded in words that symbolize them. Yam, which symbolizes Shekhinah, is spelled *yud, mem*, the same letters as *mi* (which represents Binah), but in reverse order.

Different pronouns refer to different Sefirot. *Hu*, which means "he," refers to Keter. *Ata* (you) refers to the sixth and central Sefira, Tiferet (beauty), which is also called *Rakhamim* (compassion), the Blessed Holy One (*Kudshah Brich Hu* in Aramaic and *HaKadosh Baruch Hu* in Hebrew), Heaven, sun, and king among other things. *Ani* (I) is the pronoun that refers to Shekhinah. Ani is spelled *aleph, nun, yud*, the very same letters as one of the words for Keter, *Ayin* (nothingness).

ALERT!

Sefer Yetzirah, the source of the term Sefira, states in Chapter 1, Mishnah 7: "Ten Sefirot of Nothingness, their end embedded in their beginning and their beginning in their end like a flame bound to a burning ember as the Lord is the only One and has no duality."

Though there are ten Sefirot, because of Judaism's monotheism, Kabbalists emphatically insist that they are all really one. In other words, each of the Ten Sefirot contains the others within it, but one *middah* (quality), or *panim* (face), is more dominant in each particular Sefira.

Loving Kindness (Hesed) and Power (Gevurah)

The fourth Sefira, Hesed (loving kindness, mercy), follows Keter, Chokhmah, and Binah. Hesed in certain texts is referred to as Gedulah (greatness). In the Zohar, Hesed also represents grace, the right arm of

Adam Kadmon, and is represented by the colors white and silver. Hesed is also symbolized by the biblical figure Abraham.

Abraham fathered Isaac, so Isaac in turn symbolizes the fifth and next Sefira, Gevurah (power). It is the left arm of Adam Kadmon, and is represented by the color red. In the spiritual plane of the four elements, Gevurah is fire and Hesed is water.

Hesed and Gevurah find balance in the Zohar in the next Sefira, Tiferet, which is symbolized by two biblical figures: Jacob (Isaac's son and successor) and Moses. Tiferet is represented by the color green and is also related to Shamayim (the Heavens in the biblical Creation narrative) and the written Torah.

The Last Four Sefirot

The next two Sefirot, Netzakh (eternity and/or victory) and Hod (splendor), are addressed less often in the Zohar. They represent the right and left leg of Adam Kadmon.

The ninth Sefira, Yesod (foundation), is also called *Tzaddik* (the righteous one), and *brit* (covenant). It is symbolized in the Zohar by the male sexual organ of Adam Kadmon and is represented by Joseph who, in Kabbalistic literature, represents sexual purity because he resists the insistent advances of Potiphar's wife (Genesis 39).

In Exodus 3:13 Moses says, "'I will come to the children of Israel and I will say to them: "the God of your ancestors sent me to you," and they will say to me, "what's His name?" what will I say to them?' And God said to Moses: *Ehyeh Asher Ehyeh* [I will be Who I will be], say this to the children of Israel, Ehyeh sent me to you" (3:14).

The tenth Sefira, Shekhinah (Divine Presence), receives probably the most elaborate attention in the Zohar. Shekhinah is also known as *Malkhut* (kingdom), and here again are the images of royalty uniting Keter (crown) with Shekhinah. Shekhinah is also *Knesset Yisrael* (the Assembly of Israel), moon, earth, and the oral Torah. In the Zohar, two biblical figures are particularly associated with her: King David (traditionally the paradigm of the king and from whose line the Messiah will someday come), and Rachel, who mourns for her children (that is, the Jewish people) in exile (Jeremiah 31:14).

How the Zohar Addresses Torah

For the Zohar every word in the Torah is meaningful on many levels. On the level of sod (secret, mystical) itself, there are multiple valid readings of the same word, phrase, or passage. A section in the Zohar depicts this attitude explicitly: "Rabbi Shimon said: woe to the person who says that the Torah comes to present worldly stories and mundane matters . . . all the words of the Torah are sublime words and unfathomable secrets" (vol. 3, 152a).

The Zohar continues by decribing that the Torah's appearance as merely a collection of stories is necessary so that the world can endure the power of the Torah. The author(s) of the Zohar explains this, writing that "since the Torah descended into this world, if it didn't dress itself in the garments of this world, the world would not be able to endure. Therefore, this story of the Torah is the garment of the Torah. Whoever thinks that the garment is the true Torah, his spirit will deflate and he will not partake of the world to come. . . . There is a garment apparent to everyone and fools who see a person with beautiful clothing and look no further, thinking the clothing is the body and the body is the soul. Similarly the Torah has a body which are the Mitzvot of the Torah. . . . [T]his body is clothed in the garments which are the stories of this world. Fools of the world only look at that garment which is the story of the Torah and know nothing beyond, and don't look at what lies beneath the garment. Those who know more don't look at the garment, but at the body beneath that garment" (vol. 3, 152a).

ALERT!

The peak of the Zohar's influence in Jewish life was from the 1500s through the 1700s. In the seventeenth and eighteenth centuries, some claimed that reciting the Zohar even without comprehending the words was still beneficial to the soul.

The Creation of Elohim

The first words of the Torah engendered an enormous volume of commentaries of all kinds. The poetic majesty and mystery of the Creation story inspired innumerable rabbis, Kabbalists, and philosophers alike. Part of the power of the Zohar is its reinterpretation of so much of Torah, injecting its own poetry into its refashioning of sacred myth.

In the Zohar, Rabbi Yudai asks, "What is Bereshit?" The answer in the Zohar is that bereshit means "with Chokhmah [the second Sefira, Wisdom], this Wisdom upon which the world stands in order to enter into the concealed sublime secrets. Here six grand extremities [the Sefirot from Hesed to Yesod] were engraved from which everything emerged" (vol. 1, 3b).

FACT

In the morning daily prayer service we find in the *siddur* (prayer book) the following: "The One who illuminates the earth and all that dwell upon her and in goodness renews every day perpetually the work of creation. How great are your works, YHVH, all of them are made with Chokhmah [Wisdom]."

The commentary in the Zohar goes on to explain that "from them six springs and rivers were fashioned to flow into the great sea [Shekhinah]. This is the meaning of Bereshit. [Meaning that if you divide the word in half, the first half means "he created" and the second half means "six" in Aramaic.] From here they were created. Who [Mi] created them? The unmentioned One, the concealed One, the Unknown."

Already in one of the Aramaic translations of the Torah, Targum Yerushalmi, the word *bereshit* (in the beginning) is translated as "with wisdom," though this is not referring to the Kabbalistic Sefira Chokhmah. Here in the Zohar, we see the Creation of the physical universe described in Genesis as referring simultaneously to a parallel process of emanation of one Sefira from the one above it.

In Italy in the mid-sixteenth century, there was controversy over whether or not to print the Zohar. Many rabbis felt that most people would misunderstand it. Those in favor of publishing it cited the Zohar itself, which states that through study of the Zohar the people would merit redemption. The text was ultimately printed around 1560 in both Mantua and Cremona.

Reinterpreting Genesis from Another Angle

Another rereading of bereshit from the introduction in volume 1 of the Zohar appears as follows: "Bereshit [meaning, *He*] created six. From one end of the Heavens to the other end of the Heavens, six 'sides' that expanded from the sublime secret in an expansion [He] created from the core of the first point [Chokhmah]." This commentary agrees with the previous interpretation, in which God created all of the other Sefirot from a central Sefira, which symbolized divine wisdom.

Metaphors and Symbols

It is important to remember that these rereadings of the Torah, though they can be deciphered by explaining which Sefirot are being referred to, are not meant as intellectual exercises. The Zohar is trying to articulate an experience of God's Presence using the metaphorical language of these symbols. There is always a danger of the metaphors being taken too literally and the words of the Zohar being reduced and deflated into two-dimensional symbols instead of a living relationship to the all-encompassing, all-pervading Divinity.

FACT

The great Hasidic master, Pinchas of Koretz (1726–1791), thanked God that he was born after the Zohar was revealed, for the Zohar kept him a Jew. The Ba'al Shem Tov (1700–1760), the founder of Hasidism, was quoted as saying that when he opens the Zohar he perceives the entire world.

In addition to using symbolic language in an attempt to articulate the event of Creation, the author(s) of the Zohar used symbolism to explain the name *Elohim* that refers to God. In volume 1, the text explains that "at the instant that the Concealed of the Concealed sought to be revealed It first made One Point [Chokhmah] which arose as Thought. . . . It . . . etched into the Hidden Holy Light . . . the fathomless structure that emanates from the depth of Thought and is called "Mi" [Who], the inception of the structure. It [mi] sought to be revealed and to be called by a name and clothed Itself in the garment of illuminating Glory and created Ayleh" (2a). Ayleh, spelled *aleph, lamed, hey*, literally means "these." "These" refers to the Sefirot that could be spoken of, the seven lower Sefirot that parallel the seven days of Creation.

The Zohar continues, explaining that "Ayleh ascended uniting with these [the letters *mem, yud*, spelling "mi"] and were completed in the name Elohim [the letters *aleph, lamed, hey, yud, mem*]. . . . Since Mi united with Ayleh, It [Elohim] remains a unified name eternally, and through this secret the universe exists."

Sexual Symbolism of Divine Unity

The unification of the world of the Sefirot is generally described in the Zohar through love imagery and erotic imagery. Shir HaShirim (the Song of Songs) is a frequent source of biblical quotations in the Zohar because of all the books of the Bible, it alone is full of this erotic imagery.

Shefa is a central term in Kabbalah and can mean a number of things. You can think of it as divine energy, generally depicted by images of light, water, and human seed. Shefa enters Shekhinah through its union with Tiferet by way of Yesod to continually sustain Creation.

Much attention is given to Shekhinah who is in exile from the rest of the body of the Sefirot. It is our task as humans through our consciousness, behavior, and devotion to reunify the upper worlds, specifically through the union of Shekhinah (the Queen, the bride) with her king/groom (Tiferet, or *Kudshah Brikh Hu*, the Holy Blessed One). In the Sefirotic image metaphor of Adam Kadmon (the primordial human), Yesod is represented as the male genitals and Shekhinah as the female.

A good example of this is found in a passage in volume 3 of the Zohar, which states: "Come and see, it is written [Genesis 2:10] 'And a river went out from Eden to water the garden.' This river overflows its banks at the moment that Eden mates with it in perfect [sexual] union . . . and they're drenched in desire and don't separate from one another. . . . This is the foundation [Yesod] that brings forth blessings, in order that the holy King unites with the Queen whereupon blessings are bestowed upon all the worlds, and above and below are blessed" (61b–62a).

Beyond the lush imagery in this description of harmony in God and in Creation, the standard symbolism is that of Binah as the mother, Chokhmah as the father, Tiferet as the son and king, and Shekhinah as the queen. The passage also alludes to the human role in the harmony of the divine world, which is to facilitate the unification of the Sefirot through our practice and fulfillment of the mitzvot.

The Problem of Evil: Sitra Akhra

From time immemorial, people have pondered the reason for the existence of evil in the world. The question attracted considerable attention among the philosophers of the Middle Ages and also among Kabbalists. It preoccupies the biblical Book of Job, in which God punishes the faithful and good Job by killing his family, livestock, and servants, in order to test Job's loyalty to his Lord. It is clear to most people that some innocent and very good people suffer unjustly and some people who are not good still manage to thrive. When religious thinkers believe that God is perfect and oversees the world, the existence of evil presents a problem.

Some philosophers deal with the issue through denying the existence of evil. They claim that what appears to be evil in our eyes actually is good and that we would realize that if we could see the larger picture. Others say that human beings need free will and our will would not be free if there were no possibility for doing evil.

The Zohar does not deny the existence of evil. It generally perceives the world as under the influence of God's goodness and other aberrant forces that create evil. These other forces are called *Sitra Akhra* (literally "the other side). Sitra Akhra enters the world out of an imbalance created by too much Din (divine judgment) as a result of human behavior.

FACT

In Pirkei Avot, it reads: "The world stands upon three things: The Torah, Worship, and deeds of Loving-kindness" (1:2). The Zohar adds: "The Torah—this is Jacob, Worship—this is Isaac, and deeds of loving-kindness are Abraham. These three things are the three sublime pillars" (vol. 1, 146b).

The world of the Sitra Akhra parallels the world of the Sefirot—instead of being made up of divine emanations often symbolized by light, the world of the Sitra Akhra is a world of dark emanations. There are ten Sefirot of impurity that are arranged in the form of an evil human as opposed to the perfection of Adam Kadmon. Another element related to the Sitra Akhra is the term *kelipah*. A kelipah is an outer covering or layer, a force that covers and blocks our awareness of God's will and presence. The kelipah (or kelipot in the plural) prevent the Shefa (divine energy) from flowing, obstructing our natural desire to adhere to God's commandments and draws us toward temptation. The Zohar indicates that in the world to come, the messianic era, all kelipot will disappear, the Sitra Akhra will have no place, and there will be perfect harmony with the divine energy flowing uninterrupted.

Chapter 8

Divine Immanence: The Shekhinah

The Shekhinah is one of the most striking components of Kabbalah. Though Jewish mysticism has a long history from biblical times through the era of the Second Temple and the Merkavah and Hekhalot traditions, the Kabbalistic understanding of the Shekhinah is a new presence in this literature. Prior to Kabbalah, there was never a feminine image of divinity in the Jewish tradition. The Shekhinah has been a central component of the Kabbalistic worldview since its inception.

Evolution of the Term

Shekhinah is a common term in rabbinic literature beginning with the Talmud, but its meaning is significantly different from what it came to signify in Kabbalah. Though the word Shekhinah never appears in the Bible, its root (which consists of the letters *shin, kaf, nun*) occurs with relative frequency.

The root of Shekhinah means "to dwell." The Kabbalists interpreted biblical phrases that included this root in light of their novel understanding of the word. At times these interpretations of biblical phrases offer insight into the Kabbalistic notion of Shekhinah.

FACT

"Let them make Me a sanctuary and I will dwell [*V'Shakhanti*] among them" (Exodus 25:8). This use of the same root as the word Shekhinah conveys the basic sense of God's Presence. This sanctuary became the tabernacle where the Torah and tablets of the Ten Commandments were kept. The word for tabernacle shares the same root, and is called the Mishkan.

Biblical Foreshadowings of the Shekhinah

A passage in the Book of Exodus relates to ways in which the Shekhinah will be described and understood in time: "A cloud covered the Tent of Meeting and the Glory of YHVH filled the Tabernacle. Moses was not able to enter the Tent of Meeting because the cloud dwelled [*shakhan*] upon it and the Glory [Kavod] of YHVH filled the Tabernacle [Mishkan]" (40:34–35). The "Tent of Meeting" was the place in which Moses would communicate with God during the forty-year journey through the desert on the way to the Holy Land. In addition to the words for *tabernacle* and *dwell* sharing the root of the word Shekhinah and referring to the Presence of God, the word *kavod* (Glory) mentioned in these verses also became a word referring to the Shekhinah.

Zion

Zion is the mountain upon which the First and Second Temples were built in Jerusalem. Zion, therefore, became a symbol of Jerusalem and, in turn, a symbol for all of the land of Israel. Since Zion was the location of the Temple where the tabernacle was housed, it was also seen as the most concentrated sacred space in which the Divine Presence could be sensed. A Psalm refers to "this Mount Zion, in which you have dwelled [Shakhanta]" (74:2). Both Zion and Jerusalem came to be depicted as the Mother of Israel and, therefore, they also became part of the imagery of the Shekhinah over time.

The Book of Proverbs speaks of wisdom as an entity in itself that pre-dated the creation of the universe. In an early Midrash, wisdom (Chokhmah) becomes synonymous with Torah, and God looks into the Torah in order to create the universe. The Torah is seen as predating Creation and, in Kabbalah, Shekhinah becomes symbolic of the oral Torah.

The Feminine in the Divine

In Kabbalah, the Shekhinah emerges as a feminine face of Divinity. Grammatically, the word Shekhinah is feminine, as are other words associated with the feminine face of the Divine, such as Knesset Yisrael (Assembly/Community of Israel), Malkhut (kingship/kingdom/royalty), and Torah (as in the "oral Torah"; that is, *Torah She'b'al Peh*).

FACT

The major Jewish philosophers before the emergence of Kabbalah (and contemporary with it) described God as unchangeable. It was the world that changed, but God, from a philosophical point of view, did not. The biblical image of God, however, had much more "personality." In Kabbalistic works, Ein Sof is the unchanging aspect of Divinity, while the Sefirot embody the biblical God imagery.

Shekhinah is not the only feminine aspect of Divinity, but it is the one most focused on, as the Shekhinah is the Sefira closest to Creation (as the tenth and last Sefira). The Shekhinah is the gateway to the divine level of reality. The entire collection of verses and phrases in the Bible, Talmud, and Midrashim that have central elements that are grammatically feminine are readable as referring to the Shekhinah. In addition to this there are quite a number of biblical figures who are seen as symbols of the Shekhinah.

A Bridge Between Divinity and Creation

The Kabbalistic worldview depicts God as infinite and unchangeable but connected to humankind through the dynamic nature of the world of the Sefirot. There is a constant flow of divine energy (Shefa) both down to Creation and back up toward the higher levels of divinity. The Shekhinah is the "location" of the interconnection between the physical world of Creation and the pure divine realm through which all of the life of God is expressed.

The Shekhinah is understood as the connection between the physical world and the divine universe from the very first Kabbalistic text, Sefer HaBahir. The image of the tenth Sefira as daughter, queen, and mother remain consistent throughout Kabbalistic literature.

As the bridge between the physical and the Divine, the Shekhinah is intricately connected to the fate of the Jewish people. The acts of the community as a whole and individually take on enormous importance on the one hand, and on the other hand, there is an incredible sense of intimacy with God because of this identification of the most immanent Sefira with the body of the community. There is also the sense of God being thoroughly alive in our midst and therefore accessible with the proper consciousness.

Shefa is a central term in Kabbalah and can mean a number of things. You can think of it as divine energy, generally depicted by images of light, water, and human seed. Shefa enters Shekhinah through its union with Tiferet by way of Yesod to continually sustain Creation.

The Shekhinah is the gate through which the divine Shefa flows and through which all human activity and consciousness connects to Divinity. In this scenario, the Shekhinah is in a recipient role. Divine energy flows to her and through her from the upper Sefirot. Human consciousness, when it ascends, ascends to the Shekhinah, experiencing the immanence of the Divine Presence. In the sense of not having divine "light" of her own, the Shekhinah is likened to the moon, which is beautiful and illuminated, but not by its own light.

Two Shekhinahs

The Shekhinah that is most often addressed is the "lower Shekhinah," the Shekhinah that is the tenth Sefira also known as *Malkhut*. This "lower Shekhinah" is embodied by the last letter in the name, YHVH—that is, the second *hey*. This letter appears twice in the name and the first one is representative of Binah, the third Sefira, who is also known as the Sublime Mother and the upper Shekhinah.

FACT

"All the blessings from above [the upper worlds] and from below [this world] are dependent on the seventh day [the Sabbath]. . . . Rabbi Yehuda said: 'You need to have pleasure on this day, to eat three festive meals on Shabbat in order that there will be abundance and delight on this day in the world'" (Zohar, vol. 2, 88a).

Binah, as the "upper Shekhinah," is thoroughly active in contrast to the "lower Shekhinah," which has a much more passive role in the world of the Sefirot. Binah is permanently "wedded" to the Sublime Father, Chokhmah, and gives birth to the seven Sefirot below her, the last of which is the "lower Shekhinah." These seven Sefirot are the primordial days of Creation, with Shekhinah being equivalent to Shabbat, which is the crown of the days of the week. In fact, Shekhinah is also called *atarah*, which is another word for "crown."

The Sabbath Queen

The Shekhinah, or Queen, is significantly related to the weekly observance of Shabbat. This relationship is emphasized in an important anonymous

Kabbalistic work from the fourteenth century called *Ma'arekhet HaElohut* (The "System" of Divinity), which speaks of the idea of *shalom bayit* (peace in the home), something that is particularly emphasized on Shabbat: "Peace is in the house. Then the man which is Tiferet is in his house having relations with the Queen [Shekhinah] and the bond is perfect [*Shalem*, the Hebrew word for perfect, shares the same root as *Shalom*, which means peace]. She is the blessing and the holiness that reign on Shabbat."

The Shekhinah is both a queen and the bride (*kallah*), and in Tzfat, Israel, in the 1500s the Kabbalists began a custom of going out into the fields singing Psalms to greet the Sabbath bride and queen. It is a custom for women to light two candles each on Shabbat to symbolize receiving an additional soul on this day.

Shekhinah in Exile

One of the earliest Midrashim, called *Mekhilta* (or Mekhilta of Rabbi Yishmael), quotes Rabbi Akiva as saying, "Every place that Israel is exiled, the Shekhinah, as it were, was exiled with them."

The Shekhinah became identified with Knesset Yisrael, the community of Israel, as a symbolic entity. The fate of the Jewish people, therefore, embodied and symbolized the "fate" of the Shekhinah. The ideal state, of course, is for the Shekhinah to be united with the rest of the world of the Sefirot. This would create universal harmony and bestow an abundance of Shefa (divine energy) upon the world.

ALERT!

In Jeremiah it says, "Rachel weeps over her children refusing to be consoled" (31:14). This phrase from the prophet Jeremiah became a classic image identified with the Shekhinah. Rachel, the last of the biblical matriarchs and the one most loved by Jacob (who becomes "Israel" and symbolizes Tiferet, the husband of Shekhinah), follows the people into exile.

In Kabbalistic mythology, the transgression in the Garden of Eden severed the Shekhinah from the rest of the Sefirot. The Shekhinah was expelled from the state of perfection along with humans.

Since the expulsion from Eden, the Shekhinah has been in exile from the rest of the world of the Sefirot. Human actions and behavior now determine whether there will be union between the Shekhinah and the other Sefirot or whether the Shekhinah will remain in exile.

Shekhinah and Sexual Union

The boldest descriptions of the Shekhinah as the feminine aspect of Divinity are those concerning the sexual union or, more accurately, the sacred union in which she engages with the masculine aspect of Divinity. This sacred, erotic union is the perfect harmony of the divine realm that draws down divine energy into the cosmos. The most powerful images of unity and oneness are reserved for these erotic descriptions of the divine male and female. The Zohar provides a good sample:

"Come see, behold it is said: The process of uniting everything as One, how does it transpire? Behold, it is said: He uncovered His holy arm; this is the one arm upon which salvation depends, upon which redemption depends [based on Exodus 6:6]. And why? In order to lift up Knesset Yisrael from the dust, receive her, and couple as one. And when this arousal to receive occurs, how much awe imbues the world! And then he lays his arm under her head to unite as you say (Song of Songs 2:6) 'His left arm [which symbolizes Din; that is, judgment] under my head, etc.' Then judgment [of the world] is set aside and sins are pardoned.

"Next the right arm [which symbolizes Hesed; that is, loving kindness] comes to embrace. Then jubilation saturates the world and all faces beam. Afterwards their bodies unite and all becomes one, inseparable, which is the perfection of everything, universal joy! And they are surely bound in a manner not found at other times" (vol. 3, 214b).

Human sexuality can model the divine image of union described in the Zohar. As with all other activities, our kavana (consciousness) affects the degree of holiness we may attain. At the same time, Kabbalists see all of our actions as affecting the upper worlds, which in turn may enhance or constrict the flow of divine energy into this world. The more our consciousness and behavior strive for union and holiness, the more we bring that into the world.

The Hebrew word for "woman" is *ishah* (spelled *aleph, shin, hey*), and *ish* means "man" (*aleph, yud, shin*). Each word has a letter from the divine name, Yah (*yud, hey*), in it. Remove those letters and you have the word *esh* (*aleph, shin*), which means "fire." Including those letters not only illustrates the passion, but the spiritual intensity of union.

The Shekhinah ultimately animates all of Creation. There is a spark of the Shekhinah in every living entity. We can find that spark, which is our gateway to the Immanent and Transcendent One, by going inside ourselves or by encountering that divine spark in anyone or anything else we encounter.

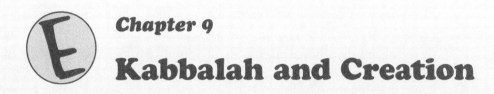

Chapter 9

Kabbalah and Creation

The Bible begins with an account of Creation. God's role in that creation, and the implications of that for a person's relationship with God, are central concerns throughout the history of Judaism. These concerns remain primary in Kabbalah, but the way they are understood is radically changed. Kabbalah is loyal to the traditional language of Scripture but reads it in a thoroughly novel way.

The Doctrine of Emanation: Atzilut

In a literal reading of the biblical text of Creation, there is a powerful Divinity bringing the universe into being in the course of six days and resting on the seventh day. Most Kabbalists throughout history have been reverent of the Jewish tradition and therefore would never negate the literal reading of the Torah. However, Kabbalists were in many ways simultaneously conservative and radical. Though they significantly reinterpreted the tradition, they insisted that they were merely sharing the true secret meaning of the Torah passed down orally throughout the generations.

Root of Emanation

One of the major examples of this reinterpretation of tradition is the doctrine of emanation. The term for "emanation" in Hebrew is *atzilut*. The root of atzilut is generally explained as related to the word *etzel* (which has the same three-letter root of *aleph, tzadi,* and *lamed*). Etzel means "close to," implying "still connected to." Atzilut means that all that emanates from Ein Sof (the undifferentiated, unchanging Eternal One) always remains connected to it.

QUESTION?

What is the relationship of the physical universe to the world of the Sefirot?
Early Kabbalists saw the physical plane as having an independent existence, but still containing Divinity within it. Without the divine life force (*khiyut*), nothing could exist. Also, all physical entities have their archetypes in the realm of the Sefirot.

The nature of atzilut is understood in more than one way through the course of Kabbalistic history, but generally Kabbalists believe the Sefirot emanated directly from Ein Sof. One way in which this is depicted is that the Sefirot eternally existed within Ein Sof and the process of atzilut brings the concealed Sefirot outward. In this manner atzilut is also a process of revelation. Ein Sof remains the hidden God and the Sefirot are the manifested, revealed God.

A Sixteenth-Century Text on Atzilut

Rabbi Meir Ibn Gabbai's book *Avodat HaKodesh* (Divine Service) from 1567 is one of the classic pre-Lurianic Kabbalistic texts (see Chapter 13 for more on Lurianic Kabbalah). Ibn Gabbai gives a very inclusive, detailed overview of Kabbalah in this work, and writes that "[t]he Atzilut of Ten Sefirot . . . is the Essence of Divinity . . . for the Emanated is not separate from the Emanator [that is, Ein Sof] and is not outside of It and is not something separate from It, but is It, Itself."

FACT

There are numerous biblical verses that serve as proof texts for Kabbalistic ideas. We find in Isaiah the phrase "I am YHVH there is no other" (45:6), which is conventionally understood to mean there is no other God. However, this phrase can also be read as "I am YHVH there is nothing else," meaning that only God exists.

The Eternity of Atzilut

According to many Kabbalists, atzilut is not an event or process that happened once upon a time in history. Atzilut is seen as a perpetual process, something that is always occurring and, therefore, our connection to Divinity is dynamic, alive, and present at all moments. At the same time, atzilut is not seen as something inherent in Ein Sof. The Kabbalists always see atzilut as a matter of divine will and love (Hesed), and not as inevitable. One question that generally came up was "Where in the divine 'scheme of things' does this divine will reside?" Keter, which is often seen as coeternal with Ein Sof, is generally considered the source of will.

Atzilut and God's Speech

Atzilut is a process that occurs within God. The Sefirot are the revealed manifestations of the Transcendent Unknowable One. For Kabbalah, which, like the rest of Judaism, sees language and words as great creative forces, atzilut parallels God's "speech." The earliest level of atzilut is comparable to God's thought, which then becomes undifferentiated sound and ultimately crystallizes as words of Torah in which all reality can be beheld.

ALERT!

Kabbalists stress that Shabbat is a higher level of existence than the rest of the week. Creation exists due to God's "speech" which continually sustains it, but the day of rest is sustained through God's "thought," whose root is higher in the world of the Sefirot.

Levi Yitzkhak of Berditchev on Creation

In the opening passage of Levi Yitzkhak's essential early Hasidic text, *Kedushat Levi*, he begins by commenting on the opening verse of the Torah: "In the beginning God created the Heavens and the earth. The principle is that the Blessed Creator created everything and is everything . . . [and] in every moment [God] emanates life-force to every living entity and everything is from [God] and [God] is whole and perfect."

Divine Nothingness: Ayin

The transitional point between Ein Sof and the emanation of the Sefirot is logically pivotal. How does this transition from the undifferentiated One to the world of Sefirot, and eventually to the world of differentiation, occur? To some Kabbalists, Keter was coeternal with Ein Sof and, therefore, atzilut really begins with Chokhmah. To others, Keter was the beginning of atzilut. This close connection between Keter and Ein Sof is reflected in the term Ayin (nothingness), which always refers to Keter. Though Ayin means "nothing" or "nothingness," in this case it would be more accurate to define it as "no-thingness," meaning a state in which there is no duality. The word *Ein* in Ein Sof derives from the word *Ayin* and is spelled with the same letters.

Ayin not only means "nothingness," but also "where." Psalm 121:1 can mean "I lift my eyes to the mountains, from where will my help come?" Or it can mean "My help will come from Ayin"—that is, all goodness, compassion, and "help" ultimately comes from Ayin. Job 28:12 can mean "Where can wisdom be found?" or "Wisdom will be found from Nothingness."

There is always the danger when speaking of these matters of letting them become cerebral abstractions, which would grossly miss the point. The experience of Ayin is a very real element of many mystical experiences. Most such experiences transcend language, while most attempts to convey them, of necessity, resort to paradoxes. The experience of oneness with all creation and the infinite presence of the Divine filling and transcending everything negates all "thing-ness," that is, all sense of being separate or distinct from the Divine disappears. "Thing-ness" is part of what the Kabbalists call the world of *yesh*, or the world of "something," the world of divisions and distinctions.

Ayin is the experience that you may have of the absolute oneness of everything, despite the appearance that we live in the world of divisions. Some of the more radical Kabbalistic formulations of this experience would say that this world of apparent divisions is an illusion. Others would say that both experiences are true; in other words, the world of division (*Olam HaPerud*) is real, but at the same time it is also ultimately a part of the world of union (*Olam HaYikhud*).

A Brief History of Ayin

The verbal expressions that attempt to communicate this experience have a history of their own. One of the primary examples of the use of the term *Ayin* is in the expression of God creating "something out of nothing," or *yesh me-Ayin*. This belief is neither obvious nor explicit in the biblical account of

Creation. In fact, this formulation doesn't appear until the end of the eleventh century in an anonymous Hebrew translation of Sa'adia Gaon's (882–942) philosophical work *Beliefs and Opinions*. Sa'adia Gaon was the first great Jewish philosopher of medieval times. His major text, *Beliefs and Opinions*, was originally written in Arabic. In the first chapter, Sa'adia argues that the world was created out of nothing. In the translation from the text's original Arabic into Hebrew, Sa'adia Gaon's idea about creation from nothing was encapsulated in the phrase "something out of nothing," or *yesh me-Ayin*.

QUESTION?

What is "negative theology"?
Negative theology is the belief that God is a being of a totally different order than all other beings. Therefore we cannot use the same categories to describe God as we would use to describe other beings. We can only say what God is not. This gave a philosophical footing to the Kabbalists' explanation of Ayin.

Maimonides accepted the formulation of Creation, "yesh me-Ayin." A similar formulation was expressed in Sefer Yetzirah possibly a thousand years earlier. In Chapter 2, Mishnah 6, the author states that "He made His Ayin, Yesh," which could be interpreted in a number of ways. It could mean "He made that which wasn't into that which is." A number of Kabbalistic commentators on this section, such as Azriel of Gerona and the fourteenth-century Kabbalist Yosef ben Shalom Ashkenazi, read this as the creation of yesh me-Ayin. However, it could also mean "he turned his No-thingness into Something."

The Kabbalists interpreted this formula of the creation of something out of nothing as the very beginnings of the process of atzilut, meaning that yesh (which symbolizes Chokhmah) emanates from Ayin (which symbolizes Keter). Though the Kabbalists adapted Maimonides' "negative theology" when speaking about Ayin, they also were much more in sync with the tone of biblical descriptions of God, which were "positive," when referring to the rest of the Sefirot.

There are a number of different words for "create" in Hebrew. A traditional explanation was that the word *boreh* refers to creating "something out of nothing." This is the root used in the opening verse of Genesis. The word *yotzer* was understood as creating "something from something."

A Psychological Perspective on Ayin

Ayin later became an important state of awareness to achieve in Hasidism. It no longer only signified a level of Divinity, but now also referred to an important mystical state of awareness. A good description of this is given in the continuation of Levi Yitzkhak's earlier passage, in which he states that "God includes everything and therefore when a person attains a state of Ayin and knows that he is nothing, he then relates to God, the Blessed One, as the [perpetually] Creating One."

The Immanent and Transcendent God

There are elements of Kabbalistic thought that are either experiences that cannot be logically conveyed or simply are axioms. Axioms are underlying principles or beliefs that cannot be logically proven without assuming them. In Western logic, a good example of this is the idea that "a" and "not a" cannot both be true. However, in order to prove this, we have to assume it.

God's immanence and transcendence are experiences essential to the Kabbalists' worldview. If God were only transcendent, the world would not be filled with God's Presence. Without God's immanence in addition to transcendence, the mystical experience of all existence pulsating with Divinity would be impossible to attain. In words, this experience sounds abstract, but it is very tangible to one who has gone through it. Most mystical theologies are attempts to give reasonable, all-encompassing explanations of existence that have begun with an overwhelming experience of God's immanent presence and transcendence.

The mystic experiences his living relationship with God as more illuminating than any logical arguments. Fundamental to this is the overwhelming sense of both the immanence and transcendence of Divinity. There are many gradations and subtleties in this sense of immanence and the Sefirot are a symbolic language that allows Kabbalists to express them.

FACT

A famous Aramaic Kabbalistic phrase from Tikkunei Zohar expressing God's omnipresence is *"Leit Atar Panui Minay,"* meaning "there is no place where God is not." The predecessor of this phrase, from a sixth-century Midrash from Israel, *Pesikta de Rav Kahana,* states that "there is no place on earth empty of the Shekhinah."

The Four Worlds

During the course of the history of Kabbalah, other "worlds" have been referred to, in addition to the world of the Sefirot, that came into being as a result of atzilut. The most prevalent of these descriptions speaks of four levels of worlds. The highest is the world of emanation (*atzilut*), the next is the world of Creation (*beriah*), followed by the world of formation (*yetzirah*), and culminating in the world of "action" (*asiyah*).

There is not a uniform way in which these worlds are spoken of in Kabbalistic works through the centuries. Various Kabbalists presented them differently, but they tended to crystallize in certain formulations.

Rabbi Azriel of Gerona spoke of the levels of beriah, yetzirah, and asiyah. In his description, they exist within the realm of atzilut. By the time of the Zohar and particularly Tikkunei Zohar, they are described as separate worlds. Rabbi Isaac of Acco in the early fourteenth century elaborates upon the details of the four worlds to a much greater extent than previous Kabbalists.

Isaiah is the foundational proof text for the existence of the four worlds. It reads as follows: "All that is called by My Name, for my Kavod [Glory] I created it, I formed it, yea I have made it" (43:7). The word *asiyah* means both "making" and "acting."

Sefirot upon Sefirot

Each of the four worlds is also composed of ten Sefirot. There are descriptions of Adam Kadmon existing in all four worlds also. Moshe Cordovero and Lurianic Kabbalah go into even greater detail concerning the four worlds. Cordovero devotes a substantial section of *Pardes Rimonim* to a discussion of the four worlds. He begins by saying that he will explain the fact that in the words of Rashbi (Rabbi Shimon bar Yokhai, traditionally believed to be the author of the Zohar and Tikkunei Zohar), we read numerous times about the Ten Sefirot of atzilut, beriah, yetzirah, and asiyah. Cordovero adds that this seems to contradict the earlier section in *Pardes Rimonim*, on the fact that there are "ten [Sefirot] and not nine, ten and not eleven."

Formation, Action, and Human Experience

The world of yetzirah (formation) is the world of the Merkavah (the divine chariot) and of the higher angels, the most important of which is Metatron. Asiyah (the world of action) is the realm of the lower angels. The world of asiyah sometimes includes the earthly realm in which we live, but in some formulations it does not.

Some Kabbalists divide the four worlds into aspects of human experience in ascending order: action (asiyah), emotion (yetzirah), intellect (beriah), and spirit/soul (atzilut). Each letter of YHVH also has been described as related to a different world with the letter yud as atzilut, and so on.

The doctrine of the four worlds essentially describes the process of Creation in an increasingly intricate way. It also conveys a more pronounced sense of distance between humans and God.

Levels of Soul

There are a number of different words referring to the soul in Hebrew. They are mentioned as early as the fifth century in Midrashic literature in Genesis (which in Hebrew is *Bereshit*) Rabbah. They are *nefesh, ruakh, khaya, neshama,* and *yekhidah.* In Bereshit Rabbah they do not refer to different levels of the soul. Biblical quotes are listed after the names to illustrate their meaning. Kabbalists interpret the different names for soul as different levels of the soul.

Genesis describes the creation of Adam: "YHVH Elohim formed the human, dust from the earth, and blew into his nostrils the breath of life and the human became a living soul" (2:7). *Formed (yitzer)* is spelled with two yud's, which is a unique spelling in the Bible and was interpreted to mean that humans have two inclinations: good and bad.

In accordance with Genesis (2:7), Kabbalists understand the soul as being of divine origin. One of the first daily morning prayers begins, "My God, the soul that you have given me is pure." The pure divine origin of the soul is what gives a person, according to Kabbalistic lore, the ability to enter a state of devekut (divine union) with God and to affect the world of the Sefirot through our actions.

There is a passage in the Zohar that describes the hesitation of the soul to enter the physical world where it fears that it will suffer at the hands of the body. In this passage, the Holy One instructs the soul that entering the physical world is the purpose of her creation (all five words for "soul" in Hebrew are grammatically feminine, with *ruakh* being conjugated both as feminine and masculine).

The Power of the Soul

Human beings through their actions can make the divine more manifest in the world. This is one way in which the Kabbalists see the purpose of mitzvot. Mitzvot are means of connecting to the divine all around us. This is particularly true of prayer, which is called *tefillah* in Hebrew.

Genesis 1:26 is among the biblical proof texts for the divine nature of the soul. In it, Elohim (God) says, "Let us make Adam in our Image after our likeness." Proverbs supplies another support: "The Neshama [soul] of a person is the candle of YHVH" (20:7). This verse in Proverbs echoes the common analogy concerning Ein Sof and atzilut, in which Ein Sof is not at all diminished because of atzilut, as in the case of a candle that is kindled from a larger fire.

The Soul in Rabbinic Literature

The Kabbalists expanded upon certain themes concerning the soul found in rabbinic literature. In Midrash Tanhuma, a Midrash of the eighth or ninth century, the soul is described as a small universe (*olam katan*). There are reflections of this perspective in even earlier Talmudic sources.

FACT

Tractate Sanhedrin in the Babylonian Talmud contains a famous quotation: "Anyone who destroys one soul, it is as though he has destroyed an entire universe. Anyone who saves one soul, it is as though he has saved an entire universe" (37a).

Kabbalists see this world as a reflection of the upper world, the world of the Sefirot. In the same manner, the "small universe" that each person is reflects the world of the Sefirot, as exemplified in the image of Adam Kadmon, the primordial human.

Neshama, ruakh, and *nefesh* are the three terms by which the soul is most commonly referred. As with most Kabbalistic ideas, there is not a standard dogma that all Kabbalists affirm, but rather there are dominant trends. Neshama is considered the highest state of the soul, ruakh next, and nefesh last. Humans are even described as having a divine nefesh and an "animal" nefesh. Everything possesses a soul, not just human beings, as everything is part of divinity. In some explanations of soul, the higher states of soul are developed as you develop spiritually. Khaya is higher than neshama and yekhidah is the highest level of all according to most Kabbalists who write on the subject. It is very rare for a person to reach the level of yekhidah.

Moshe de Leon on the Soul

In one of his Hebrew Kabbalistic books, *Shekel HaKodesh*, Moshe de Leon writes that "The 'intelligent' form that's in a person, that is what is called human, for the skin, flesh, and bones are a human's clothing. . . . On the likeness of the [Divine] throne [Ezekiel 1:26] was the likeness as the appearance of a human above upon it. What is this 'likeness of a human?' The three levels connected as one, which are Nefesh, Ruakh, and Neshama" (33).

The Soul and the Sefirot

Kabbalists ultimately see the different levels of soul as having their source in the world of the Sefirot. Neshama, which is the highest, has its root in Binah. Ruakh has its root in Tiferet, and nefesh has its root in Shekhinah.

Having the root of one's soul in the world of the Sefirot implies that we have a huge responsibility to live holy lives in order to enhance the presence of the Shekhinah in this world. Every one of our actions contributes or detracts from this presence. Hasidic masters taught that we must turn our *ani* (ego) into Ayin (nothingness) [both words are made up of the same three Hebrew letters, but arranged differently] in order to truly accomplish this holy work of making the Divine Presence felt in this world.

Chapter 10

The Human Role in the Cosmos

The desire to communicate the insights of a mystical experience strains language to its limits. As we discussed in the previous chapter, there are underlying principles of Kabbalah based on such insights, rather than logic. The Kabbalist who undergoes moments of union with the divine experiences both the infinitesimal significance of our existence and the majesty of it.

The Cosmic Influence of Our Acts

Part of what may account for Kabbalah's impact on Judaism and its prominent position for a number of centuries is that it invigorated the everyday acts of people by attributing cosmic influence to them. Kabbalists understand kavana, meaning a person's focus and consciousness, as having an effect beyond the immediate obvious influence of our actions. Though people have always had to grapple with the clear lack of connection between a person's moral qualities and their fate and fortune in this world, Kabbalah teaches that our actions have an impact, nevertheless, in ways that are not plainly evident. (The biblical Book of Job is a perfect example of the antiquity of the attempt to confront this issue.)

A central Kabbalistic doctrine is that every action on this plane that we inhabit has its parallel, and therefore repercussions, in the upper worlds. This is applicable no matter how apparently trivial the action. Traditional Judaism tends to be very exacting in its requirements for ritual behavior. There is a lot of attention to detail. Someone on the outside would probably think that this preoccupation with precision is going way overboard. Kabbalists, on the other hand, claim that these fine points matter enormously because everything we do affects the upper worlds. Plus, the attention to detail focuses your consciousness, and consciousness and intention, or kavana, make a vital difference.

Levi Yitzkhak of Berditchev quotes the Ba'al Shem Tov's interpretation of Psalms: "YHVH is the shadow of your right hand" (121:5). God behaves like a shadow does with a person. Everything that a person does, the shadow also does. The sixteenth-century Kabbalist Meir Ibn Gabbai used the analogy of the strings of two instruments. When one vibrates it activates the other's vibrations.

The two main schools of Kabbalah (see Chapter 11) approach the issue of the cosmic influence of our acts differently. For the Ecstatic Kabbalists, the mystical experience, the state of union with God, is the supreme end toward which we should strive. This state is sought for its own sake and not with the ulterior motive of achieving any other goal. Theosophical Kabbalah, on the other hand, had a much stronger orientation toward affecting the harmony of the upper worlds and consequently affecting the state of this world.

Kabbalah sheds a new light on all activity on the plane of this world. Though Kabbalists never negate the significance of the acts we do on Earth, they see these same acts as potentially catalyzing events in the divine realm. One of the most striking examples of this is evident in the history of Messianism in Judaism.

Messianism

Much of the earliest Kabbalah dealt with the redemption of the individual through knowledge of, and connection to, God. It was not really until the Zohar that individual redemption and national and even universal redemption became seriously combined. The tragedy of the Spanish expulsion in 1492 intensified the focus on this concern.

QUESTION?

What does *messiah* mean?
The Hebrew word for messiah, *mashiakh,* means "the anointed one" and refers to a king. Though there are biblical prophecies of a messianic era of peace (for example, Isaiah's "the lion lying down with the lamb"), Messianism, with the image of a divinely appointed person bringing about this era, became more prominent during the Roman conquest of Israel and after.

After the expulsion, there developed a desire and drive to force the hand of Heaven, that is, to precipitate the messianic era. People believed that their pious actions could create the right conditions for the Messiah to come. Though the Zohar encouraged such activity, it wasn't until the Kabbalistic flowering in Tzfat, Israel, that numbers of people seemed to really act on this desire. Some people took to ascetic disciplines of self-denial hoping to purify themselves so that they might be able to affect change in the cosmos. The belief that a community of pious mystics could be even more effective also grew. Ultimately this led to the tragedy of the Sabbatean movement that gathered around the false messiahship of Shabbtai Tzvi in the mid 1600s.

During the 1600s, a large number of Jewish people began to believe that a Turkish Kabbalist, Shabbtai Tzvi, was the Messiah. When Shabbtai Tzvi had an audience with the sultan of Turkey in 1666, the sultan demanded that the would-be messiah convert to Islam or be put to death. Shabbtai Tzvi chose to convert to Islam rather than die a martyr. Many of his followers were devastated to discover that they had put their faith in a false messiah, but others converted to Islam as well believing that this was somehow part of the process of redemption. Still other Jewish people remained secret followers of Shabbatai Tzvi while continuing to live traditional Jewish lives.

The Power of Prayer

Prayer is another important example of our cosmic influence. For Kabbalists, prayer is not merely the literal words that are traditionally said. Instead, the words of prayers are understood as containing multiple levels of meaning that are capable of creating unifications in divine realms. The Ba'al Shem Tov said that each word of prayer is a world in itself. Each word of prayer can also work as a ladder to the Divine.

In Genesis Jacob dreams "a ladder is standing on the earth and its head reaches heavenwards and behold! messengers of God ascending and descending upon it" (28:12). Jacob realizes that "YHVH is in this place and I didn't know" (28:16). Until we experience the immediate presence of the Infinite One, we are not truly aware that God is every place at every moment.

The most powerful words of prayer are those said purely in praise of God. These are the words that have the potential to reach the most sublime states of our awareness of the Divine. They are the words that take us as far away from our material and social wants and as close as possible to our inner need for connection to the Eternal One.

The Mystical Meaning of the Sh'ma

The central prayer in the Jewish tradition is the *sh'ma* (literally "hear," "listen," "understand"), which comes from Deuteronomy: "Hear Israel, YHVH is our God, YHVH is One" (6:4). In fact, no English translation can convey the many meanings of the prayer because those levels don't survive in the English version.

ALERT!

The Zohar on reciting the Sh'ma: "At the moment that Israel unifies the secret unification of 'Sh'ma Yisrael' with perfect Kavana, immediately one light is emitted from the unfathomable upper world. . . . Then the Queen adorns herself to enter the wedding canopy with her Groom . . . with one desire to be One and never parted" (vol. 2, 133b).

In the actual Torah scroll the last letter of the word *sh'ma* (which is an *Ayin*) and the last letter of the word *ekhad* (one), which is a *dalet*, are enlarged, spelling *ed*, which means "witness." Reciting this prayer implies bearing witness to the oneness and unity of God. From a Kabbalistic perspective, reciting this prayer with great intention can help bring about unification in the upper worlds, which is the greatest function of prayer.

Being and Doing

The two major streams in Kabbalah play out their relationship to "being" and "doing" differently. For Ecstatic Kabbalists, the main focus of activity, of "doing," is to achieve the highest level of "being" of which we are capable. Meditation is that act that comes closest to pure "being." It attempts to lead us to a state where we cease our activity and bask in "being"—both the divine being that is within us and the oneness of the being that transcends us.

Obviously it is impossible for human beings to survive without "doing." However, the acts that we engage in can be done with various levels of consciousness. Consciousness is our connection to pure being, meaning to the presence of God. Meditation is an attempt to enable us to not only dwell in a state of pure "being," but also to allow the consciousness that meditation cultivates to spread into the other activities of our lives and connect us more closely with the Divine Presence.

The Theosophical Kabbalistic Approach

The theosophical Kabbalistic approach to the question of "being" and "doing" tends to focus more on the aspect of our activities. As decribed in specific Kabbalistic texts, certain forms of prayer have a lot in common with meditation. Kabbalistic prayer attempts to dwell in the words of the prayers, particularly those prayers that praise God, turning the prayers into extended forms of meditation.

Prayer, Meditation, and Intention

Ecstatic Kabbalists tend to separate their meditation from prayer. They use techniques of concentration focused on names of God and permutations of the letters within these names. In the meditational aspects of theosophical Kabbalistic prayers, the individual words are transformed into vehicles reaching far beyond the words themselves.

Kavana can also mean a specific mystical intention often recited before rituals, such as sanctifying the wine on Shabbat or waving the *lulav* (palm branch) and *etrog* (citron) on Sukkot (one of the three pilgrimage holidays). It begins: "For the sake of uniting the Blessed Holy One and His Shekhinah with love and awe behold I am (then the act is named)."

Every activity has the potential of serving as a catalyst to our consciousness of God. This requires, first of all, having the appropriate kavana for the act itself. Traditional Judaism, with its highly ritualized lifestyle, enables

Kabbalists to use the various ritual activities to focus on the goal of unifying the upper worlds.

In order for your practice of the traditional rituals to be most effective and done with the maximum kavana, you need to understand their deeper meanings. Grasping the purpose of these activities is a central task, particularly for the Theosophical Kabbalists.

The Divine Commandments: The Mitzvot

Related to the drive toward theurgy is the vast Kabbalistic literature concerned with the mystical meaning of the mitzvot. The position that every act has potential cosmic significance readily explains the fact that most Kabbalists were also deeply concerned with halakhah (Jewish Law). Outstanding examples of this combination of mystic and "legalist" are Yosef Karo, Nachmanides, and the Vilna Gaon.

There are many different types of Jewish laws, for example *dinim, mishpatim*, and *khukim*. Khukim, for example, are those laws that have no rational explanation as, for example, the dietary laws whose only justification in the Torah is "to make you holy." Early in the history of Kabbalah, only certain mitzvot were explained according to their sublime significance. By the time of the Zohar, about 100 years later, all the mitzvot were commented upon according to their esoteric significance.

FACT

The *sukkah*, the temporary booth traditional Jews dwell in during the holiday of Sukkot, is a reminder of the years the Jewish people wandered after the Exodus. The word *sukkah* (spelled *samekh, vav, kaf, hey*) embodies the union of YHVH, whose gematria is 26 (spelled *kaf, vav*), with Shekhinah, whose divine name, Adonai, has the gematria of 65 (spelled *samekh, hey*).

Entire books were written elucidating the Kabbalistic significance of the mitzvot. In contrast to this, the medieval Jewish philosophers' works did not particularly stimulate the practice of the mitzvot because they focused more on the intellectual contemplation of God, largely ignoring the practice of physical rituals. The Kabbalists, on the other hand, saw the practice, the physical actions, as creating a flow of Shefa (divine energy) from the upper worlds.

An Esoteric Explanation of Mitzvah

Levi Yitzkhak of Berditchev explained that the word *mitzvah* comes from the same root as *tzavta*, which means "together." In other words, the practice of mitzvot creates unifications in the divine realm. He also taught that the word mitzvah (spelled *mem, tzadi, vav, hey*) was related to the divine name, YHVH. First, both words share the letters *vav* and *hey* as their last two letters. Secondly, he used the exegetical tool of atbash (where the first letter, *aleph*, of the Hebrew alphabet is replaced by the last letter, *tav*, and where the second letter, *bet*, is replaced by the second to last, *shin*, etc.). According to Atbash, *mem tzadi*, the first two letters of mitzvah, come out as *yud hey*.

Interpretive tools such as atbash and gematria are outside of the framework of rational thought. Applying the rules of logic to a nonrational system makes the system seem absurd. By remaining open to the message revealed by these nonrational methods, it is possible to see beyond the limitations of rational thought.

Levi Yitzkhak explains that there are two aspects of God in relationship to our existence: the aspect of Ayin (nothingness) and the aspect of yesh (somethingness). The Ayin aspect controls everything that transcends nature and the yesh aspect operates in nature. It is through the practice of the mitzvot that we connect the Ayin and yesh components together.

Levi Yitzkhak goes on to explain that there are two parts of a mitzvah, the part whose power is revealed to us and the part that is concealed. The revealed part is the part symbolized by the last two letters of the word mitzvah (vav, hey). The concealed part is the part symbolized by mem, tzadi (which conceal the letters yud and hey within themselves as revealed through the method of Atbash).

The Zohar teaches at length about the cosmic influence of our actions. "Whoever gives *Tzedakah* [usually translated as "charity," though its root comes from the word *justice*], to the poor makes the Holy Name whole above as is proper"(vol. 3, 113b).

In Lurianic Kabbalah, the mystical understanding of mitzvot is tied to the concept of *Tikkun*. Mitzvot are an essential part of the process of Tikkun, restoring and healing the world and the divine realm. Your kavana when performing mitzvot continues to be an important factor in the Tikkun you may help bring about.

The Holiness of the Sabbath

Shabbat, the Sabbath, has always held a place of great importance in Judaism. It is described in the Talmud (Tractate Brakhot 57b) as one-sixtieth of the "World to Come." In rabbinic literature there was a belief that if everyone observed one Shabbat as prescribed, it would bring the Messiah.

There are a number of components of traditional Shabbat observance. One, of course, is refraining from work. This is often misunderstood because we impose the connotation of the English word *work*. However, the kinds of work meant observance of Shabbat come from the thirty-nine categories of work that were done during the building of the ancient Temple in Jerusalem. As spiritually important as the building of the Temple was, this activity ceased on Shabbat. Other aspects of Shabbat observance are prayer, study of Torah, and the simple pleasure of the day, a day in which we cease trying to impose our will on the world.

The Zohar says that Shabbat is equal to the entire Torah and "whoever observes Shabbat is as though they kept the entire Torah" (vol. 2, 47a). It goes on that Shabbat is a "delight for everything, a delight for the soul and the body, a delight for the upper worlds and the lower worlds."

ALERT!

When we look at Shabbat as a day of restriction, it feels like an anchor (in Hebrew, the word for "anchor" is *ogen*, spelled *Ayin, nun, gimmel*). However, when we experience the spiritual freedom and joy of the day we turn the ogen into *oneg*, meaning "delight," spelled with the same letters: Ayin, gimmel, nun, in a different order.

The Zohar remarks that "all six supernal days [which can be interpreted as the Sefirot Hesed through Yesod] are blessed from Shabbat" (vol. 2, 88a). Shabbat is the seventh day and Binah, which is seven Sefirot above Yesod and is the upper Mother (as Shekhinah is the lower Mother), pours forth the blessing of Shefa, divine energy, to all the Sefirot below her. There is also a traditional belief that for the duration of Shabbat we acquire an "additional" soul (*neshama y'teirah*).

Study of Torah

The study of Torah along with prayer and meditation are generally the pillars of the spiritual life in Kabbalah. Since Kabbalists see Torah as the blueprint of the universe and as one with God (as the saying goes: "the Blessed Holy One and Torah are One"), engagement with Torah is a supreme activity. The meaning of Torah is very broad, encompassing all valid spiritual teaching, including Kabbalistic writings.

Shimon the Tzaddik, a high priest of the Second Temple, used to say: "The world stands on three things: Torah, worship, and deeds of loving-kindness" (Pirkei Avot 1:2). Prayer is traditionally called "worship from the heart" (*avodah she'ba'lev*).

Through study of the Torah one can catalyze unifications in the divine spheres. There are many passages in the Zohar about the Kabbalistic companions studying passages of Torah. Getting up in the middle of the night to learn Torah is considered very powerful as it's written in Joshua: "You shall contemplate it day and night" (1:8). The Zohar says that the "voice" of the Shekhinah praising the Blessed Holy One at midnight is the voice of those who rise at midnight to study Torah.

According to Lurianic teaching, each person has her own letter in the Torah. In other words, each person is able to read Torah in a totally unique way. Each person has something only he or she can teach about Torah.

Torah Study for Its Own Sake: Torah Lishmah

Studying Torah has always been the most highly esteemed activity throughout the tradition. But studying Torah does not necessarily lead to holy behavior. Studying as a purely intellectual activity without the intention of acting on what you've learned is not highly regarded.

Torah Lishmah (Torah study for its own sake) means studying Torah for the love of it and not for some external reward, such as recognition, esteem, or money. It does not mean studying Torah without the intent of practicing in your life what the teaching has given you.

FACT

Much of the way in which Kabbalah, Midrash, and even to a degree Jewish philosophy, made their points was through the device of interpreting Torah. It was rare, particularly in Spanish Theosophical Kabbalah, to offer insights without grounding them in the interpretation of various verses of the Torah.

Torah as an Entry Point into Understanding

Zohar Chadash gives a clear sense of how Torah is an entryway for understanding the great mysteries of existence: "One should know how to contemplate the secrets of his soul. . . . Today you are here, tomorrow in the grave. One [should] know how to contemplate this world and comprehend the world in which he exists and how it is perfected and afterwards the sublime secrets of the upper world in order to know his Creator. All of this a person contemplates from the inner secrets of the Torah" (Midrash Song of Songs 18a).

Already in Talmudic times it was taught that the study of Torah increases peace in the world (Babylonian Talmud, Tractate Brachot 64a). In Kabbalistic thought, Torah study brings about unity in the upper worlds, increasing the flow of divine energy into our world.

Embodied Spirituality

Judaism in general puts a great emphasis on living in community and pursuing your spiritual life in the context of the larger social group. All of the spiritual heroes are generally social and political heroes as well. Moses is the ideal example of this devotion to community. He has his first encounter with the Divine alone and deep in the wilderness. He experiences the voice of "Ehyeh" commanding him to return to Egypt to free his people from slavery.

The prophetic tradition illustrates the powerful combination of connection with the Divine and ethical, social, and political consciousness. Though people often have their visions and mystical experiences in seclusion, they always return to the community.

ALERT!

In biblical and post-biblical times there was a type of ascetic called a *nazir*. Some people took a nazirite vow for a month during which they would not shave, cut their hair, or drink wine. In this way they attempted to express greater devotion to God. There were some people who would be lifelong Nazirites.

Minyan

Prayer, which may at times be more elevating for the individual in private, is encouraged to be done with a *minyan*, a group of ten or more people considered adults in the eyes of the tradition. (The age of majority in the Jewish tradition is thirteen for men and twelve for women. The orthodox world only counts men in a minyan with the explanation that since women are not obligated to do mitzvot that must be done at a specific time, such as prayer, they should not be counted. Nonorthodox Judaism counts both men and women in a minyan.) Certain prayers can only be recited with a minyan and, likewise, the Torah can only be read publicly with a minyan.

Worship Through the Physical: Avodah BaGashmiyut

Though there is a strong component of Kabbalah that emphasizes meditation and transcending physicality, there is always the prevalence in Judaism of living your spiritual life through the body. Sex, for example, is a holy act when performed under proper, loving conditions. Eating is consecrated through the dietary laws. Shabbat, one of the holiest times in Jewish life, is a day in which we enjoy festive meals, sing, study Torah, and make love.

In Kabbalah, embodying your spirituality and tying in your spiritual peaks through mitzvot is very important, as the great Hasidic master Rebbe Nachman taught, so that your body has an instinctual memory of them. Our body's memory is often much longer lasting than our mind's memory. There is a tendency in Kabbalah, though, to avoid indulging in the pleasures of the senses for fear that they may seduce us away from our focus on God.

Annihilation of the Ego: Bittul HaYesh

The transcendence of the ego is called *bittul hayesh* in Hebrew. Our egos often interfere with our ability to do things for their own sake, and they can become an idol that we worship unconsciously. At the same time, the desire to rid ourselves of ego can become a very egocentric preoccupation, thereby achieving the very opposite of what we originally intended.

FACT

The Hebrew word *Shiviti* (I set), the first phrase of Psalm 16:8 ("I set YHVH before me always"), became the center of a chart called a Shiviti. Used in synagogues and homes beginning in the eighteenth century, the charts were composed of Kabbalistic and biblical phrases, names of angels, and so on, aesthetically arranged to encourage contemplation of the Divine.

A possible solution to this dilemma of ego is the idea that the greater our kavana—that is, the greater the focus of our consciousness on wherever we are or whatever we are doing—the easier it is to transcend the ego. The more aware we are of God's Presence, the more our ego recedes during those moments.

The Maggid of Mezeritch, the great Hasidic master and disciple of the Ba'al Shem Tov, describes in his book, *Maggid D'varav L'Ya'akov*, the task of the Tzaddik in the world: "In the Gemara (Tractate Ketubot 5a) [it says] the work of the Tzaddikim is greater than the creation of Heaven and Earth. The meaning is that the creation of Heaven and Earth was Yesh [something] from Ayin [nothing], while Tzaddikim make out of Yesh, Ayin [nothing]. In everything that they do, even the most physical [activities] such as eating, they elevate the holy sparks from the food. Likewise, in every situation they transform Yesh to Ayin."

The Tzaddik, the model for our behavior, connects to the Divine in everything and brings it back to its source in Ayin. He turns every possible moment into a moment of connection with the Divine, a moment of living on a much higher spiritual level, transforming the world around him. During these periods, the Tzaddik lives in a state of bittul hayesh.

Chapter 11

The Many Faces of Kabbalah

Kabbalah developed in a number of different forms. The two major schools were Theosophical Kabbalah and Ecstatic, or Prophetic, Kabbalah. In addition there were other Jewish mystical movements occurring around the same time period. Mystical activity flowered in Spain, France, Germany, Italy, Israel, and other parts of the Middle East.

Theosophical Kabbalah

The opening Mishnayot (the plural of Mishnah) of Sefer Yetzirah sets the stage for the major trends in Kabbalah. It mentions the thirty-two wondrous paths of wisdom through which the universe was created and the Ten Sefirot and twenty-two letters of the Hebrew alphabet. The two major schools of Kabbalists generally divide along these two focal points.

Theosophical Kabbalists focus on the world of the Sefirot and the Ecstatic or Prophetic Kabbalists focus on the mystical secrets of the Hebrew alphabet and the divine names. Theosophical Kabbalists write on a number of concerns, but rarely in a sustained systematic way. They contemplate the workings of the world of the Sefirot and Creation's relationship to the divine realms. Since humans are part of Creation, this understanding gives specific meaning to a person's life. Though Judaism, for millennia, has had a clear framework for how a person should live (doing mitzvot and studying Torah), the Kabbalistic perspective modifies how we see these actions. This will, in turn, affect how we actually carry out these activities.

Most of the Kabbalistic texts that exist are by Theosophical Kabbalists. These books generally avoid describing personal mystical experiences, but they are not dispassionate and intellectual in content. Rather, they are filled with a combination of heart and mind.

In Exodus (35:35) there is the expression "Chokhmat Lev" (wisdom of the heart), in reference to Bezalel and his helpers who beautifully craft the Tabernacle. The heart was seen as the seat of true wisdom rather than the head. The head can help understand where the heart must journey and think critically about what the heart experiences.

Varieties of Kabbalistic Texts

There are a number of types of Kabbalistic works in the tradition of the Theosophical Kabbalists. Because the Torah is divided into portions read weekly (so that the entire Five Books of Moses are completed every year), it was common for commentaries on the Torah to follow the order of the portions. Not every Kabbalistic text approached the Bible from only a Kabbalistic perspective. Some commentaries expressed a few viewpoints simultaneously. Nachmanides' commentary, for example, primarily explained the pshat, the plain, literal meaning of the text.

In a Hasidic text, *Sefer Ba'al Shem Tov* (the book of the Ba'al Shem Tov, the founder of modern Hasidism in the 1700s), which reads much like a theosophical Kabbalistic work, there's a seventy-page discussion on prayer when commenting upon the Torah portion of Noah. Its take-off point is the phrase in Genesis (6:16), "Make a window for the Ark." The word that's normally translated as "window" or "opening," *tzohar*, also means "brightness." So the Ba'al Shem Tov reads the phrase as not only referring to Noah and the Ark, but also as referring to prayer because this phrase can also be understood to mean "make your word shine." He understands the Torah's phrase as meaning prayer should be filled with words that shine, that bring light and illumination into your life, and that Kabbalists should bring that intensity and intention to each *tayva*—to each word—so that it illuminates and brings them closer to the Eternal One.

ALERT!

The Hebrew word *tayva* has a few crucial meanings. It's the word for the Ark that Noah built and it's also the word for the basket in which the infant Moses was sent down the river to be saved from the Egyptians. Finally, it also means "word." This allows for interpreting the biblical stories as representative of the power of language.

Another aspect of theosophical Kabbalistic literature is the exploration of the purpose and meaning of the mitzvot. Usually, Theosophical Kabbalists aim to explain the cosmic purposes behind the mitzvot and how they interrelate with and affect the divine realms. This is largely related to the area called *theurgy*, or (according to *Merriam-Webster's English Dictionary*) how human action can affect the spiritual world. A fairly standard Kabbalistic belief is that if a person lives in a state of purity, has great sincerity, and understands the workings of the divine realm (the Sefirot), he or she can bring an abundance of goodness into the world. That person would have to act, of course, with great kavana, meaning focus and intention. While Kabbalists have a grand cosmic image of God as transcendent, they also have an equally immediate sense of God as present and as close to you as you are to yourself.

There was another genre of spiritual literature that was often written by mystics and Kabbalists called *mussar* literature—meaning, ethical literature. Though, on first thought you might assume that Kabbalists would be preoccupied with their relationship with God, at the same time they were very careful to live scrupulously ethical lives.

FACT

There are many ways in which mitzvot are categorized and analyzed to help us understand them and encourage a spiritual lifestyle. Mitzvot are often divided according to those between humans and God and those between humans and other humans. The interhuman activity takes precedence. Kabbalists are very careful to live extremely ethical lives and to understand the subtleties in human interaction.

Kabbalistic Ethical Texts

There were quite a number of Kabbalistic mussar texts. A book written by Bahya Ibn Pakuda in the eleventh century initiated this type of literature. The book is called *Chovot HaLevavot* (Duties of the Heart). Bahya was a prekabbalistic Jewish mystic. Beginning around the middle of the 1500s in Tzfat, Israel, there began a period of a few hundred years in which Kabbalistic mussar texts were very influential. Rabbi Moshe Cordovero wrote *Tomer Devorah* (The Palm Tree of Deborah). Other classic texts in this genre were *Reshit Chokhmah* (The Beginning of Wisdom), by Elijah de Vidas, and *Shnei Lukhot HaBrit* (The Two Tablets of the Covenant; that is, the Ten Commandments), by Isaiah Horovitz.

Moshe Cordovero begins *Tomer Devorah* by saying that every person should resemble the Creator in the secret of the sublime "form." He explains that being created in the "image and likeness" of God means that our behavior has to be like that ascribed to God. Chapter by chapter he goes through the Ten Sefirot discussing what ethical qualities characterize each Sefira. Cordovero begins with the first Sefira, Keter (crown), which he says is characterized by the thirteen *middot* (ethical qualities) of supreme compassion that are implied in the biblical Book of Micah (7:18–20). God is merciful, forgiving, and compassionate, and we must behave in the same manner. In the same chapter he goes on to explain that our souls are intertwined with each other, meaning that each of us has part of our neighbor in us and our neighbor's good fortune should be as desirable to us as our own, for we truly are interconnected.

ALERT!

Proverbs states: "In all your ways know 'Him'" (3:6). These few words contain two central elements of the Kabbalistic focus: living a God-centered life, and "knowing" or being united with God. In *Shnei Lukhot HaBrit,* Rabbi Horowitz elaborates that your kavana should be "for the sake of Heaven," whether you are eating, sleeping, making love, or doing other activities.

Delving into the Sefirot

Explanations and explorations of the Ten Sefirot was another focus of theosophical Kabbalistic works. The various categories of texts always overlapped. A book whose main focus was teachings concerning the Ten Sefirot would generally incorporate explanations of biblical verses as they exemplified the author's points. Similarly, ethical statements would be found throughout the text.

Another category of theosophical books is those that explained the secret teachings of Nachmanides, which he alluded to in his Torah commentary and elsewhere. Nachmanides himself discouraged this, but after a couple of generations his disciples' disciples began to write about his esoteric teachings.

Ecstatic or Prophetic Kabbalah

The other major form of Kabbalah is best known as Ecstatic, or Prophetic, Kabbalah. The most dominant Kabbalist of this orientation was Abraham Abulafia. It is primarily concerned with the attempt to experience God as intimately as possible and to transcend our conventional states of consciousness. The ultimate goal is to achieve a state of union (devekut) with God. The major means of achieving this is through meditational techniques using the Hebrew alphabet and names of God.

Exploring the Hidden Voice of Torah

Both of the two major Kabbalistic paths explain hidden meanings of the Torah, but their methods of doing so differ. The Theosophists tend to interpret the Torah using Kabbalistic symbolism, whereas the Prophetic school tends to use the techniques of gematria, plays on the words of the text, and other means such as notarikon (taking the first or last letters of words to form other words or taking the letters of a word as an acrostic for a phrase).

FACT

The term *ecstasy* comes from the meaning "to stand outside one's self." In religious language it applies to intense experiences in which one stands outside one's normal perceptions. It is generally accompanied by a feeling of exhilaration. In Kabbalah it is often connected with a sense of union with God.

Mystical commentaries on Scripture are a major part of theosophical Kabbalah, whereas they are not in Prophetic Kabbalah. The Sefirot themselves are not a focal point in Prophetic Kabbalah and Abulafia himself saw it as an inferior method, at best useful as a starting point before fully engaging in his system of practices.

The elaborate meditational system that Abulafia taught focused on divine names and the permutations of the letters and vowels of the names. He incorporated breathing exercises, music, color imagery, and head movements all geared toward breaking free from conventional ways of experiencing the world and entering the realm of the One God that underlies and unifies it all. In addition to the Ecstatic Kabbalist's quest for union with God was the goal of achieving a state of prophecy.

Prophecy and Kabbalah

Prophecy in the Jewish tradition has a number of meanings. In the Bible, the prophet was essentially a person of intense spiritual awareness. This spiritual awareness led the prophet to have a powerful moral vision that compelled the prophet to speak of the consequences of people's actions upon their lives in the future. Moses is considered the greatest of all prophets. For the Ecstatic Kabbalists, the prophetic state meant attaining revelations as a result of their intimacy with God. It meant a merging of the Kabbalist's consciousness with divine consciousness.

The prophet Mikha wrote: "[God] told you, human, what is good and what YHVH requires from you—doing justice, loving mercy, and walking humbly with your God" (6:8). These three qualities of justice, mercy, and humility are pillars of the ethical life along with love of both God (Deuteronomy 6:5) and your fellow human (Leviticus 19:18).

Among Abulafia's many "prophetic" books is *Khayei HaOlam HaBa* (The Life of the World to Come). He sets the tone for the book with the following words: "I have come with these words said in truth to forewarn all who come to the gate of this book not to be hasty in spirit to approach the Holy at any time until purifying his consciousness from the vanities of the day and cleansing himself from pride and anger which are the major Kelipot [*obstacles*, in this case] preventing entering and having a vision of the splendor of YHVH. To visit His Hekhal [palace] he needs to humble himself before all people. . . . His Kavana should be for the sake of Heaven and he should have compassion even on those who hate him. His intention should be for the sake of true wisdom and not to take pride in himself."

This could just as well have been written by a Theosophical Kabbalist. There are many overlapping qualities to both orientations. Both were very committed to the traditional life of Torah and mitzvot. Where the paths begin to part is in how the mitzvot are addressed. Much of the theosophical Kabbalistic orientation is in carrying out the mitzvot with an expanded consciousness and grasping the cosmic dimension of the mitzvot. The Ecstatic Kabbalist's meditational activities stood largely outside of that framework.

There were a number of Kabbalists who combined elements of both orientations. Prominent examples are Rabbi Isaac of Acco, Moshe Cordovero, and Isaac Luria. We don't see explicit descriptions, such as Abulafia's, of ecstatic union with God again in Jewish literature until early in the Hasidic movement in Eastern Europe in the late 1700s.

"Practical" Kabbalah: Kabbalah and Magic

There was a segment of Kabbalah that was relatively minor in its impact, called *Kabbalah Ma'asit*, which translates as "Practical Kabbalah." Most of it was what we would call "white" magic, meaning that it was an attempt to affect change for the better in people's lives. It would generally use divine names and names of angels on amulets and for incantations. There was a significant difference between the way Practical Kabbalists would use divine names and names of angels and the way other Kabbalists or earlier Jewish mystics would.

FACT

While most cultures use amulets as a source of spiritual power, Jewish amulets differ from others in that they often focus on the written word, as in the names of God or angels, and not as much on a shape or symbol.

The names of God are used by "mainstream" Kabbalists in order to draw closer to God either because that is the highest good that a person can attain in life (according to the Ecstatic Kabbalists) or in order to affect the entire state of Creation for the good. Though most Practical Kabbalists practice their craft to bring about some good in another person's life or to rid that person of disease or the like, they often work on a very individual level rather than a cosmic one. Some of them undertake these tasks only if circumstances are particularly bad and intervention seems warranted. It would be particularly frowned upon if someone attempted to engage in magic for his or her own gain.

Most mainstream Kabbalists avoided this completely and disapproved of it, though they believed that it was effective. Abulafia was particularly strong in his condemnation of it. The Zohar states that the power of Practical Kabbalah came from the leaves of the tree of knowledge.

Some of the magical practices that constitute what is known as Practical Kabbalah began in Talmudic times and had a folk religion air to them. The making of amulets was often part of this practice. Folk remedies that included calling upon angels by their esoteric names also played a role.

There is a vast difference between the use of esoteric angelic names to guide the Merkavah mystic, for example, in his spiritual journey and the Practical Kabbalist's use of similar names. The mystical journey is one that attempts to connect to the transcendent elements of existence, whereas the magical wants to take that vast power and use it on the mundane level.

Kabbalah and the Occult

Other occult "sciences" were also on the fringes of Kabbalah. Astrology, for example, fell into this category. There is a long history of the acceptance or dismissal of astrology in Judaism. It's not explicitly mentioned in the Bible. While the Talmud addresses astrology, it does not present a clear opinion on whether astrological signs are important in Judaism. There is a Talmudic quote, *"Ayn Mazal L'Yisrael,"* which can be understood in two ways. One way is that Jews are not governed by the stars; the other is that Jews don't have good luck. The Talmudic understanding is the former; the folk/comic understanding is the latter. The opposing opinion in the Talmud was that stars truly do have an effect on a person's fortune.

Among Jewish philosophers of the Middle Ages only one completely dismissed astrology, and that was Maimonides. In Kabbalah it was often believed to be a genuine science, but it was marginalized in the Kabbalistic worldview. The Zohar states that the stars had their power over people's fortunes and destinies until the giving of the Torah, which enabled people to not be subject to the fate of their stars.

ALERT!

The expression *mazal tov* (in the Sephardic pronunciation) or *mazel tov* (in the Ashkenazic pronunciation), which is used in the sense of "congratulations!" literally means "good constellation," or "good star."

Kabbalah and Alchemy

Alchemy also had a minimal connection with Kabbalah. The symbols of the two systems did not coincide. For alchemists the ultimate symbol of perfection was gold, whereas for Kabbalists gold was a symbol for the Sefira of Din, which means "judgment" (another name for this Sefira was Gevurah, "power"). Silver, on the other hand, represented a higher Sefira, that of Hesed (loving kindness or mercy). A very important Kabbalist, Chaim Vital (1542–1620), Isaac Luria's main disciple, spent two years during his youth studying alchemy. He repented of this in his old age.

Kabbalistic Interpretations of Scripture

Commentaries have long existed to accompany the study of Torah, and they occur in various guises. Some are straightforward commentaries, the most influential of which are Rashi's (1040–1105) commentaries on the entire Bible and Talmud. The earliest translations of the Torah (the Septuagint into Greek, Onkelos into Aramaic, etc.) are also commentaries or interpretations of sorts. All translation requires choosing between possible meanings, and that is a form of interpretation. One of the main avenues for communicating Kabbalistic thought was through interpretations of Scripture.

A good example of a Kabbalist commentary comes from the Zohar on the *Parashah of Lekh Lekha*. Lekh Lekha is the third Torah portion and is concerned with Abraham, beginning with God's telling him to leave his country and to go to the land of Canaan and ending with the promise of the birth of Isaac followed by Abraham's and Ishmael's circumcisions.

The Hebrew phrase *lekh lekha* is generally understood to mean "get your-self out." *Lekh* is the command form of the verb "to go," and *lekha* in this context means "yourself." But the Zohar indicates that on a deeper level it means "go into yourself" in order to know yourself and to prepare yourself for the new land that God will show you, meaning a higher plane of existence.

FACT

The Torah is divided into fifty-four weekly portions so that the entire Torah is read over the course of a year. Each portion is called a *Parashah*. The name of each Parashah comes from the first important word in it. For example, the first is called *Bereshit*, the second *Noakh* (about Noah), and so forth.

Another commentary expands upon this by explaining that the next word in the verse, which conventionally means "from your land" (*m'artzekha*), can also be understood to mean from your physicality into your spirituality. That's how you will come to see the land that God will show you. This is a universal message true of everyone at all times.

One of the great Torah commentaries containing much Kabbalistic material is that of Bakhya ben Asher, who lived in Saragossa, Spain. Rabbeinu Bakhya (our teacher/Rabbi Bakhya), as he is called, wrote his commentary in 1291 and it was the first Kabbalistic text to be printed with its complete text intact (in 1492 in Naples). Bakhya was a disciple of Rabbi Solomon ben Abraham Adret who was the main disciple of Nachmanides. Bakhya wrote a lot of what he had learned of Nachmanides' Kabbalistic teachings from his teacher and also incorporated the insights of other Kabbalistic works.

ESSENTIAL

The Torah says the entire nation experienced a divine revelation at Mount Sinai. Some sages later said they heard "I am YHVH your God," [the first commandment.] Others said only the first word: "Anokhi" (I am) was heard. A mystical commentary suggests only the first letter of the first word—the silent aleph—was heard.

Other Schools of Medieval Jewish Mysticism

Jewish mysticism flourished in the Middle Ages in other forms in addition to Kabbalah, though Kabbalah became dominant. The most important of these was the movement known as Hasidei Ashkenaz. These medieval German Hasidim who flourished in the twelfth and thirteenth centuries in Germany had a lot in common with Kabbalists. They had a very strong focus on mystical prayer and an understanding of the universe and God that was comparable to the Kabbalists.

The medieval German Pietists were generally an ascetic sect. They deprived themselves of many social and sensual pleasures. Consistent with Jewish tradition, however, they were committed to marriage and reproduction.

FACT

In Pirkei Avot, a Hasid is defined as one who says, "What is mine is yours and what is yours is yours" (5:13). The term *Hasid* means someone who is pious. It also shares a root with the word *hesed*, which means "loving kindness" or "mercy." So, a Hasid was someone who was loving, merciful, and pious.

The medieval Hasidim were particularly fervent in their enthusiasm toward the mitzvot and prayer. The term *Hasid* had always implied going beyond the normal standards of piety. Their worldview was characterized by the sense of the infiniteness of God and God's simultaneous closeness. There is a verse in the Torah (Deuteronomy 7:21) that says that YHVH your God is in your midst, which was interpreted as meaning within you.

The most important text of Hasidei Ashkenaz was *Sefer Hasidim* (The Book of the Devout), written by Yehuda the Hasid (died 1217), though there were many other texts authored by its main teachers. Along with their ascetic practices, they felt that the source of prayer, for example, was a joyful heart and love of the Omnipresent. Historically this movement thrived despite the devastation and persecution of the Jewish community during the Crusades.

Much of medieval Hasidism's literature was ethical in nature and much attention was given to interpreting the Torah. Hasidei Ashkenaz used the interpretive techniques of gematria and notarikon (reading the letters of a word as though each letter stood for a different word) much more than Theosophical Kabbalists tended to. There was contact between the Spanish Kabbalists and the German Hasidim and both groups influenced each other, but the height of activity for Hasidei Ashkenaz was the period of 1150 to 1250. The Hasidim themselves, much like the Kabbalists, claimed that their teachings were handed down orally for generations.

ALERT!

A good example of notarikon is the explanation that the word *amen* in Hebrew, which is generally understood to mean approximately "I agree," comes from three words: God is a trustworthy ruler (*El melech ne'eman*), with each letter of amen standing for a different word.

Another medieval Jewish mystical movement was a type of Hasidism in Egypt whose main figure was Abraham, the son of Maimonides. This group was not as influential as the Kabbalists or the medieval Hasidim.

Last, but not least, is the group often referred to as the Circle of Contemplation. They also existed in the early 1200s and have a mystical theology quite distinct from the Kabbalists. The most influential texts of this group are *The Books of Contemplation* and *The Fountain of Wisdom*. Their impact continued to be felt in later Jewish mystical circles. Rabbi Moshe Cordovero in the late 1500s considered *The Fountain of Wisdom* (*Ma'ayan HaChokhmah*) as one of the few most important mystical texts, and the Maggid of Mezeritch, probably the most influential disciple of the Ba'al Shem Tov (the founder of Eastern European Hasidism), attested to studying it with the Ba'al Shem Tov in great detail.

Christian Kabbalah

An interesting phenomenon known as Christian Kabbalah began to develop in the fifteenth century. It took hold among mystically oriented Christians who were primarily exposed to Latin translations of Kabbalistic works. The existence of Kabbalah was apparently unknown to these seekers before this, and its "discovery" evoked great interest. Christian Kabbalah attempted to reconcile Kabbalistic teachings with the beliefs of Christianity.

A number of early translations of Kabbalistic texts into Latin were undertaken by Jewish converts to Christianity. Christian Kabbalists generally took the position that the hidden truths contained in Kabbalah confirmed their beliefs in Christianity. Jewish Kabbalists, on the other hand, perceived Christian Kabbalah as full of mistranslations and misreadings of Kabbalistic texts.

Christian Kabbalists saw Kabbalah as an ancient lost tradition of divine revelation that had suddenly been rediscovered. They also believed that it would reveal secrets of Christianity as well as illuminate the works of Plato and Pythagoras.

FACT

The Medicis in Florence supported the opening of a Platonic academy. This was the beginning of serious Christian Kabbalistic thought. The main force behind this school of Christian Kabbalah was Giovanni Pico della Mirandola (1463–1494). He had Kabbalistic works translated into Latin.

While Christian Kabbalah didn't begin with any conversion agenda toward the Jews, over time this developed. As time passed, Christian Kabbalists had less and less knowledge of the original Kabbalistic texts and the Jewish component of Kabbalah became less evident. It was not uncommon for Christian Kabbalists to engage in Kabbalistic theorizing without knowledge of the original sources. In other words, what they knew of Kabbalistic thought without reading actual Kabbalistic texts became the springboard for their own speculations.

There was a tendency, beginning in the seventeenth century, to bring alchemical ideas into Christian Kabbalah. The seventeenth century also saw a significant growth of Christian Kabbalah because of the spread of the book *Kabbalah Denudata* (the most famous and influential translation of Kabbalah into Latin).

Chapter 12

Abraham Abulafia: Ecstatic Mystic

Abraham Abulafia is far and away the most influential Kabbalist in the school of Ecstatic (or Prophetic) Kabbalah. In fact, though he was clearly influenced by mystical and philosophical predecessors, he essentially founded this Kabbalistic orientation. Abulafia's biography is full of fascinating elements. His personality was powerful, his ideas were radical and controversial, and his influence has been long lasting.

Abulafia's Life and Work

Abulafia was born in Saragossa, Spain, in 1240. He spent his first twenty years in Spain before beginning a life that was often characterized by wandering. His rabbinic education was good, but far from outstanding. On the other hand, his knowledge of philosophy was quite extensive.

FACT

Barukh Togarmi was a Kabbalist and a cantor who was Abulafia's teacher probably during the three years Abulafia lived in Barcelona (1270–1273). Togarmi, who wrote a commentary to Sefer Yetzirah, used the methods of gematria, notarikon, and temurah in his quest for mystical knowledge of the Name of God. Abulafia made great use of these methods of interpretation also.

Like other prominent Kabbalists of the time, such as Moshe de Leon and Yosef Gikatilla, Abulafia took an interest in Maimonides' philosophical work *Moreh Nevukhim* (Guide of the Perplexed) before he became a Kabbalist. Unlike Moshe de Leon, the main author of the Zohar (who, incidentally, was also born in Spain in 1240), he never ceased to feel a great affinity with Maimonides. In fact, Abulafia wrote three Kabbalistic commentaries on Maimonides' *Guide,* and for a few years made a living teaching it.

In Search of a Mythical River

Abulafia's father died when Abraham was only eighteen, and two years later, Abulafia journeyed to the land of Israel in search of the mythical river Sambatyon. A journey of this length, particularly in those days, was quite an ordeal. According to legend, the Ten Lost Tribes of Israel dwelled beyond the Sambatyon. Talmudic legend characterized the Sambatyon as a very rough river during the six weekdays, but what was particularly unusual about this river was that it rested on the Sabbath.

Abulafia left the Land of Israel because of warlike conditions between the Muslims and Christians in the region. He took a boat from Acco to

Greece and spent the next ten years in Greece and Italy. Scholars speculate as to whether he made contact with Sufis (Islamic mystics) in the land of Israel because some of his meditational methods seem comparable to those of Sufis. Abulafia also focused on breathing techniques during meditation and scholars wonder whether he may have been indirectly influenced by Yoga via Sufism.

ALERT!

Sufism is traditionally understood to be the inner, mystical, and esoteric teachings of Islam. Sufis particularly stress the importance of love as central to the essence of God, and focus on reducing the ego and seeing the beauty in the seemingly ugly and the good in what appears most evil.

Barukh Togarmi initiated Abulafia into the secrets of Sefer Yetzirah. Abulafia himself eventually wrote a commentary to Sefer Yetzirah called *Gan Na'ul* (The Locked Garden). In 1271, at the age of thirty-one, Abulafia had his first transformative experience. He understood the experience as that of attaining prophetic inspiration and he began teaching his methods and insights to a small number of chosen students. Yosef Gikatilla, who became a well-known and influential Kabbalist in his own right, was Abulafia's foremost student. Gikatilla, who later became close with Moshe de Leon, wrote important works both in the theosophical Kabbalistic vein and in the "Way of the Names," as Abulafia called his own Kabbalistic system.

Prolific Author

Abulafia wrote close to fifty works. A little more than half were Kabbalistic texts of various sorts. In addition to commentaries on Sefer Yetzirah and Maimonides' *Moreh Nevukhim*, he wrote numerous books in which he explains his meditation techniques, teaches the secrets of the various names of God, and writes his insights into the Torah and the mitzvot.

Abulafia also wrote another type of work, which he called his prophetic books. Of the more than twenty that he wrote, only one has survived, *Sefer*

HaOt (The Book of the Sign; the word *Ot*, however, also means "letter"). These emerge more out of his immediate experiences.

Going to See the Pope

In the summer of 1280, Abulafia went to Rome to see Pope Nicholas III, to speak on behalf of the Jewish people and to persuade the pope to improve the difficult conditions under which they lived.

In medieval Europe the Church at times subjected Jews to "disputations" in which they were forced to defend Judaism against Christianity. If in the course of the disputation the judges decided that a Jew had blasphemed against Christianity, he would be put to death. A famous disputation in Paris in 1240 resulted in the public burning of the Talmud.

The most famous disputation that ever occurred was the one imposed upon the Ramban, Nachmanides, in 1263. This debate, which occurred in Barcelona, was attended by many church officials and by the king of Aragon himself. However, unlike most public disputations, Nachmanides was promised by the king that he could speak freely and would not be accused of blasphemy if he denied that Jesus fulfilled the messianic predictions in the Bible.

During the course of the four formal debates with a Jewish convert to Christianity, Pablo Christiani, Nachmanides was generally considered to have argued more persuasively and the king honored him. However, the king told Nachmanides afterward that he could no longer guarantee his safety, and Nachmanides, at the age of sixty-eight, underwent the journey to Jerusalem.

During the disputation Nachmanides said that an indication of the messianic era would be when the Messiah would go to the pope to represent the Jews. Abulafia clearly had messianic ambitions, as he went to Rome for the purpose of representing the Jewish people. Pope Nicholas III, hearing of Abulafia's intentions, ordered him arrested and put to death by burning.

Though Abulafia was forewarned about this, he ignored the warnings and continued his journey, entering Rome, only to be imprisoned. However, that night the pope suddenly died. Abulafia was kept for a month in the College of the Franciscans and was subsequently freed.

Continued Controversy

After his release, Abulafia went to Sicily and remained there for most of the rest of his life. During this period of time he composed the majority of his books. He attracted a number of people to his teachings and created a stir as a result of his belief in himself as the Messiah. People of the community who opposed his claims wrote to the most influential rabbi of the times, Rabbi Shlomo ben Abraham Adret, also known as the Rashba, who lived in Barcelona.

FACT

There is a body of literature known as *responsa* consisting of questions and responses by rabbinic authorities. Responsa are already mentioned in the Talmud, but this form of literature became very important in the Middle Ages and collections of individual rabbis' responses concerning scriptural interpretation, Jewish Law, philosophy, and innumerable other topics have been published.

In a collection of the Rashba's responsa we find a very harsh reply to Abulafia's messianic claims. The Rashba was a Kabbalist himself, in fact he was the main disciple of Nachmanides. He essentially said that Abulafia was a charlatan. Abulafia responded to this criticism in a letter to a colleague of the Rashba's in Barcelona, Rabbi Yehuda Salmon, who had been a student of Abulafia's in the early 1270s. This letter, which has been printed under the title "*V'Zot L'Yehuda*" (And This Is to Yehuda), contains some of Abulafia's criticisms of Theosophical Kabbalah. Generally, Abulafia respected the "Way of the Sefirot," considering it good for beginners, while seeing his own form of Kabbalah, the "Way of the Names," as enabling a person to achieve true knowledge of, and union with, God.

The Rashba was a Theosophical Kabbalist in the vein of his teacher Nachmanides and was very critical of Abulafia's claims to prophecy. As a result of this controversy and the criticism he was drawing over his messianic aspirations, Abulafia was forced to flee Sicily. In his few remaining years he continued to write, and he died in 1291.

Abulafia, Maimonides, and Sefer Yetzirah

Abulafia saw the foundations of Kabbalah in Maimonides' *Guide of the Perplexed* and in Sefer Yetzirah. Maimonides believed philosophy was the path to attaining prophecy. Even the nonkabbalistically oriented student of the Guide recognizes that there are many elements of Maimonides' work that are esoteric. For Maimonides, the contemplation of God and Torah, the highest truths, is the greatest goal of philosophy. At its peak, this activity, when undertaken by a person of outstanding moral, spiritual, and intellectual qualities, leads to the attainment of a state of prophecy.

The biblical image of the prophet is of a person of great spiritual and moral stature. The prophet offered moral and spiritual teachings, criticized the people, including royalty, of their failures, and warned of future consequences. Moses was considered the greatest of all prophets. Prophecy was generally believed to have ceased with the destruction of the Second Temple in Jerusalem.

Reading Maimonides Esoterically

Abulafia believed that the true way to understand Maimonides' *Guide to the Perplexed* was to read it esoterically. Furthermore, this reading of the *Guide* should be taught orally, just like most esoteric teachings. Even those who wrote Kabbalistic texts generally believed that the true understanding of such works must be communicated orally by a teacher or attained through direct experience. This belief is explicit in the Talmud regarding the teachings of the mystical knowledge of Creation and of the Merkavah.

The *Guide* taught an allegorical way of reading Scripture. Maimonides was very insistent, for example, about the incorporeality of God, meaning that God has no physical form. Therefore all of the expressions in the Bible that refer to God's hand, mouth, etc., can only be understood properly as metaphors.

To the philosophically inclined, Maimonides' attempts to reconcile Aristotle and Torah were generally very appealing. Ultimately, if there was an irreconcilable conflict between the two, Maimonides accepted the Torah's position as divinely revealed truth.

FACT

In one of Abulafia's commentaries to the *Guide*, *Sitrei Torah* (Secrets of the Torah), he refers to the chapters of the *Guide* by the term *Gan Eden* (Garden of Eden), whose gematria is the number of chapters in the *Guide*. Gan Eden refers to Paradise in Hebrew, and is echoed in the word *Pardes* (orchard), which refers to mystical knowledge.

Abulafia claimed that he learned the Kabbalistic teachings of the *Guide* from great teachers of his generation who transmitted these secrets to him orally and from God (through his own experiences). Though Abulafia mentions elsewhere his teacher Rabbi Hillel of Verone with whom he studied the *Guide*, there is no historical evidence that Rabbi Hillel read it esoterically. Abulafia didn't name the Kabbalistic mentors who taught him how to read the *Guide*.

Essentially, Abulafia absorbed two main elements from his study of Maimonides. Maimonides' metaphysical explanation of reality (his definition of God as the "Active Intellect" and as "the Knowledge and the Knower") provided a vocabulary and framework to describe Abulafia's experiences of union with God. Furthermore, Maimonides' explanation of prophecy as the prophet's attaining inspiration and vision from "the Active Intellect" fit with Abulafia's understanding of his own mystical experiences.

The Guide Alone Is Not Enough

Despite the high esteem in which Abulafia held the *Guide*, he felt that there was a crucial element lacking in it. This was the true knowledge and experience of "the name," which you could achieve through the mystical practices taught in Sefer Yetzirah. Once you have immersed yourself in this practice, you will return to the *Guide* and understand it ever more deeply.

ALERT!

Controversy surrounded the writings of Maimonides. Many strongly criticized both his towering code of Jewish Law, *The Mishnah Torah,* and the *Guide.* Theosophical Kabbalists generally opposed Maimonides' rationalization of the mitzvot, feeling it undermined their spiritual foundation. They, on the other hand, offered the hidden spiritual bases for the mitzvot in their books.

Abulafia as a whole was concerned with the spiritual life of a person rather than the correct interpretation of a text. He believed that the experience of "the name" was an attainment greater than any intellectual achievement. Abulafia consistently treated the *Guide* as a work that contained thirty-six secrets. The knowledge of the thirty-six secrets contained in the three sections of the *Guide* would bring a person redemption, *geulah* (spelled *gimmel*, whose gematria is 3, representing the three sections of the *Guide*, and *aleph, lamed, hey*, whose gematria is 36). To explain these secrets, Abulafia used methods, such as gematria and notarikon, that Maimonides himself did not take seriously.

Language and Mysticism

The power of language is a constant theme throughout the Jewish tradition and particularly throughout Jewish mysticism. However, Abulafia's understanding of language and his use of it differs significantly from Theosophical Kabbalah's orientation.

Abulafia saw the letters of the alphabet as the gateway to a deeper experience of God than that provided by "the way of the Sefirot." He reinforces this by noting that the gematria of the phrase "Permutation of Letters" (*Tzeruf HaOtiyot*) equaled that of the "Work of the Chariot" (*Ma'aseh Merkavah*). In other words, this method is the true Ma'aseh Merkavah.

Abulafia believed that his meditative methods (which you will learn more about in Chapter 16) using the Hebrew language could give you a deeper understanding of reality than philosophy could. Contemplating the letters and meditating with them would unlock secrets inaccessible by any other means. To Abulafia, the structure of the Hebrew language itself contains within it the secrets of the natural universe.

Functions of the Hebrew Language

For Abulafia, language had two essential functions. The conventional one was communication of our thoughts. The second function was for the attainment of prophecy.

Pirkei Avot (5:1) states that the universe was created with ten utterances. This statement stems from Genesis, in which God says, "Let there be . . . and there was . . . ." In its first chapter, second Mishnah, Sefer Yetzirah speaks of "Ten Sefirot of Nothingness and twenty two Foundation Letters" and goes on to distinguish the three categories of letters: "Three Mothers, Seven Doubles, and Twelve Elementals." A relatively short section of Sefer Yetzirah is devoted to the Sefirot and the majority of the rest is devoted to an esoteric examination of the letters of the Hebrew alphabet.

Hebrew was believed to be the original language, the language in which Adam named all the animals, the language through which Creation came about. All other languages were understood as in some way coming from it. Another belief was that there were seventy languages. In ancient times, some people took this literally, but by medieval times it was seen as a reference to all the other languages and to all knowledge that humans possess collectively.

ALERT!

A classic Midrash on Exodus (*Sh'mot Rabbah*) 5:9 in describing the divine revelation at Mount Sinai says that the divine voice became seventy voices so that all nations of the world could hear. Abulafia noted that the gematria for "combining of the letters" (*Tzeruf HaOtiyot*) was equal to that of the words "seventy languages" (*Shiv'im L'shonot*).

Those, like Abulafia, who philosophized about human language in general tended to think that language came about through human convention, but that Hebrew, the language of divine revelation, reflected reality on a different level. Some saw it as a revealed language, others as a language whose nature made it the ideal medium for communicating revelation.

For Theosophical Kabbalists, contemplation of the Sefirot was the means of understanding God. For Abulafia, the names of God were the vehicle for this knowledge and meditation on the names revealed a deeper level of this knowledge than the Sefirot could possibly reveal.

The Kabbalistic Meaning of Letters

Abulafia wrote that different aspects of the Hebrew alphabet were filled with mystical meaning. The shapes of the letters themselves were not a matter of human convention, but were provided through prophetic insight by those who communicated God's revelation. The names of the letters were deeply significant. The first letter of the Hebrew alphabet, the aleph, for example, is spelled *aleph, lamed, pheh*. The name of the aleph, therefore, has the gematria of 111, which emphasizes its standing for "unity" (the gematria of the aleph itself is 1). In addition to the visual form and the names of the letters both being meaningful, the numerical equivalents of the letters were highly significant.

Abulafia saw the combining of letters as the construction of something, much as any living being is put together with different parts of the body. Sefer HaBahir had said that the vowels were the souls of words and Abulafia agreed with this perspective. The vowels provided various pronunciations of YHVH when using them as a meditation technique with this name. Also, the vowels indicated the head movements and breathing exercises that Abulafia practiced to accompany the pronunciation and meditation on the divine letters.

FACT

Interpretations of the significance of the shapes and names of the letters of the Hebrew alphabet occur in the Talmud and Midrash. They become even more common in the Middle Ages, particularly in theosophical Kabbalistic works.

Music and Mysticism

The Bible, especially the Psalms, has many references to the playing of music in a spiritual context or as part of religious ceremonies. King David, traditionally held to be the author of the Psalms, played the harp. His music was believed to calm the soul. The Levites played various instruments in the ancient Temple, such as the lute, drums, and the harp, in addition to singing.

ESSENTIAL

In the Second Book of Kings, the prophet Elisha says, "And now, bring me a minstrel; and it came to pass when the minstrel played, the hand of YHVH was upon him" (3:15). Abulafia, in reference to prophecy, also quotes the Talmud, which says that "the Shekhinah only dwells where there is joy" (Tractate Shabbat 30b).

Music played an important role in Abulafia's meditational techniques. He saw many parallels between the technique of letter combination and music. Abulafia offered the analogy of sympathetic tones occurring between different instruments, or different strings in the same instrument, with a comparable process resulting from letter combination. This technique, he says, just like music, brings great joy to the soul. Also like music, the technique of letter combination occurs outside the soul, but has a great affect on a person's internal life.

A person who makes himself into an instrument of sorts, capable of being played upon by the Shekhinah, may thus become a vessel of prophecy. The Midrash Mekhilta on Exodus refers to prophets as analogous to instruments. Music is also used in the process of letter combination when the practitioner recites the letters in a melodic way. This is comparable to the traditional reading of the Torah scroll and other parts of the Bible. They are always accompanied by melodies that are indicated by cantillation marks.

Abulafia explains that the term *Gan Eden* (the Garden of Eden, paradise) has the same letters as *ad nagen* ("while playing") and the same gematria as *eved nagen* ("a playing servant" or "a servant of playing"). Music could both induce the state of prophecy and prepare you for receiving it as the Shekhinah moves through you like sound rising from an instrument.

Permutations of the Divine Names

There are many elements to Abulafia's techniques of letter combinations. He primarily worked with YHVH and with the seventy-two-letter name of God. When using YHVH, he combines each letter individually with the aleph and uses five different Hebrew vowels (according to Sephardic Hebrew grammar) in changing combinations. So he might begin with aleph and yud and vocalize them with the same vowel and then proceed with different combinations from there. The vowels he uses are the *kholam* (pronounced oh), *kamatz* (pronounced ah), *khirik* (pronounced ee), *tzereh* (pronounced eh), and *kubutz* (pronounced oo). With great care and concentration, Abulafia put each set of letters together with every possible combination of vowels.

ALERT!

Rashi's commentary on the Talmudic passage about the "Four Who Entered Pardes" in Tractate Chagigah says they entered Pardes "by means of a [divine] Name" (14b). The usage of divine names for meditation is clearly much older than Abulafia's technique. Methods similar to Abulafia's were also used among the Hasidei Ashkenaz.

Abulafia saw the divine name as reflecting the structure of reality and also as being embedded in a person's soul. The manipulation of the letters and vowels of "the name" would consequently change a person's soul and consciousness. Therefore it was especially important that a person undertake these processes with maximum awareness, to avoid causing harm to oneself.

An unusual element of Abulafia's method was that he would often utter the letters, vowels, and their permutations out loud. This was generally forbidden by the Kabbalistic tradition. Other Kabbalists, such as Issac of Acco, who also used YHVH as a focus of meditation, avoided any attempted utterance of the name. The Mishnah (Tractate Sanhedrin 90b) explicitly says that whoever intentionally pronounces the divine name has "no place in the world to come." Abulafia apparently felt the exact opposite, that the attainment of the "world to come" was only possible through his method of letter combinations and their verbalization.

FACT

Pirkei Avot states: "Turn it [the Torah] and turn it, for everything is in it" (5:25). This is a classic expression of the traditional belief that all knowledge can ultimately be found in the Torah. Abulafia added to these words: "and all of it is in you and all of you is in it."

Abraham Ibn Ezra (1089–1164)—poet, biblical commentator, and philosopher—wrote a commentary on the verse 10:21 of the biblical book of Daniel regarding prophecy, which can be understood as saying that humans are the vessel for the divine message. Abulafia believed that the process of permutation of letters could provide you with access to that prophetic voice that comes from the depths of your soul. If you were able to reach that level you would be met and taught there by a spiritual teacher. Abulafia adopted the term *intellect* that Maimonides used to refer to this highest level of the soul. He understood, again following Maimonides, that prophecy was when this highest level of the human soul merged with the divine "Active Intellect." Abulafia also referred to the "Active Intellect" as "the Splendor of the Shekhinah."

The Hebrew term for letter combining, *tzeruf otiyot*, also means "purification of the letters." In Abulafia's book *Imrei Shefer* (Sayings of Grace or Beauty), he says: "Know that Tzeruf Otiyot is the first thing that a Kabbalist teaches another Kabbalist given that he possesses good qualities, and awe of Heaven, hate of greed, love of truth, pursuit of peace, humility, generosity, modesty, fleeing transgression, protecting Mitzvah, wise, understanding, educated, loving study, diligent, striving to know the Torah for its own sake."

Abulafia's Enduring Influence

Though Abulafia encountered much opposition to his teachings during his lifetime and even had to flee Sicily because of the controversy surrounding him, he ultimately had a powerful impact on Kabbalah. In addition to influencing major Kabbalists of his own era such as Yosef Gikatilla and Isaac of Acco, he had a strong impact on the most important Kabbalists in Tzfat almost three centuries later.

Cordovero and Abulafia

Moshe Cordovero quotes Abulafia extensively in his classic work *Pardes Rimonim* and records Abulafia's meditational techniques of permutations of the letters and of the divine names. He also taught Abulafia's breathing techniques. Cordovero has an entire section in *Pardes Rimonim* devoted to the letters, one devoted to vowels, and another devoted to tzeruf (combinations). An Italian disciple of Cordovero's, Rabbi Mordekhai Dato, wrote of Cordovero practicing these forms of meditation.

Dato writes further that Cordovero was a successful practitioner of this method of meditation and that he taught it to his disciples. In other words, Cordovero combined both a profound knowledge of Theosophical Kabbalah and an intense practice of Ecstatic Kabbalah.

Abulafia, Luria, Vital, and Hasidism

Isaac Luria and his main disciple, Chaim Vital, also show the influence of Abulafia. This is particularly evident in their meditation techniques. First of all, both Vital and Luria were students of Cordovero until he died. The fourth chapter of Vital's *Sha'arei Kedushah* (Gates of Holiness), which contains meditations with divine names, is very Abulafian.

The practice of *hitbodedut* (meditation) by Hasidim and the many writings that speak of devekut as a union with God are another example of Abulafia's powerful influence hundreds of years after his death. The attainment of a state of ecstasy, which Abulafia understood as prophecy, remained a focal point of meditation for hundreds of years after Abulafia and was incorporated into parts of the Hasidic movement.

Modern-day Kabbalists continue to practice Abulafia's techniques. Though some of his books have finally found their way into print in recent years, people still continue to go to the effort of copying his unpublished works from libraries, such as the manuscript section of Hebrew University in Jerusalem.

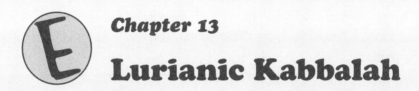

Chapter 13

Lurianic Kabbalah

After the expulsion from Spain in 1492, the Jewish world was traumatized. Kabbalah, whose center had been primarily in Spain, was deeply affected by this upheaval. Approximately fifty years after this cataclysm, a new Kabbalistic center emerged in northern Israel in the town of Tzfat (often called Safed in English).

Kabbalistic Community in Tzfat

According to the Kabbalistic tradition, the Zohar was written by Shimon bar Yokhai when he lived in a cave for thirteen years in Meron in northern Israel while hiding from the Romans. Slightly southeast of there is the town of Tzfat, which became a Kabbalistic center in the 1500s. Some of the giants in the history of Kabbalah lived there, including Isaac Luria, Moshe Cordovero, Yosef Karo, Shlomo Alkabetz, Chaim Vital, and many more—all in the same time period.

ALERT!

Tzfat was the site of the first printing press in the Middle East. In 1578 the first Hebrew book was printed there. Contemporary Tzfat has seen a revival of mystical activity. The graves of Isaac Luria and Moshe Cordovero, for example, are visited by tourists and the devout alike, as are the synagogues in which they and others prayed.

On Friday evenings toward sunset Kabbalists would walk through the fields outside of town dressed in white, singing specific prayers and psalms, greeting Shabbat the Queen. This is the origin of the Kabbalat Shabbat (receiving or welcoming Shabbat) service that has become a part of synagogue services on Friday evenings. The most famous part of this service is the song "L'kha Dodi" (Come My Friend to Greet the Bride, Shabbat), which was composed by the Kabbalist Shlomo Alkabetz.

Moshe Cordovero

Moshe (Moses, in English) Cordovero (1522–1570) was a great synthesizer of Kabbalistic thought. He had an encyclopedic knowledge of the Kabbalistic writings that preceded him. While only in his twenties, he wrote one of the most influential Kabbalistic works, *Pardes Rimonim* (The Pomegranate Orchard), in which he systematically presents much of the Kabbalistic thought that came before and contributes his own thought and experience. He wrote a major multivolume commentary on the Zohar called *Or Yakar*

(The Precious Light) and a classic work on Kabbalistic mussar (ethics) called *Tomer Devorah* (The Palm Tree of Deborah).

Cordovero, also known as the Ramak (an acrostic for Rabbi Moshe Cordovero), studied both the Ecstatic and the Theosophical Kabbalah and wrote about both. He was Isaac Luria's teacher for about half a year before dying in 1570 at the age of forty-eight. Cordovero's thought had a significant impact on Hasidism and he would probably be even better known if it weren't for the unprecedented impact of Luria.

FACT

Moshe Cordovero sought to commune with the souls of departed Tzaddikim (plural of Tzaddik). He would lie down on their graves and meditate to receive their teachings. He also had the practice, shared with his teacher Shlomo Alkabetz, of voluntarily wandering in exile from home in sympathy with the Shekhinah's exile, seeking revelations from the Shekhinah who dwells in the heart.

Cordovero was an accomplished student of Talmud and wrote a manual for pious conduct. He was a student of philosophy also, but felt that Kabbalah was superior. To Cordovero, Kabbalah resolved the problem of the existence of a physical, finite world created by the "infinite perfect God." The Sefirot and the concept of emanation explained this transition. Cordovero was not only a master synthesizer of previous thought and a serious thinker in his own right, but he was also a committed practitioner of Kabbalistic meditation and a prolific writer. He dominated the Kabbalistic circles in Tzfat until his death and left a number of disciples, some of whom were major Kabbalists themselves.

Yosef Karo

Yosef Karo (1488–1575) was an important Kabbalist, but much better known as one of the most influential figures in the nonesoteric (*nigleh*) tradition. Karo was the author of the authoritative code of Jewish Law called the *Shulkhan Arukh* (The Set Table"). He is also well known for his book

Maggid Mesharim (Preacher of Uprightness). *Maggid Mesharim* is the published part of a spiritual diary in which Karo records the teachings given to him by his maggid. A maggid in this sense is a heavenly disembodied voice that comes to someone spiritually and ethically worthy either in a dream state or while awake, emanating from the person's own throat.

Yosef Karo understood his maggid as being the Shekhinah taking the form of the Mishnah. Karo would establish contact with his maggid by reciting Mishnayot (Mishnaic passages). There is a famous letter written by Shlomo Alkabetz (circa 1505–1576), who was the teacher (and later the student and also the brother-in-law) of Moshe Cordovero, to the Kabbalistic community in Salonika, Greece, in which he tells of his experience with Karo when they stayed up all night on the evening of Shavuot studying Torah, prophets, Mishnah, and Kabbalah. As they were studying Mishnah, Alkabetz and others present witnessed a resonant voice emerging from Karo's own throat teaching them.

From Karo and Alkabetz's all-night vigil studying Torah, Mishnah, and Kabbalah on the first night of Shavuot, the custom began of observing this vigil, called *Tikkun Leil Shavuot*, on that night every year. *Shavuot* means "weeks" and marks seven weeks after Passover. Though initially an agricultural holiday, Shavuot became associated in rabbinic times with the receiving of Torah at Mount Sinai.

Chaim Vital

Vital was born in 1542, probably in Tzfat. He plays an eminent role in the history of Kabbalah primarily because he became the main disciple of Isaac Luria and the author of the most influential books of what are known as *Kitvei Ha'Ari* (The Writings of the Ari, the acronym by which Isaac Luria was known). Vital was a proficient student of Talmud and was ordained. He began his Kabbalistic studies at the age of twenty-two as a disciple of Moshe Cordovero. After Cordovero's death he became Luria's main disciple. In addition to authoring *Etz Chaim* (The Tree of Life), the most important text of

Lurianic Kabbalah, he wrote numerous other works including a work on ethics and meditation called *Sha'arei Kedushah* (The Gates of Holiness), a commentary on the Zohar, and a spiritual autobiography called *Sefer HaKhezyonot* (The Book of Visions). He died in 1620.

Vital did not want any of his writings on Luria's teaching to be published or distributed outside of his small circle of students. However, when he was seriously ill in Tzfat in 1587, his younger brother was bribed to allow hundreds of pages of his manuscripts to be copied. These are what eventually were published and led to the dissemination of Luria's ideas, which ultimately became the dominant form of Kabbalistic thought.

Isaac Luria: The Ari

Rabbi Isaac Luria (or Yitzkhak Luria in Hebrew), is known also as the "Ari" (the holy "Lion"), an acrostic for the divine (meaning "mystical master"). Rabbi Luria was born in Jerusalem in 1534 of an Ashkenazi father and a Sephardi mother. His father died when he was very young and his mother then raised him in his uncle's house in Egypt. He was an excellent student in the nigleh tradition that is in Talmud and halakhah (Jewish Law) and he began studying Kabbalah also. Eventually he moved back to Israel, settling in Tzfat either in 1569 or 1570, where he studied with Cordovero until the latter's death in the fall of 1570.

A plague in Israel between Passover and Shavuot killed 24,000 of Rabbi Akiva's students. The day the plague ceased, *Lag BaOmer*, became a semiholiday. It is also the date of the death of Shimon bar Yokhai, who is believed to be buried in Meron where there has been a celebration at his gravesite on that date since 1522.

Luria taught a small number of disciples, probably not many more than thirty. He first attained fame as a poet. Since his Kabbalistic thought was not publicly known and he preferred to keep it that way, it was his personal charisma and saintly behavior that was recognized during his lifetime. Luria died on July 15, 1572, during an epidemic. Within a number of years after his death, legends about his life abounded. A book called *Shivkhei Ha'Ari* (Praises of the Ari), written about thirty-five years after his death, is a biography of Luria's life. It contains factual information embellished with legends about his saintliness.

Part of the power of Luria's personality is attested to by the fact that within a matter of months of moving to Tzfat, where there was already a cluster of stellar Kabbalists, he became by far the dominant figure. Luria's Kabbalistic system has a few central issues, and like most Kabbalistic thought, there are a few major themes: understanding Creation, redemption, and our relationship to the Divine and the world in which we live. Included within this is always the problem of the existence of evil in a world created by a perfect God.

Divine Self-Limitation: Tzimtzum

Up until Luria, Creation was described in Kabbalah as a direct emanation (atzilut) from Ein Sof of the divine realm of the Sefirot, eventually culminating in the physical universe. In earlier Kabbalah, the exploration of the transition point from the undifferentiated divinity that is Ein Sof to a world of apparent differentiation raised important questions. The emanation of the world of the Sefirot largely addressed this. Then the question arose as to whether the Sefirot are the essence of God or vessels for divinity leading to the creation of the universe.

Moshe Cordovero said that the Sefirot were both essence (*atzmut*) and vessels (*kelim*). He further explained, following Nachmanides, that there was a necessary tzimtzum (contraction) of the divine "light" to make creation of the physical universe possible. Each successive Sefira, therefore, was a slightly less intense level of pure divinity than the Sefira above it. This tzimtzum is necessary because the intensity of the divine Shefa (energy) would be too much for Creation to tolerate, just as an overabundance of light is blinding. This is the earliest meaning of the term *tzimtzum* in Kabbalah. There is an interrelationship between revelation and concealment. For some element of revelation to be possible, there must be some concealment, because total revelation would be overwhelming.

The idea of tzimtzum also exists in the Midrash, which describes God contracting in order to enter a finite space such as the Holy of Holies in the ancient Temple in Jerusalem or the Shekhinah contracting itself to fit between the cherubs on the Ark.

ALERT!

The question of whether or not tzimtzum was meant literally remained an issue for at least 200 years. Many Kabbalists claimed that it was not literally true, but human minds needed the metaphor of tzimtzum to grasp to some degree the divine process of Creation. Others insisted that it was, in fact, meant literally.

In pre-Lurianic Kabbalah, there is generally an unbroken connection from Ein Sof to the physical universe we inhabit. However, for Luria the process was much more complicated and significantly different. Luria's use of tzimtzum implies a contraction of Ein Sof away from the space left empty to make room for Creation. The understanding here is that Ein Sof without tzimtzum could leave no room for anything that is not Ein Sof. Into this empty space created by tzimtzum, Ein Sof sends divine light, which fills the empty space with the Ten Sefirot.

There are a number of slightly different versions of tzimtzum described in various books. In another version, instead of divine light, what enters the empty space is the yud of YHVH. In this description, Ein Sof, which contains all of the Sefirot undifferentiated, uses the roots of Din (the Sefira that is judgment, boundaries, and limitation) to bring about tzimtzum. Tzimtzum itself leaves a residue of divinity in the empty space called *reshimu*, a process analogous to the residue of wine left in an empty bottle. Into this empty space the roots of *Rakhamim* (compassion, mercy) pour the divine yud. The divine reshimu becomes the source of vessels that would receive the light that would ultimately lead to Creation.

The Shattering of the Vessels: Shevirat HaKelim

After tzimtzum, the process that followed is quite complex. Emanation sent divine light into the tehiru, which is the primordial space left after tzimtzum. This emanated light from Ein Sof, which was intended to assemble the reshimu (the residue of divine light left behind from the process of tzimtzum), and the elements of Din that were driving powers behind tzimtzum, came in two forms: concentric circles (*iggul*) and a line (*yosher*).

FACT

Isaac Luria had a number of disciples who wrote somewhat different versions of his system. There are, therefore, differing views of tzimtzum and "the breaking of the vessels." Among these writers are Chaim Vital, Yosef Ibn Tabul, and Moshe Yonah. Though Vital is considered Luria's main disciple, within Vital's own writings there are discrepancies in the presentation of elements of Luria's system.

The line of light (yosher) comes straight from Ein Sof and therefore its essence is slightly "higher" than that of the circular light whose shape is a response to the empty space left from tzimtzum. According to Luria's system, emanation first forms the level of Adam Kadmon. Here Luria differs from earlier Kabbalistic systems. It is only after Adam Kadmon that the levels of existence known as atzilut (emanation), beriah (Creation), yetzirah (formation), and asiyah (action) come into being.

The first act of emanation is the Ten Sefirot taking the form of Adam Kadmon in concentric circles with the highest Sefira, Keter, on the outermost circle surrounded by Ein Sof. After this the Ten Sefirot rearrange themselves in the form of a line, which symbolically is represented in the form of a human.

The next step in the symbolic description that ultimately leads to our existence is that the head of Adam Kadmon radiates huge amounts of light that take various forms. The forms are elements of the Hebrew language and components of the Torah such as letters, cantillation marks, and even the crowns that adorn certain letters in the Torah scroll. The symbolic systems of light and language are fused here. Each vessel has an inner light and an encompassing light; each emanated light has a circular and a line aspect. At each successive step of emanation, the vessel containing the light becomes less subtle and less sublime.

The Talmud says that Torah speaks in the language of humans (Tractate Brakhot 31a). Similarly, Kabbalah gives visual metaphors for abstract, nonphysical experiences. This is related to the debate over whether tzimtzum is literal or metaphorical. The imagery of light, circles, and lines is an attempt to provide symbolic language for experiences that language cannot quite communicate.

Cosmic Cataclysm

All of the Sefirot had "vessels" in which their light was contained. The first three vessels, which received their light individually, were able to contain the light. At this point it is worth remembering that Cordovero, who was Luria's teacher for the first six months of Luria's residence in Tzfat, said that the Sefirot were both essence and vessels. Here we see this expressed in Luria's system.

The next six Sefirot, Hesed through Yesod, which were often seen as a separate grouping from the first three and from the last Sefira, received their light all at once; they could not contain it, and each shattered successively. The vessel for Malkhut also could not withstand its abundance of light and cracked, but not as severely as the six Sefirot above it.

Kelipot

What happened to the light in the vessels? Part of it returned to its source, but part of it descended along with the shattered vessels, vivifying the kelipot (outer shells). The light that is "trapped" in the kelipot is the source of their life. Otherwise they would be dormant forms like Adam without the breath of life blown into him (Genesis 2:7). The kelipot are the root of evil according to Luria's system.

Concealing of the Divine Light: Or Ne'elam

After the Shattering of the Vessels, according to most versions of the Lurianic creation story, nothing in the cosmic order was the same as originally planned. The kelipot pervaded all levels and worlds. At the same time, the kelipot, which are in virtually all physical existence, contain within them divine light. Every kelipah is sustained by the divine light within it. Everything that exists in the physical universe that we inhabit has a spark of divinity within it, no matter how deeply buried it is by the kelipah in which it resides.

Pirkei Avot states that "Everything is foreseen [by God] and free will is given" (3:15). On the surface this seems like a contradiction. However, if you recognize that for God the past, present, and future are all "present," it is comparable to the fact that our knowledge of history does not negate the free will of the people who took part in that history.

There is a difference between the free will of humans choosing their actions and Ein Sof emanating the universe. From an ethical point of view, the essence of human behavior is the ability to do good out of choice rather than being preprogrammed to do so. On the other hand, God, who is perfect, cannot make mistakes or miscalculate. God, who is all-knowing and all powerful, foresees the results of all actions and therefore must choose this entire process of tzimtzum and the Shattering of the Vessels for a reason, even if the reason is not fathomable to our minds. The end result of this scenario is that human beings have both a cosmic mythological explanation for the existence of evil in the world, its connection to the physical realm, and its potential conversion back to goodness. Bound to all of this is our human role in redeeming the entire cosmos and bringing about an era of redemption and perfection (the messianic era).

Redeeming the Divine Sparks: Nitzotzot

From the beginnings of Kabbalah, human activity was seen as having cosmic impact, but much of it tended to be geared toward achieving individual redemption through uniting with God. With Lurianic Kabbalah, the mythology of the hidden divine sparks created a foundation for a broader form of redemption, one that would affect all of humanity. It's true that elements of this were in evidence in earlier Kabbalah such as the Zohar, but it didn't attain centrality until Lurianic Kabbalah.

In Tzfat a community of Kabbalists shared a sense that they could bring about the messianic era through their concerted effort. They believed their activities, prayer, meditation, performing of mitzvot, and their unification of the divine realms through their consciousness could change everything. Every element of life and the physical universe contained divine sparks (*nitzotzot*) that needed to be released and redeemed so that our existence could reach a higher state.

ALERT!

Hiding the divine sparks in all earthly things are the kelipot, or shells, surrounding them and preventing the flow of Shefa (divine energy). The performance of mitzvot erodes these barriers, and by exposing all of the divine sparks Kabbalists hope to bring redemption and perfection to the world and harmony in the Divine realms.

This perception of the divine spark in everything included the realm of evil. Who was capable of redeeming the divine spark contained in evil? Only a Tzaddik of such consciousness that he would not be susceptible to the evil and could come in contact with it in order to raise the holiness hidden deep within. In Luria's day people understood that only a truly rare individual was capable of such spiritual feats. In later days, such as during the time of Shabbtai Tzvi and his spiritual offspring, this orientation degenerated greatly, leading people to defy ethical standards with the excuse of redeeming the divine sparks hidden in the forbidden acts.

Mystical Prayer: Kavanot

The term kavana in Kabbalah and in Judaism in general had a number of meanings, but the central one was that of intention and mental focus. Yitzkhak Luria used the term to refer to specific Kabbalistic meditations accompanying the traditional prayers.

In pre-Lurianic Kabbalah the kavanot (plural of kavana) that were prevalent were focused on the Sefirot. In other words, specific prayers would be used as meditations to connect the person praying with the Sefira associated with that prayer. Kabbalistic prayer was generally very meditative and probably the major means of attaining union with God. The seminal Kabbalist Azriel of Gerona spoke of Kabbalistic prayer as penetrating to the nothingness of each word. Each word had the potential to connect you directly to God.

Lurianic Prayer Books

Luria's system of kavanot changed the focus of kavana to the use of mystical names of God associated with particular words throughout the prayer book. There are many Kabbalistic prayer books, which are manuals of mystical prayer. After Luria the publication of such *siddurim* (prayer books) increased. A prayer book based on Luria's teachings often contained specific names of God written into the expanded letters of words. Another element was taking the ultimate name YHVH and giving it different vocalizations by putting a particular set of vowels under each letter of YHVH, each set of vowels having a specific significance. These methods had much in common with Abulafia's meditational system.

Kabbalistic prayer with kavanot combined the communal aspect of prayer with the highly individualized meditations added to it. Though there were Kabbalistic prayer groups, individual Kabbalists could also practice their kavanot in the context of a larger community.

In earlier Kabbalistic kavanot the main focus was on achieving a state of devekut with the Omnipresent, but in Luria's system the goal of raising the divine sparks in ourselves became an additional important element.

Unifications: Yikhudim

Isaac Luria's relationship with his disciples was unique. He would give them a "reading" of their soul and its *gilgulim* (reincarnations). When walking through the hills surrounding Tzfat he would point out to them the burial places of ancient Tzaddikim (saints) with whom they would commune. Luria would individualize the meditations of his disciples based on his perceptions of the roots of their souls.

The Ari had a system of *yikhudim*, which were meditations on various letter combinations of YHVH or variant vocalizations of the name. For example, the name could be written out spelling each of the letters individually in different combinations. The letter *hey* could be spelled as a hey alone or as hey aleph, or hey yud, etc. Each of these possibilities would spell the name of the letter and each had its own significance. These meditations were believed to help effect a Tikkun (a healing, repairing) in the upper and lower worlds.

Repairing the Cosmos: Tikkun Olam

There is a strong messianic element in Lurianic Kabbalah. The entire view of reality that Luria puts forth that includes tzimtzum and Shevirat HaKelim (the Shattering of the Vessels), culminates with Tikkun, the repairing, healing, and realigning of all the worlds.

Our Role in Achieving Tikkun

Tikkun began immediately after the Shattering of the Vessels with the lights radiating from the forehead of Adam Kadmon. These lights are the main power bringing about Tikkun. However, an element of Tikkun is left in human hands. It is through our consciousness, our actions, yikhudim, kavanot, and mitzvot, that we are able to bring about the finishing touches of Tikkun that will usher in the age of perfection which is the messianic era.

What are Yikhudim?
Yikhudim are a form of Jewish meditation focusing on variations of the Divine Name and often various vocalizations of it in order to bring about union and Tikkun of the soul, cosmos, and the Divine Name itself.

The Shattering of the Vessels disrupted the original vision of Creation resulting in the worlds of atzilut, beriah, yetzirah, and asiyah being at a "lower level" than they were intended to be. The world of asiyah itself, in which we dwell, is not at the spiritual level that it should be and has descended to the level where there are kelipot. In the messianic era, which our actions are meant to bring about, asiyah can once again be freed from all kelipot and all Creation will live in harmony with the One.

Psychological Elements of Tikkun

Tikkun and the other Lurianic terms such as tzimtzum and kelipot have profound psychological applications as well. They operate on the macrocosmic and microcosmic levels equally. Probably every individual has some brokenness and is in need of Tikkun, which in this case can mean psychological and emotional healing. At times we need to do some tzimtzum of our egos in order to bring about an ultimate Tikkun. Luria's system inspires deep spiritual, psychological, and social activity, all of which are necessary to bring about a messianic era.

Chapter 14

Dancing with the Divine: Hasidism

The last major development in the history of Kabbalah and Jewish mysticism is the Hasidic movement, which began around the middle of the 1700s. It revolutionized both Kabbalah and the Jewish world and brought mysticism to a huge portion of the Jewish population. Though Hasidism has changed significantly since its beginnings in the eighteenth century, it has continued to be a powerful movement in Jewish religious life.

The Ba'al Shem Tov

Yisrael ben Eliezer (Israel the son of Eliezer), better known as the Ba'al Shem Tov, was the founder of Hasidism. He lived from 1700 (or according to some accounts, 1698) to 1760 in the Ukraine. There is an abundance of legends about him, but we possess hardly anything that he himself wrote with the exception of a few letters. Fortunately for our study of him, his disciples quote him regularly and there are collections of his sayings gathered from their books. Among his disciples was his grandson, Moshe Chaim Ephraim of Sudylkov, the author of *Degel Machaneh Ephraim* (The Banner of the Camp of Ephraim, a title taken from Numbers 2:18), a classic Hasidic text that contains many quotations from his grandfather.

The Ba'al Shem Tov was a very charismatic personality and a mystic of deep insight and experience. There are many stories of people who became his disciples despite initially being closed to his teachings. Often these people were very learned rabbis themselves. There are also accounts of his powerful personality by people who remained opposed to him.

The Ba'al Shem Tov did not fit the typical profile of spiritual leaders in his time. He was not the product of a traditional *Beit Midrash* (House of Study), nor does he appear to have had great knowledge of Talmud. His background does not stand out in any way. He was the child of older parents who were quite poor. He eked out a living at first as a Hebrew tutor for young children and later in life he assisted his wife in running an inn.

The Ba'al Shem Tov's Main Disciples

The Ba'al Shem Tov's two main disciples were Dov Ber, the Maggid of Mezeritch, and Ya'akov Yosef of Polnoye. Each initially was critical of the Besht (an acronym for Ba'al Shem Tov) based on what they had heard about him, but after experiencing him in person each was thoroughly won over. The first Hasidic text, *Toldot Ya'akov Yosef* (The Generations of Ya'akov Yosef) by Ya'akov Yosef of Polnoye, was published in 1780—close to thirty-five years after the beginnings of Hasidism. Both Ya'akov Yosef and the Maggid of Mezeritch were already steeped in Kabbalah, but their encounter with the Besht enabled them to see the same texts in a thoroughly new light.

A *Ba'al Shem* is literally a "master of the Name," implying a person who uses the divine name to heal or perform miracles. Ba'al Shem Tov (Master of the Good Name) is a variation of this term. The term Ba'al Shem was used in the Middle Ages and Ba'alei Shem (the plural) became increasingly common from the thirteenth century onward.

According to the legends concerning him, the Besht began his public career at the age of thirty-six and had a small number of disciples. The Maggid of Mezeritch was the most influential of these because the Maggid had possibly 300 disciples himself of whom quite a number mentored future significant leaders. The Maggid was a great organizer and he sent some of his prize students out into different parts of the Jewish world in order to spread their teachings to a wider public.

Teachings of the Ba'al Shem Tov

The Besht was an ecstatic mystic and preached joy as it is written in Psalms: "Worship YHVH with joy, come before 'Him' with glad song" (100:2). The main expression of this was his orientation toward prayer. The Besht taught that prayer said with true kavana (heartfelt intention) was more effective than prayer said using the esoteric kavanot of the Kabbalists who followed the teachings of the Ari (Isaac Luria). Other elements of great importance to him were equanimity (*hishtavut*), union with God (devekut), and humility (*shiflut*).

The opening paragraphs of the book *Tzava'at HaRibash* (The Testament of Rabbi Yisrael Ba'al Shem), published in 1794, illustrate a number of the Besht's major concerns, stating that "it is essential to study moral lessons every day whether great or small and to see to it that one is always imbued with good moral qualities and upright behavior and not to permit a day to pass without doing a Mitzvah whether great or small . . . [as it says] 'Be care-ful [*Zahir*] with a light Mitzvah as with a weighty one' [Pirkei Avot 2:1], [Understand] Zahir [as in the phrase] 'the enlightened shall radiate' [Daniel 12:3]." This verse from the biblical book of Daniel is the very verse from which the Zohar derives its title. What the Besht is saying, in other words, is that your soul will radiate and shine from a "light" mitzvah as much as from a "weighty" one, because the heart that loves and longs for God invests much more meaning in whatever we do than the weightiness or lightness of the act itself.

Hitlahavut (ecstasy) is a central Hasidic value. This passionate engagement with life, God, and the joyous performance of mitzvot is especially characteristic of early Hasidism. Sometimes the behavior of Hasidim in expressing these values drew the criticism of those who opposed Hasidism.

Another principle central to the Besht was "Shiviti YHVH L'Negdi Tamid," from Psalms (16:8), which means "I place YHVH before me always." When you truly place YHVH before yourself, meaning when you are constantly conscious of God's presence, then you will attain a state of equanimity (in Hebrew, *hishtavut,* which has the same root as *shiviti*)and what others think of you (whether it be praise or ridicule) will be irrelevant.

Of the few surviving letters of the Besht, one was meant to be hand-delivered by Ya'akov Yosef of Polnoye to Gershon Kitiver (also known as Abraham Gershon of Kitiv), the Besht's brother-in-law. Gershon Kitiver was a Kabbalist and Talmudist and had studied in the Kabbalistic community (the *Klaus*) of Brody in the Ukraine. Originally he opposed his sister's marriage to the Ba'al Shem Tov, but later became a close disciple.

Gershon Kitiver immigrated to Israel in 1747, first settling in Hebron and later moving to Jerusalem. In Jerusalem he developed ties with the Sephardic Kabbalistic community of Bet El. In fact, Gershon Kitiver is the one link between these two vibrant eighteenth-century Kabbalistic communities. The letter was never delivered because Ya'akov Yosef failed to complete his journey to Israel. He later published the letter in his book *Ben Porat Yosef.* The letter is largely about the Besht's visions during a mystical experience, which he called an *aliyat neshama* (an ascension of the soul), a practice that the Besht seemed to regularly undertake.

ALERT!

There are often variant spellings of Hebrew or Yiddish words or names when transliterated in English because there were differing accents and pronunciations in various parts of Eastern Europe. This is particularly common regarding names of places; for example, *Kitiv* may be written as "Kutov" or *Bratzlav* as "Breslov."

An Abundance of Masters

In a period of about fifty years or less there emerged an enormous number of outstanding spiritual leaders in the relatively small geographical region where Hasidism flourished. Many of them wrote books, so the library of Hasidic texts is considerable. A short list beyond those already mentioned would have to include works by Levi Yitzkhak of Berditchev, Nachman of Bratzlav, Elimelekh of Lizensk, Menachem Mendel of Kotzk, Schneur Zalman of Lyady, Barukh of Kossov, Abraham of Kalisk, Pinkhas of Koretz, Barukh of Medzebozh, the Seer of Lublin, Menachem Nahum of Chernobyl, Menachem Mendel of Vitebsk, and Yisrael of Rizhin to name just a few. This abundance of spiritual giants, very few of whose works have been translated into English, even surpasses the great Kabbalistic community of Tzfat in the 1500s.

ESSENTIAL

The spiritual master is called a *rebbe* or a *Tzaddik* (righteous or saintly person). The *rebbe* or *Tzaddik* would become established in a particular community after which they were named and their *Hasidim* (devotees) would gather round them and study and pray with them. The devotees studied not only Torah, but how the rebbe lived, for the rebbe embodied Torah.

The Besht's teaching emphasized that God was ever-present and accessible to everyone as in the words of Isaiah: "[T]he whole world is filled with God's Glory" (6:3). He taught that the way to experience God was through our devotion, ecstasy, and joy in praying, fulfilling mitzvot, and studying Torah. Not everyone, however, was capable of achieving the mystical heights of which the Ba'al Shem Tov spoke, and though the movement attracted some truly exceptional people, it remained small until its message of each individual's access to the Divine Presence became modified.

Mysticism as a Mass Movement

Hasidism in its earliest stages, contrary to popular myth, appealed primarily to young scholars who were drawn to mysticism, not to large masses of the Jewish population. Though the Besht himself was often found among the less-educated members of Jewish society, the people who became his disciples were elite students of Torah and Kabbalah. This was similarly true for the Maggid of Mezeritch. It was only in the next generation of spiritual leaders, or rebbes, that the conscious decision was made to try to spread the teachings to a much wider public. This necessitated the lowering of the spiritual standards of devotion that had originally been a major element of Hasidism.

A major shift occurred in Hasidic life as a result of this. The average Hasid was no longer expected to strive for direct encounters with God and to be in a state of devekut as much as possible. Rather, the Hasid would now attempt to commune with God through the Tzaddik or rebbe, who himself would have direct experience of God. The institution of Tzaddikism became a major characteristic of Hasidism as time went on.

The Hasidic "Court"

Most Hasidic masters had disciples who developed their own following of Hasidim. A community often formed around the early Hasidic masters, and their successors in turn perpetuated those communities and teachings. The successors to the earliest masters were not chosen based on hereditary relationships. Though the Besht had a son, for example, his son did not succeed him. The same is true with the Maggid of Mezeritch and many of the early masters. As time went on and Hasidism evolved, the position of rebbe became institutionalized and his immediate descendent generally took his place. There was a great emphasis therefore on preparing the successor from a very tender age, helping him develop those qualities desirable in a rebbe. The child had to be trained to be learned in the traditional texts, to have a deep spiritual sensitivity, and to be able to provide spiritual, psychological, emotional, and practical guidance and counsel to his Hasidim. The responsibilities of a rebbe are enormous because his Hasidim live their lives in accordance with his counsel.

FACT

There was an organized reaction against Hasidism by people called *Mitnagdim* (opponents). The most significant Mitnaged, the Vilna Gaon (an important Kabbalist of his era), considered Hasidim rebellious against Judaism and "excommunicated" them. He refused to meet with Menachem Mendel of Vitebsk in 1772 and Schneur Zalman in 1777, who hoped to convince him that Hasidim were loyal to tradition.

The Triumph of Hasidism

Despite strong reactions against it, Hasidism ultimately triumphed, becoming a very popular movement among Eastern European Jewry. It reinvigorated Orthodox Judaism by bringing an intense fervor to religious life. Even those who opposed it were indirectly reinvigorated by it because they had to intensify their own commitments in order to present appealing alternatives to hold on to those among them who were attracted to Hasidism. In the yeshiva (advanced Talmudic academy) world of Lithuania, a very strong movement developed emphasizing moral perfection. This movement was called the mussar movement, which is showing signs of revival today and is expanding beyond the yeshiva world.

Hasidism was also attacked from the other end of the social spectrum. In the turbulent, difficult times in which Hasidism arose there was much poverty and anti-Semitism. The Jewish world was still recovering from the vastly popular following surrounding the false Messiah, Shabbtai Tzvi. At the same time there was a strong movement toward secularization, science, and rationalism called the haskalah (enlightenment) movement. The haskalah movement was very critical of Hasidism and attacked it as superstitious and irrational.

The vast majority of the Hasidic world was wiped out by the Nazis during World War II. The small group of survivers tried to re-establish themselves in the United States or Israel and have been remarkably successful. There are large Hasidic groups today such as Lubavitch/Chabad, Satmar, and Bobov in the United States and Belz, Ger, Bratzlav, and others in Israel.

The first studies of Kabbalah and Hasidism in the nineteenth century suffered from an antimystical bias. Given this constellation of factors, it is all the more amazing that Hasidism has survived and even thrived for almost 300 years. Hasidism has had a significant impact on the revival of Jewish mystical thinking outside the orthodox world since the 1960s.

Hasidic Teachings

In order to truly understand any particular Hasidic group a number of factors are involved. You need to know their teachings, their tales, their style of prayer, and their niggunim (music).

Though Hasidism has developed many different sects during the course of its almost 300-year history, there are certain teachings that remain central to all. Worshipping God joyously is one of these. The centrality of music and dance to Hasidism is an expression of this. The powerful and enigmatic Rebbe Menachem Mendel of Kotzk took a famous rabbinic statement and used it to illustrate this point. In the Talmud it says that "when the [Hebrew] month of Av [during which both ancient Temples where destroyed] arrives we diminish our joy; when the month of Adar [in which we celebrate the festive holiday of Purim and a month after which we celebrate Passover] arrives we multiply our joy." The Kotzker Rebbe adds, "but always joy" (Tractate Ta'anit 29a).

The phrase in Proverbs (3:6) "In all your ways know Him [God]" is fundamental to Hasidism. Included in this verse are two major themes. One is the goal to live in a state of union (devekut) with the Divine as much as possible. The other is to sanctify your entire life through your activities. This is called *avodah b'gashmiyut* (worshipping God through the physical). In this manner we can raise the sparks (*nitzotzot*) of Divinity and holiness that are in everything.

Menachem Mendel of Kotzk reinterpreted the verse of Psalm 81:10 that "you should have no strange god among you" to also mean that "God should not be a stranger to you."

The perspective that there are sparks of divinity in everything affects the way we relate to the world. It gears the intention of our actions and thoughts toward raising up those sparks. It renders all of our actions of vital, even cosmic, importance, for we can bring holiness into the world and hasten the messianic era through our attention to the Divine that fills everything. Just as any person we encounter might be the Messiah, the Divine spark is in everything even if it is not obvious to us.

Hasidism emphasizes, as does Judaism in general, the spiritual life that is lived in community, as Hillel is quoted in Mishnah Pirkei Avot: "Do not separate from the community" (2:5). Hasidism, with few exceptions, tends to avoid asceticism.

FACT

Ya'akov Yosef of Polnoye had ascetic tendencies when he met the Besht. The Besht told him a parable about once driving a carriage with three horses, none of which was neighing. A peasant told him to loosen the reins, which he did, and the horses began to neigh. Ya'akov Yosef understood that the soul too needs to have the "reins" loosened.

While Hasidism discourages self-denial, it also frowns upon overindulgence in the physical. It attempts to sanctify our physical activities by focusing on the spiritual through them. There is also the ideal of totally transcending the physical, which is called *hitpashtut hagashmiyut*. This may occur most easily through prayer, music, dance, or the study of Torah for its own sake (*Torah Lishmah*, which means to study Torah not to achieve anything such as recognition or reward, but to study purely for the love of God and Torah).

Chanting, Dance, and Divinity

Music is an essential part of Hasidism. Each Hasidic sect, of which there were and are many, developed its own music both in terms of formal prayers said in the synagogue and in less formal settings. The development and use of niggunim, melodies, both with words and without, is an important part of the contemplative and ecstatic life of the Hasid.

A niggun is often sung without words and the two or more musical motifs in the particular niggun are repeated, often for as long as twenty minutes or more. There are also *tish niggunim* (table melodies) sung in between teachings of the rebbe at communal meals. The niggunim are a form of meditational chanting. Some are referred to as *devekus niggunim* (mystical union melodies), *makhshove niggunim* (contemplative melodies), and *moralishe niggunim* (moral melodies).

ALERT!

Through the writings of the Mitnagdim, those who most opposed Hasidism, we learn much about Hasidism itself. In their writings, the Mitnagdim criticized the importance of singing and dancing among Hasidim and the displays of ecstatic behavior. Some Hasidim were known to even do somersaults in the streets of their towns.

Along with niggunim, dance is a very important part of Hasidism. Both music and dance can express and induce elements of ecstasy and contemplation that are different from traditional prayer and study. Often a formal prayer session will end with a dance.

There are also many tales in which music plays a role. The Besht apparently sang to the children when he brought them to *kheder* (their study "room"). There are a number of niggunim sung to this day attributed to the Besht, to Rebbe Nachman of Bratzlav, to Schneur Zalman, and to other early Tzaddikim. Rebbe Nachman taught that every truth in the world has its own niggun.

Contemplative and Ecstatic Prayer

Prayer is a highly developed art in Hasidism and styles of prayer vary from sect to sect. Generally there were two major trends, one to be very still when *davenen* (a Yiddish word, meaning "praying"), the other to be so filled with ecstatic passion (hitlahavut) as to find it difficult to be still. In fact, both orientations were intended toward the same goal: facilitating kavana (focus and intention) and attaining a state of devekut (union with God).

FACT

Yiddish, which has a common ancestry with Medieval German and a significant Hebrew component, was the language of Eastern European Jews and remains the spoken language of most Hasidim. Hebrew is considered the Holy Tongue, the language of formal prayer and *sforim* (spiritual books).

Hasidim tend to be much more flexible with times of prayer than traditional orthodoxy, which has very fixed times and even requires that certain prayers be recited by certain times of the day. Hasidim look back to the Mishnah, which noted that the Hasidim in ancient times took an hour for meditation before beginning their prayers. In justifying their prayer habits in response to criticisms from Mitnagdim, they would cite the Talmudic account of Rabbi Akiva who, when praying in private, would start in one corner of the room, but be so moved in ecstasy that he would be in the completely opposite part of the room by the end of the prayer. Another favorite biblical reference that Hasidim used to defend their practices was the biblical description of King David dancing in ecstasy before the Ark (Second Book of Samuel 6:14–16).

Every Word Counts

The Besht was quoted as saying that each word of a prayer is a world in itself and you need to put all of your strength into it. Without putting ourselves into every word of a prayer, the change in the effect of the prayer would be as dramatically noticeable as a person missing a limb. He added that it is only through God's gracious love that we survive after truly praying since we have poured all of our self into it. This pouring of oneself into prayer was part of *Hitpashtut HaGashmiyut*, transcending one's physicality. Prayer was probably the most common act among Hasidim for achieving Hitpashtut HaGashmiyut and, therefore, it took precedence over even Torah study.

QUESTION?

What is Hitpashtut HaGashmiyut?
Hitpashtut HaGashmiyut is the act of transcending the physical world. In other words, it means to strip yourself of concerns about material possessions, the material world, and even your own physical body during prayer.

Hitbodedut

Rebbe Nachman had a unique method of meditative prayer called *hitbodedut*. He advised his Hasidim to take an hour a day, alone in nature, and pour out their hearts in the language they're most fluent in (which for them was Yiddish).

Though the Hasidim were loyal to traditional Judaism in its prayers and observances, they added their particular fervor, music, and joy to prayers and to practices in general.

The Hasidic Tale

One of the most striking elements of Hasidism is the Hasidic tale. Much Hasidic teaching, beginning with the Ba'al Shem Tov, was communicated via parables and tales. There are a few paradigms of the tales. The first is represented by the book *Shivkhei HaBesht* (Praises of the Ba'al Shem Tov) published in 1814–1815. Much of this book is based on accounts of people who knew the Besht; most of our biographical knowledge of him comes, in fact, from this book. The publisher of the book pieced it together from various manuscripts. Explaining his reason for publishing the book, he quoted the Besht as saying that "one who engages in praises of the Tzaddikim [the righteous or saintly] is as though he engages in Ma'aseh Merkavah [contemplation of the divine chariot]."

The Besht's grandson, the author of *Degel Machaneh Ephraim*, says that one of the amazing things about his grandfather was that he would worship the Eternal One even through the telling of non-Torah stories, clothing his great wisdom in simple folk tales.

The earliest stories of the Ba'al Shem Tov as found in *Shivkhei HaBesht* tell much of his travels and his teachings. It was primarily in the anthologies of Hasidic tales that began to emerge long after the deaths of the praised Tzaddikim that miraculous stories became more commonplace.

There are many stories in which the prayers of someone totally unlearned are more meaningful and powerful than those of scholars, stories in which a sincere tear brings one closer to God than most prayers. Rebbe Nachman of Bratzlav was quoted as saying, "Nothing is as whole as a broken heart."

Another story found in numerous versions concerns the tradition of the thirty-six hidden Tzaddikim for whose sake the world exists.

QUESTION?

What is a lamed vavnik?

Lamed vavnik translates as the number "thirty-six," which, besides being twice the gematria for *khai* (which means "life"), refers to a legend stemming from the Talmud that there are thirty-six righteous souls (Tzaddikim) in each generation who keep the world in existence. A lamed vavnik is a person believed to be one of these hidden thirty-six Tzaddikim.

Time and again, these stories reveal that the main individual in the story is not at all what he appears to be. Someone who initially seems to be the antithesis of a Tzaddik is ultimately revealed as a lamed vavnik, exposing a truth hidden beneath the surface.

Rebbe Nachman of Bratzlav

A unique type of Hasidic tale is that told by Rebbe Nachman of Bratzlav (1772–1810). Rebbe Nachman was the great-grandson of the Besht. At the end of his short life he decided that he would do his teaching through the form of tales, creating thirteen stories that he told to his disciples from 1806 to 1810. The most famous of the tales was the last, entitled "The Seven Beggars." The tales are filled with Kabbalistic symbolism, narrative drama, and autobiographical elements incorporated into the fiction of the stories.

Rebbe Nachman's tales were originally told in Yiddish and most books have them written in Hebrew and Yiddish, although some English translations exist. Nachman's followers were (until recently) the only group of Hasidim who refused to appoint a successor, feeling that no one could replace Rebbe Nachman.

Nachman's tales are often tales within tales that explore the difference between reality and appearance. In each segment of "The Seven Beggars," a beggar tells his story. Over the course of each story, the beggar contradicts his initial appearance, once again revealing a spiritual truth at the conclusion of the tale. The beggar who stutters, for example, is in reality extremely eloquent. He appears to stutter because the words of this world are not worth saying unless they have to do with the Holy One. Nachman does not reveal the story of the seventh beggar, the legless dancer. Instead, he makes readers wait for his appearance at the wedding feast just as they must wait for the Messiah.

Parables, Anecdotes, and Aphorisms

Levi Yitzkhak of Berditchev was known as a great, original teacher, a defender of the people and friend to all. Once when encountering a *Maskil* (a believer in the *Haskalah*, the Jewish enlightenment movement) Levi Yitzkhak said, "the God you don't believe in, I don't believe in either." In another encounter with a Maskil who was publicly breaking the laws of Shabbat by smoking, Levi Yitzkhak said, "surely you've forgotten it's Shabbes [the

Yiddish pronunciation of Shabbat].” The Maskil replied that he knew very well what day it was. Levi Yitzhak continued, “then you must be unaware that smoking is forbidden,” to which the Maskil replied that he knew all “their” rules. Levi Yitzkhak then addressed the Eternal One: “Riboyno Shel Oylam [Master of the Universe], he may break some of your command-ments, but no one can make him lie.”

Another classic story is that of Reb Zusya, a disciple of the Maggid of Mezeritch, about whom it was said that he claimed he wasn’t worried that after he died the Eternal One would ask him why he wasn’t Moshe Rab-beinu (Moses our Teacher), but rather that the Master of the Universe would ask him why he wasn’t Zusya.

The Mystic as Communal Leader

Though great mystics and Kabbalists have been community leaders (as teachers) throughout their history, Hasidism introduced the widespread phenomenon in which the mystic (the Tzaddik or rebbe) was the active head of the community. Rather than living a cloistered life, the rebbe took on the burden of the difficult lives that his followers, his Hasidim, endured.

The house of the Tzaddik often became more of the spiritual center than even the synagogue, since according to Hasidic belief, every moment of the day was a moment that should be filled with a connection with God. The rebbe has audiences with individual Hasidim as a regular part of his day or week, during which the Hasid may seek advice or guidance on his most per-sonal spiritual or survival concerns.

A common Hasidic custom is the *tish* (table), often held by the rebbe at the special third Shabbat meal (*Seudah Shlishit* in Hebrew) and last-ing for hours. The tish usually entails teaching, chanting traditional nig-gunim (melodies) of the particular Hasidic sect, and the blessing over food by the rebbe, who takes a morsel and divides the *shirayim* (left-overs) among the Hasidim.

The rebbe's goal in his community is to completely devote himself to the people, following the model of Moses. The people are to be spiritually elevated through him. He is their greatest advocate and defendant. After the incident of the Golden Calf in Exodus, for example, God wants to wipe out the Jewish people and start a new people from Moses. Moses pleads on their behalf, saying, "If now you will forgive their sin, but if not, please blot me out of the book [the Torah] that you have written" (Exodus 32:32).

Chapter 15

Foundation of the Universe: The Tzaddik

A Tzaddik, in the plainest sense of the word, is a person who is righteous. In a more technical sense, a Tzaddik is a person who is always striving to go beyong fulfilling the letter of the law. The Tzaddik as a pillar of justice and compassion supporting society and as a Sefira channeling the flow of divine energy into this world is found everywhere in Kabbalistic works.

Tzaddik: The Ninth Sefira

The human and divine versions of the Tzaddik are mirrors of each other and the image of the Tzaddik serves as an ideal of human holiness. Proverbs (10:25) says, "And the Righteous [Tzaddik] is the foundation of the world" (*Tzaddik Yesod Olam*, in Hebrew). This could also be translated as "the righteous is an eternal foundation," because the word olam means "world," "universe," or "eternal." The ninth Sefira is generally referred to by the term Yesod, which means "foundation," but Yesod is so strongly associated with Tzaddik that both terms are common when referencing the ninth Sefira.

In the chapter on the ninth Sefira in his book *The Gates of Light (Sha'arei Orah)* written around 1290, Yosef Gikatilla writes that "this attribute [Middah] is called 'Yesod,' for just like a house leans upon the foundations, the Middah [which is another word for Sefira] Adonai [the divine name associated with Shekhinah] leans upon the Middah of Yesod." He continues by stating that "in the Gemara . . . [the sages] said: 'what does the world stand upon?' 'On one pillar which is the Tzaddik, as it is said . . . and Tzaddik is the Foundation of the Universe'" (Proverbs 10:25).

FACT

Ya'akov Yosef of Polnoye wrote in 1780 that "there are leaders of the generation [meaning, Tzaddikim] who are capable of opening a channel for awe in the world and then awe becomes a common thing and there [are those] who are capable of opening a channel for love in the world."

As the ninth Sefira, Tzaddik or Yesod receives all of the divine energy (Shefa) that has emanated from the higher Sefirot. This includes emanations of Hesed (love) and Din (judgment). No Sefira can bestow Shefa on the world without the mediation of Yesod. There can be no harmony in the upper worlds without the union of the male and female elements of the Sefirot and this can only occur through the Sefira of Tzaddik. This union, described in sexual love imagery, creates the reign of harmony, peace, and perfection in the cosmos.

Rabbi Moshe de Leon in one of his Hebrew Kabbalistic works explains the phrase "Moses took the bones of Joseph with him [to the Promised Land]" (Exodus 13:19) as meaning that because Moses [who symbolizes Tiferet, the "husband" of Shekhinah] could not unite with Shekhinah except by way of Joseph (who represents Tzaddik), and because "The Land of Israel" is a symbol for the Shekhinah, he had to take the bones with him to facilitate the union of Tiferet with Shekhinah in sexual embrace. The phrase "the bones of" can also be read as "the essence of."

Righteous, Justice, and Charity: Tzaddik, Tzedek, Tzedakah

The words righteous, justice, and charity all have the same root in Hebrew (*tzaddi, dalet, kuf*). What we think of in English as being charitable is considered doing what is "just," such as taking care of those less-fortunate than ourselves is our obligation as humans. Justice should not be confused with "judgment." Justice means being committed to what is right, and it is important to keep in mind that there is a large measure of compassion in determining what is indeed right.

"Justice, justice you shall pursue" (*Tzedek, tzedek tirdof*; Deuteronomy 16:20). There are numerous interpretations for why the word *justice* is mentioned twice in this verse. One is that you should be just in your words and in your actions. Another interpretation is that you should pursue justice in a just manner.

Three Names as One

Gikatilla explains that you must "know that there are three names: Tzaddik, Tzedek, and Tzedakah. The Middah [Sefira] of *El Khai* [the living God] is called Tzaddik; the Middah of Adonai is called Tzedek [justice]; and since the Tzaddik bestows his blessing upon Tzedek [Shekhinah] that Shefa and

Emanation [atzilut] is called Tzedakah [charity]. These three names come together as one: Tzaddik gives, Tzedek receives, and Tzedakah is the mystery of bestowing, union, and unifying. According to this secret it is said 'the memory of the Tzaddik is a blessing'[Proverbs 10:7]."

The word *memory* (*zekher*) could also be read as *zakhar*, meaning "male," because Yesod/Tzaddik is the Sefira that represents the male organ of Adam Kadmon.

The Healing Power of Tzedakah

Proverbs offers the statement that "Tzedakah saves from death" (10:2). Gikatilla picks up on this verse to emphasize how wonderful *tzedakah* (giving charity) is, for when a person does an act of tzedakah, not only is she doing an important act on this plane of existence, but she simultaneously facilitates union between the Sefirot Tzaddik and tzedek (justice), which brings life into the world.

When the act of Tzedakah is given graciously it connects us to others, even people that we don't know. In fact, in human terms it is important for the dignity of the receiver of charity that the giver and the receiver don't know each other. Giving tzedakah is an expression of our bond with and responsibility for the lives of others. As it says in Genesis, "I am my brother's keeper" (4:9), which means that we are each responsible for caring for the other.

Tzaddik and Sexuality

Because of the association of the Sefira of Yesod with Tzaddik and its representation of the male organ of Adam Kadmon, the image of Tzaddik was strongly associated with sexual conduct that met sacred standards.

The biblical character most closely associated with Tzaddik and the Sefira of Yesod was Joseph. Joseph resisted the sexual temptation of Potiphar's wife (Genesis 39) and described succumbing to it as a great transgression and a sin against God. For this reason, he symbolized holy sexual behavior in contrast to simply following our passions. Because so much imagery of union in the divine realm is expressed in erotic terms and the male organ is represented by the Sefira of Yesod, much emphasis is placed on creating the right kavana when having sex. Every action in this world affects the state of the upper worlds. This certainly includes our sexual behavior.

FACT

Sefer Yetzirah reads: "Ten Sefirot of Nothingness as the number of fingers, five facing five with a unique covenant intentionally in the middle as in the circumcision of language and the circumcision of the flesh" (1:3). The covenants of language and flesh are closely related here. In Kabbalah both divine "speech" and sexual union with Tzaddik are associated with the Shekhinah.

The Holiness of Sexual Union

Humans' ability to procreate mirrors the creation process of the world of the Sefirot. The Song of Songs, which is filled with erotic imagery, was often interpreted kabbalistically as referring to the union of the Tzaddik and the Shekhinah, or the ninth and tenth Sefirot (but simultaneously of the mystic and the Shekhinah).

ALERT!

The Hebrew term for "the Holy of Holies" is *Kodesh HaKodashim*. The term for marriage in Mishnaic Hebrew is *kiddushin*, which derives from the same root as "holiness." On the Ark of the Covenant in the Holy of Holies in the ancient Temples in Jerusalem there were two angels who were depicted in intimate embrace whenever Israel was devoted to God.

The Zohar offers a striking teaching on the Tzaddik and sexuality: "Young Rabbi Yesa was in the presence of Rabbi Shimon and said to him: 'It's written "blessings upon the head of the Tzaddik" [Proverbs 10:6], shouldn't it have said *to* the Tzaddik? What is the meaning of *head* of a Tzaddik?' [Rabbi Shimon] said to him: 'The head of a Tzaddik is the holy crown. . . . That place of the [covenant] is called *head of a Tzaddik* from which springs flow. . . . Thus the head of a Tzaddik is that place which when emitting springs into the female [Shekhinah] is called head of a Tzaddik, Tzaddik is first [the word *rosh* means "first" and "head"] because all blessings reside there'" (vol. 1, 162a–b). The Zohar continues, noting that "the seed isn't drawn down except at the moment when the female is ready and the desire of both is as one, one union with no separation."

Shefa HaBrakha

The term *Shefa*—which literally means an overflow and abundance of the divine life–force—easily lends itself to erotic imagery, which is particularly employed in certain descriptions in the Zohar. There is a *Shefa HaBrakha* (an abundant flow of blessing) that emanates from the divine realm to the world of Creation by means of the sacred union of Tzaddik (Yesod) and Shekhinah.

Righteous, Wise, and Pious: Tzaddik, Chakham, Hasid

Three ideal religious models have dominated the Jewish tradition. These are the Tzaddik, the *chakham*, and the Hasid. The profile of the Tzaddik and Hasid has changed significantly over time, while the chakham has remained consistent for at least the last 2,000 years.

The chakham, which literally means the "wise," generally implies a scholar, at least from post-biblical times. Outside of the Jewish tradition it implies a philosopher; within the Jewish tradition it means someone who has a deep knowledge of the Torah and Talmud.

FACT

"A Chakham is greater than a prophet" (Babylonian Talmud, Tractate Baca Batra 12a). By the period of the Talmud, the official era of prophecy was considered over. A "prophet" is someone who has knowledge from direct experience of the Divine; a chakham is someone who has acquired knowledge through mastering the canonized texts of the Jewish tradition.

The sages of the Talmud are referred to as the *chakhamim* (plural of chakham). The preference of the chakham over the *navi* (prophet) is the result of a conservative element in the Jewish tradition. A navi is someone whose vision, rather than scholarship, gives them authority. This vision can introduce something radically novel. If the prophet's vision is too inconsistent with the Jewish tradition, it is rejected and considered "false prophecy."

The Dominance of the Scholar

The dominance of the chakham in the Jewish tradition remains largely intact to this day. Originality is the province of the prophet and the mystic much more than of the scholar. Scholars solidify the tradition and support its customs by providing insight into the original sources that gave birth to those customs. The conflict between the scholar and the charismatic leader was a crucial division that occurred from the outset of Hasidism.

It is a common misconception that Hasidism arose as a reaction by the masses against the domination of Jewish society by scholars. In fact, many of the great Hasidic masters combined charisma with great intellectual achievements. Their authority stemmed much more from their charisma than from their scholarship, but the combination of both qualities enabled them to offer radical new visions into the Torah.

Early Image of the Hasid

The traditional image of the Hasid, until the advent of eighteenth-century Hasidism, was that of the very pious person whose religious practice was much more extreme than the societal norm. The Tzaddik during much of this same time period generally represented the ideal of the norm, which was someone who followed the Torah and mitzvot and lived a good, moral life. According to Maimonides, the strict definition of a Tzaddik was someone whose good deeds outweighed the bad, while the definition of a *rasha* (a wicked person) was someone whose bad deeds outweighed the good.

The Hasid was classically seen as on a much higher spiritual level than the Tzaddik because of the intensity of his involvement in spiritual practices. A Hasid not only fulfills the letter of the law, but strives for the spirit of it. The Hasid is described in the Talmud as the one who meditates for an hour before beginning his prayers. In the Middle Ages in Germany, the mystics who had pronounced ascetic habits were called *Hasidim*. Over time there has been a blending and blurring of definitions that has been particularly influenced by the qualities associated with the Kabbalistic use of the term *Tzaddik* in reference to the ninth Sefira, Yesod.

"A Tzaddik is called a mirror because every person sees themselves in him as in a mirror. In truth every Tzaddik includes within himself the general aspects of the world and all people" (Likkutei Amarin, 35b).

The Evolving Image of the Tzaddik

In Kabbalistic literature, the Tzaddik began to take on a connotation of a person whose life aids the upper and lower worlds to function properly. Just as the ninth Sefira, Tzaddik, is the channel through which divine energy emanates into the world in a balanced manner, so the Tzaddik on the human plane fosters balance in the upper and lower worlds.

Over time, the image of the Tzaddik acquired more and more of the spiritual luster that the term *Hasid* had held since Talmudic times. By the time we reach the late eighteenth century, the terms Tzaddik and Hasid have largely reversed roles. The leader of a group of devotees within a generation or so of the emergence of Hasidism came to be known as a Tzaddik (or rebbe in Yiddish). The Hasid, in turn, acquired a meaning very close to what Tzaddik had denoted in Talmudic times, someone who lived a life of Torah, mitzvot, and high moral standards.

FACT

A *mokhiakh* was usually a traveling preacher who would wander through villages trying to inspire the local population to live righteous lives devoted to Torah and mitzvot, both in relationship to God and to their fellow humans.

The Tzaddik who led a group of Hasidim had much of the mokhiakh in him. Most of the early leaders of Hasidism functioned in their society, more as a mokhiakh than as a traditional rabbi. They combined these characteristics with the Kabbalistic understanding of Tzaddik.

The Tzaddik as Spiritual Leader

In the earliest days of Hasidism, the term Tzaddik was not used to refer to the charismatic spiritual leader, though this came about within a generation or so. The movement evolved considerably over time and the charismatic leader soon became an institutionalized component of Hasidism. The centrality of the Tzaddik began quite informally. People naturally gravitated toward a person who seemed to exist on a higher spiritual plane because such a person was a living embodiment of people's spiritual aspirations and a great inspiration and teacher.

ALERT!

With the growth of ethical (mussar) literature, the phenomenon of the mokhiakh became increasingly common in eastern European Jewish society. Much of mussar literature had Kabbalistic foundations.

Zohar on the Tzaddik

The Zohar states that "this Light [the special light that came into being on the first day of Creation and was hidden away ever after for the righteous in the world to come] the Blessed Holy One sowed in the Garden of Eden and made rows and rows of through this Tzaddik, who is the gardener of the Garden. He took this light and seeded it, the seed of Truth, rows and rows in the Garden. And it gave birth, and flowered and made fruits from which the world is nourished. This is what's written (Psalms 97:11): 'Light is sown for the Tzaddik'" (vol. 2, 166b).

Here in the Zohar, the Tzaddik is a figure that nourishes the entire world spiritually. The Tzaddik figure is symbolic of the process of emanation flowing from the world of the Sefirot to this world, but it is understood that the figure of the Tzaddik, such as Rabbi Shimon in the Zohar itself, is also the tender of this seed of truth. The spiritual ideal of a Tzaddik tending the fruits created from the divine light becomes fundamental to the spiritual image of the Hasidic leader.

One kind of Tzaddik "is always in a state of devekut and does the work that is his lot, but is only a Tzaddik for himself and doesn't bestow his righteousness on others. This Tzaddik is like a Cyprus tree that bears no fruit"(from *Or Torah, The Light of Torah*).

Spiritual Qualities of a Charismatic Leader

The Hasidic Tzaddik combines all the earlier characteristics of the Talmudic Hasid and Tzaddik and the Kabbalistic image of the Tzaddik. The Tzaddik enters the social sphere in order to raise its spiritual level. Though the Tzaddik strives to be in a perpetual state of devekut with the Eternal One, he must descend to the level on which society operates in order to spread new insights and share them with others.

The Tzaddik as a charismatic leader existing in the midst of a community has to nullify his own personality in order to serve the community. He has to empty himself of his ego in order to become a vessel for the divine Shefa to flow through and spiritually vivify those around him.

Strengths and Weaknesses of the Institution of the Tzaddik

The institution of the Tzaddik became, without doubt, the backbone of Hasidism within a few generations. This brought the spiritual intensity of Kabbalah to a much larger community of people. Throughout Eastern Europe during the peak of its influence, a large percentage of the Jewish population was familiar with mystical ideas, if not necessarily with mystical experiences.

FACT

In addition to the kind of Tzaddik who is a Tzaddik for himself but does all of his righteous work, "there is also a Tzaddik who brings forth the precious from the vile, and he multiplies and makes flower the good in the world" (from *Or Torah, The Light of Torah*).

Tzaddik as a Model of Spiritual Life

The Tzaddik was an accessible model who lived in the midst of his community and was considered the "living Torah." In other words, the Tzaddik was the model of how to live a pious, even ecstatic life. The Tzaddik brought much hope and meaning to the existence of people who were often subject to much poverty and persecution. It would be unrealistic to say that these difficult conditions ceased to have a punishing affect on people's lives, but despite these challenges, the Tzaddik brought together a community buoyed by religious fervor that maintained high standards of ethics and public responsibility. While it is part of the Torah's commandments to take care of the needy people in society, having a charismatic figure at the center of the community, reminding its members what their moral and religious obligations were, inspired adherence to those tenets of the Torah.

Although prayer has always been the most powerful spiritual practice among Hasidim, having the Tzaddik as part of the praying community intensified the fervor, depth, and focus of the community's prayer experience.

Tzaddik Has Many Social Roles

The Tzaddik also played the role of social worker, therapist, counselor, mentor, and model to virtually everyone in the community. He (or she—there were a few women who played the role of Tzaddik or rebbe in certain Hasidic communities) would hold private meetings with his Hasidim regularly, in which he would listen to their needs for hours at a time. His Hasidim perceived the Tzaddik as their direct link with God because of his elevated spiritual stature. This dynamic and these practices continue to the present day.

The role of the Hasidim and their relationship with the Tzaddik is also significant, because essentially the community chooses whether the Tzaddik will be their leader. Even when it largely became a matter of hereditary descent and succession, the community still had to choose to accept the new Tzaddik and recognize his worthiness.

ALERT!

The Tzaddik or rebbe is believed to contain a spark of Moses in him. Moses is described in the Bible as the most modest person (Numbers 12:3). The Tzaddik, in order to represent this element of Moses, has to empty himself of his ego and be selfless. Part of his power then comes from the strength his followers invest in him.

Changing Patterns in Hasidism

In the first few generations of Hasidism, the spiritual ideals of the movement, such as devekut (union with God), were perceived as goals for every Hasid. Over time, as Hasidism became increasingly popular, these ideals were no longer seen as realistic for the individual. In its place, the Hasid would be bound to the rebbe, who would, in turn, have an intimate relationship with God.

One of the negative aspects of Tzaddikism (as it came to be called by non-Hasidic scholars) was the dependence on the Tzaddik in so many aspects of the average Hasid's life. Critics saw this as stunting the emotional and psychological growth of the individual. One of the major spiritual criticisms that opponents of Hasidism have expressed is that having a mediator between the individual and God was not a Jewish pattern. Judaism was seen as always promoting every person's ability to have a direct relationship with God. In its beginnings, Hasidism not only promoted anyone's opportunity to directly relate to God, but it also raised the expectations of how close any person could be to the Eternal One.

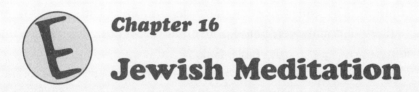

Chapter 16

Jewish Meditation

Meditation has a long history in Judaism. Most of the meditative components of Judaism come from the Kabbalistic tradition, though we do find mention of it before the advent of Kabbalah. As in the case of the mystical tradition in Judaism, meditative techniques were kept among an elite minority until the emergence of Hasidism, which made these techniques more accessible to the masses. In the last twenty years, meditation has spread even more widely in Jewish circles of all denominations.

What Is Jewish Meditation?

There are two Hebrew words that are primarily used to refer to the act of meditation. The first word is *hitbodedut*, and the second word is *hitbonenut*. Hitbodedut literally means "being alone with oneself" and is used throughout Kabbalistic literature. Hitbonenut comes from the word Binah, which literally means "understanding." Hitbonenut refers to the activity of going deeply into oneself and reflecting to achieve understanding.

Other words are also used in certain contexts to refer to meditation, though they are not commonly used to mean this. Kavana, which is a word of great importance in the history of Kabbalah, usually means "intention" or "direction of thought." Occasionally, however, it is used as a term for meditation, as discussed in earlier chapters. Devekut, a word that often means "union" or "uniting with" (and is frequently translated as "cleaving"), is also sometimes used to mean meditation, especially in the phrase "uniting of thought" (*Devekut HaMakhshavah*).

There is no explicit mention of meditation in the Bible, but Kabbalists interpret certain passages as referring to it (the Kabbalists, of course, always saw their own doctrines encoded in the Bible). There is a verse in Genesis (24:63) in which Isaac went out into the field toward evening. The verb used in the verse is *lasuakh*, which is sometimes translated to mean "to meditate."

In clarifying the meaning of this word *lasuakh*, Rashi explains that it's an expression used in reference to prayer. The word for prayer in Hebrew, *l'hitpalel*, is a reflexive verb. Rather than being a word that implies an outward action, the verb "to pray" in Hebrew, grammatically, implies an inwardly focused activity.

What is a tallit?
The tallit is a prayer shawl often placed over your head during meditation to facilitate kavana. Each corner has a fringe (called *tzitzit*) tied in knots as reminders of the 613 Mitzvot. The Bible (Numbers 15:38) instructs that each tzitzit needs a blue cord among the white ones. These colors became those of the flag of the modern state of Israel.

The Bible and Meditation

Another biblical phrase that the Kabbalists referred back to with regularity appears in Psalms: "I set YHVH before me always" (16:8). This was understood as the very prescription for, and description of, meditation. YHVH, as the most sublime name of God, is a major focus of meditation. Another biblical verse that was understood as a meditational reference because of its specific mentioning of God in connection with silence was the phrase *kol d'mamah dakah* (the subtle sound of silence) in the Elijah story in I Kings (19:12). Both of these phrases repeatedly resurface in Kabbalistic texts as proof books for meditational activity.

Kavana as Meditation

Throughout the history of Judaism from Talmudic times onward there is a lot of reflection on the proper manner of prayer. The key word concerning this is *kavana*. Kavana comes from the same root as the word for "direction" (*kivun*). Essentially, kavana is the directing and focusing of your consciousness. Kavana can have a number of additional meanings depending on the context. Kabbalistic and Hasidic literature repeatedly focus on kavana, particularly in reference to prayer, but also when exploring the spiritual aspects of all human activity.

Isaac Luria, in the early 1570s, taught very specific kavanot (plural of kavana), or "intentions," used during the prayers. Prayer was not something to be thought about or spoken as normal speech. Rather, the words were to be treated meditatively, experientially. There were special Kabbalistic prayer books that were written to provide specific kavanot for particular words in the traditional prayers. This practice has continued to this day in the Kabbalistic yeshivot in Jerusalem.

Most of the Kabbalistic kavanot in the prayer book connected particular prayers and even particular words in prayers to specific Sefirot. The various names of God used in the prayer book refer to different Sefirot. The entire service, in fact, was seen as an ascent from universe to universe (from the world of asiyah to yetzirah to beriah, and finally to the world of atzilut through the Sefirot).

There are three prayer services a day: morning, afternoon, and evening. Legend has it that each was instituted by a patriarch, specifically by Abraham, Isaac, and Jacob. The complete service, including important prayers and reading the Torah, can only be done if there are ten adults present. In orthodox circles, these ten adults (above the age of thirteen) must be male.

Meditative Prayer and Merkavah Mysticism

The conventional prayer service became transformed into a Kabbalistic parallel to the ascent of the Merkavah mystic toward the divine throne. Instead of the Merkavah mystic's characteristic inner journey, the Kabbalist would make the inner journey ascending to the world of the Sefirot. In this way the Kabbalist was able to use the same essential prayer service that everyone utilized, but employ it for very esoteric aims. Since it was a fundamental Jewish principle to not separate yourself from the community, this satisfied both the need to take part in prayer with the community and the need to focus on individual meditation.

The word *Mishnah* itself comes from a root that means "to learn through repetition." Originally, the Mishnah was taught orally and memorized. There was great hesitation in writing down words intended for oral transmission. Consequently it was written in a very concise manner, almost as an outline, serving as a springboard for teaching the rest of the oral tradition.

In contrast to the Merkavah mystic who had his own meditative techniques for attaining ecstatic visions and trance states to enter the realm of the divine glory (Kavod), the Kabbalist strove to enter the realm of divinity itself and commune with or attain union with God via various meditations. There were a number of dominant methods that were used. One common method was the repetition of a particular Mishnah over and over in a mantralike manner.

Candle-Staring and Divine Light

In early Kabbalistic texts both candle-staring (gazing at a flame for a prolonged period of time) and visualizing divine lights were meditational methods. Light was a common symbol of both knowledge and the Divine Presence. Many Kabbalistic texts have light in their titles because of its symbolic significance in the Jewish tradition. A very short list of examples would include:

- **The Bahir** (Illumination)
- **The Zohar** (Enlightenment, Radiance)
- **Sha'arei Orah** (The Gates of Light)
- **Or HaGanuz** (the Hidden Light)
- **Or HaSekhel** (the Light of the Mind)

The *Or Ein Sof*, "the Light of the Infinite," is a common Kabbalistic term for the divine "light" that emanates down to the creation of the physical universe, vivifying all that exists.

The imagery used to express the divine emanation that culminates in the creation of the universe is often that of light. This parallels the Creation story (*Ma'aseh Bereshit*) in Genesis in which light is formed on the first day: "Let there be light, and there was light."

FACT

Every synagogue has an "eternal light" (*ner tamid*) in front of the Ark where the Torah scrolls are kept that symbolizes God's eternal Presence. The Ark reflects the Ark of the Covenant, where the Ten Commandments were kept, and the eternal light was the westernmost branch of the Menorah in the First and Second Temples that was kept aflame continually.

Azriel of Gerona on Meditation

Rabbi Azriel of Gerona (a small town near Barcelona, Spain) was a Kabbalist of great influence and insight who wrote about meditation in the first half of the thirteenth century. In his Commentary on Talmudic Aggadot (Midrashic legends) he explains that one's consciousness expands in meditative prayer and ascends to the place of its source (in the divine realm of the Sefirot), beyond which it cannot go. Each word of the prayer book, in addition to its commonly understood definition, also contains divine energy that can be connected to through meditative prayer.

Yosef Gikatilla

Yosef Gikatilla (1248–1325), another prominent Spanish Kabbalist, was unique in that he was Abraham Abulafia's most outstanding student and subsequently became a major voice among Theosophical Kabbalists. Gikatilla and Moshe de Leon became well acquainted and part of the same Kabbalistic community. Gikatilla's most influential book, *Sha'arei Orah* (The Gates of Light), is constructed of chapter-by-chapter ascension through the world of the Sefirot. He elaborates upon the symbolism of the Sefirot, explaining which names of God refer to which Sefira and what characterizes each Sefira, essentially mapping out the spiritual terrain for the reader. The purpose of the book is to facilitate the spiritual journey the practitioner of Kabbalah would wish to make. It leaves the reader to individually turn their prayers into a meditation.

Meditation and Contemplation

Meditation and contemplation are related, but distinct activities. Contemplation generally refers to thinking intensively about a subject. It is a very focused intellectual, cerebral activity—though, like all activities it has an emotional component. Very often people use the terms meditation and contemplation interchangeably. Meditation, though it is a mental activity, is not an intellectual activity.

Meditation is the focusing of one's consciousness on something, but not the act of thinking about it. That is why, occasionally, the term *kavana* is used to refer to meditation—because kavana is the directing of one's awareness and intention.

Maimonides and Meditation

Maimonides, the most influential Jewish philosopher and Talmudist of the Middle Ages, was a great proponent of intellectual contemplation. Though he uses similar language at times to the Kabbalists by advocating a constant awareness of God, his method is one of contemplation, meaning thinking about, rather than "being" with, God.

Maimonides (1135–1204) was born in Muslim-controlled Cordoba, Spain. Most of Spanish Kabbalah was written in the Christian-controlled part of Spain. While the Spanish Kabbalists generally didn't know Arabic, a number of the Spanish Jewish philosophers wrote texts in Arabic. Maimonides wrote his famous philosophical book, *Guide of the Perplexed*, in Arabic, which most Kabbalists read in Hebrew translation.

Maimonides' book *Guide of the Perplexed* exerted a huge influence on the Jewish thought of his time and continues to do so to this day. At the same time he was a very controversial figure and the disagreement surrounding his teachings continued for generations. Some Kabbalists saw him as a fellow mystic, while others opposed what they perceived as his excessive rationalism (which they felt missed the deeper truths of Torah that transcend rational thought). Most had deep respect for his Talmudic knowledge.

Knowledge of God's Name

Maimonides spoke of divine secrets and of being focused on God as often and continuously as possible. For Maimonides this was an intellectual activity. It began with studying philosophy and grasping the nature of reality through philosophical reasoning and continued with a more abstract kind of contemplation.

Kabbalists spoke of holding God's name in the "mind's eye" and using it as a focus of meditation. Maimonides wrote of "knowledge" of God's name, which meant apprehension and understanding. Both Kabbalists and Maimonides referred back to Psalm 16:8 ("I set YHVH before me always") to illustrate their point, but they understood the very same verse in different ways.

FACT

Maimonides studied in Morocco after fleeing Spain and briefly lived in the Holy Land of Israel before settling in Egypt, where he remained until his death. In Egypt, Maimonides was the physician to the Sultan of Cairo and wrote his work *The Mishnah Torah*.

Maimonides lays out his ideal of a contemplative life in *Moreh Nevukhim* (*Guide of the Perplexed*; sec. 3, chap. 51). Here he even speaks of union with God, much as the Kabbalists do. However, union appears to mean for him an apprehension rather than what it is usually understood as, which is as a mystical experience. For Maimonides, this apprehension at its peak was what constituted a state of prophesy.

Meditation in Talmud and Sefer Yetzirah

Even though there are short entries in the Talmud that discuss mysticism, such as the Merkavah mysticism that was the basis of the story of the "Four Who Entered Pardes," there is no description of the meditative techniques used to arrive at such a state. Our knowledge of that comes from reading the surviving fragments of the Merkavah and Hekhalot texts themselves. However, there is a highly revealing entry in the very first volume of the Mishnah, called Tractate Brakhot (Tractate Blessings), that is primarily concerned with prayer.

Chapter 5, Mishnah 1, begins: "One doesn't stand to pray unless one is in a serious state of mind. The earliest Hasidim [pious ones] used to meditate an hour and then pray in order that they would direct their hearts to the Omnipresent [to the Makom]."

As in other Talmudic references to activities of this nature, no detailed description is given. A commentary on the passage explains that the person empties his mind from all distracting thoughts so that his consciousness and his kavana will be pure in his prayer. Maimonides also explains that during prayer, a person should see himself as standing before the Shekhinah (the Divine Presence).

The name *HaMakom* [the Omnipresent or, literally, "the place"] for God was frequently used in Talmudic times. A Midrash found in a few collections, including Bereshit Rabbah, asks: "Why is the Blessed Holy One [*HaKadosh Baruch Hu*] called 'Makom?' Because 'He' is the 'place' of the universe, but the universe is not his 'place,'" meaning that God also transcends the universe.

A Meditative Guide from Antiquity

Fairly contemporary with the previous Mishnah was an entry in the book Sefer Yetzirah (The Book of Creation), which is about the actual process of meditation. This passage, as all the passages in this short classic, is written in the form of a Mishnah. Chapter 1, Mishnah 8, reads as follows: "Ten Sefirot of No Thingness—Restrain your mouth from speaking and your heart [mind] from thinking. And if your heart [mind] races, return it to the Makom which is why it's said (Ezekiel 1:14) 'the Khayot run and return.' And concerning this a Covenant is made."

This short entry requires a significant amount of explanation because of the cryptic nature of its style. Silence and stilling the mind are two fundamentals of meditation. You can still the mind by focusing on a particular object of meditation such as a divine name, the ineffable aleph (the aleph, which is the first letter of the Hebrew alphabet, is a silent letter), a candle flame, or even nothingness. But it is the nature of the mind to race toward other thoughts (which, if we note the thoughts without dwelling on them, reveals to us what is going on inside ourselves). The next step, as mentioned here in Sefer Yetzirah, is to bring your consciousness back to the Omnipresent ("the Makom"). This process of bringing consciousness back to the Omnipresent helps strengthen our spiritual "muscles" and develops our ability to have kavana (intentional focus).

FACT

Aleph is an excellent focus of meditation. It is silent and is the first letter of every first-person future tense verb (for example, "I" will . . .). It is the first letter of the Ten Commandments and of both words for "I" (*Anokhi* and *Ani*), which implies that silence, meaning humility, should be the first component of "I."

A passage such as this one in Sefer Yetzirah is very difficult to translate because there are a number of levels on which the words can be understood. Even the phrase "restrain your mouth" is not as straightforward as it seems. The word translated as "restrain" (*blom*) has as its root the same three prime letters of the word or words for "no-thingness" (*blimah*, or sometimes written as two words, *bli mah*). So "restrain" really incorporates into it the idea of dwelling in nothingness through silence.

The word *khayot* in this passage requires clarification. In the original biblical passage in the Book of Ezekiel, khayot is often translated as "living creatures" and is understood as a kind of angelic being. However, the same consonants can spell *khiyut*, which means "life force" and that's usually how it's understood in the Kabbalistic tradition. The passage about the khayot or khiyut running and returning is often used as a fitting description of the nature of mystical awareness and experience. On the one hand the experience is generally fleeting. On the other hand, you have a timeless moment in which you feel thoroughly united with the Infinite One. It leaves, but it can just as unpredictably return. Meditation is on the one hand an exercise of one's spiritual "muscles" and kavana and, on the other hand, a readying of the consciousness for the experience of union with the One.

A Covenant of Silence

The last phrase of this Sefer Yetzirah section also deserves attention, as it too contains a double meaning. The literal meaning is "concerning this a Covenant is made." The covenant is the pact, the connection, between the Jewish people and God that's first mentioned in the Bible with the patriarch Abraham. The sign of the covenant was circumcision, which in Hebrew is called *brit milah* (or *bris milah* if you use the Eastern European pronunciation of Hebrew). The word for "covenant" is *brit,* and *milah* means "circumcision." Milah has another meaning as well; it also means "word." So there is the covenant of circumcision and the covenant of speech. (There is an expression in the Jewish tradition of having "a circumcised heart," which means being sensitive and caring. In contrast, having "uncircumcised lips," means not speaking well—see Exodus 6:12, 30.) In fact, the phrase in Sefer Yetzirah translated as "concerning this" also means "concerning this *word*." So the phrase also means "concerning this word a Covenant is made." But what is that "word"? Silence!

Meditation and Prophetic States

Abraham Abulafia's meditational school was very different from other Kabbalistic meditation of his era. He would take the letters of the divine name and write or imagine them in many combinations and with many different vocalizations using all of the possible vowel combinations. Abulafia called this method *tzerufei otiyot* (the combinations of letters) or *chokhmat ha-tzeruf* (the wisdom of combining). The term *tzeruf,* however, also means "purification." Abulafia's method implied simultaneously combining and "purifying" the divine letters to connect to their divine energy.

For Abulafia, and Kabbalists in general, the Hebrew alphabet is not merely a set of symbols representing the sounds of language. Kabbalists understand the Hebrew alphabet as the very foundation blocks of Creation. The letters of the main divine name, YHVH, are the most powerful combination conceivable.

Abulafia primarily worked with the seventy-two-letter name of God (which stems from the three verses of Exodus 14:19–21, each verse of which contains seventy-two letters) and the ineffable name YHVH (called *Shem HaMeforash* in Hebrew, which literally means "the explicit name"). One's consciousness was completely absorbed in the divine name until, hopefully, one reached an altered state of awareness. Abulafia's system was experientially oriented and meditation was the key to it.

Abulafia, following the pre-eminent Jewish philosopher of the Middle Ages, Maimonides, saw the goal of the contemplative person as the attainment of a state of prophecy. To Abulafia, the state of awareness that you could achieve using his meditational techniques was the true state of prophecy. He wrote quite a number of manuscripts based on his "prophetic" experiences, only one of which has survived.

Medieval Meditation Manuals

Abulafia also wrote numerous meditational manuals describing his methods, none of which were printed until very recent times. It was possible, however, to get a manuscript copied, and they were passed among the serious seekers. We see his influence upon other Kabbalistic authors in Europe and as far away as the land of Israel.

ALERT!

An anonymous Kabbalist wrote a text called *Sha'arei Tzedek* (The Gates of Righteousness) in 1295 in Israel, which contains an autobiographical section describing the author's spiritual and visionary experiences using what seem to be Abulafia's techniques. This manuscript illustrates both the widespread influence of Abulafia and provides a glimpse into the inner world of those who practiced his meditational teachings.

Rabbi Moshe Cordovero from Tzfat quoted Abulafia extensively in his classic work *Pardes Rimonim* (The Pomegranate Orchard), holding him in high esteem. Cordovero believed that meditation made the Divine Presence more palpable wherever the righteous engaged in it.

Chaim Vital on Meditation

Isaac Luria's main disciple, Rabbi Chaim Vital, recorded the most important versions of Luria's teachings that we have. Vital wrote a classic book of Kabbalistic mussar (ethical) literature called *Sha'arei Kedushah* (The Gates of Holiness). *Sha'arei Kedushah* is also a text on mystical techniques and meditations. Its fourth and concluding section, which is the section primarily devoted to elaborating on these techniques, was historically left out of printings of the book. The original publisher wrote that "since this fourth section . . . is entirely [divine] names, permutations, and esoteric secrets it is not appropriate to bring it to the altar of the printing press."

Within the last decade, however, this fourth section has been published in Jerusalem (as have a number of manuscripts by Abulafia). A few selected quotes from it illustrate both some of the techniques and how earlier mystical teachings were absorbed by later Kabbalists.

Vital writes about spiritual attainment: "A person should seclude himself so nothing disturbs his thought. He should meditate to the utmost and strip his physicality from his soul as though he no longer sensed that he has a body, but is purely soul. . . . [S]ublime holiness doesn't rest on a person if he's too attached to the physical." Regarding someone who wants to seriously meditate, Vital advises that he "first must repent from any sins and afterwards be careful not to continue to do those sins. Afterwards he should become accustomed to rid himself of the negative qualities ingrained in him like anger, sadness, irritability, idle conversation, and the like . . . meditate in a secluded place, wrap yourself in a Tallit, sit, close your eyes, divest yourself of your physicality as though your soul has left your body and ascended to the Heavens. After this recite one Mishnah numerous times successively with the greatest rapidity that you can while still speaking clearly."

Meditation on the Divine Name

The name YHVH is unique in Semitic languages. Other names for God such as *Elohim*, *El*, or *Eloha*, for example, share a root with other Semitic words such as the Arabic word for God, Allah. YHVH, according to the Jewish tradition, was pronounced only once a year on the holiest day, Yom Kippur. It was pronounced by the high priest who was a direct descendent of Aaron, Moses' older brother, in the Holy of Holies in the First and Second Temples. The high priest would take days preparing himself for this profound occasion.

Not pronouncing the name contributes to its unique power. Among the Ten Commandments is the commandment not to take God's name in vain. To say this name with appropriate kavana is an almost impossible task. Instead, its silent presence contributes to its power in meditation.

In Pirkei Avot we read: "Shimon [the son of Rabbi Gamliel] says: All my days I grew up among the wise and I've never found anything better for a person than silence. And it's not the theory that matters most, but the practice" (1:17).

Isaac of Acco, in the late thirteenth century or early fourteenth century, wrote a text entitled *Me'irat Einayim* (The Illumination of the Eyes), which contains specific instructions concerning meditating on the explicit name, YHVH, to achieve union (devekut). A passage from this text articulates clearly this meditational technique: "If one wants to know the secret [Sod] of binding his soul to the Sublime realm and the union of his consciousness to God . . . [he] should place in his mind's eye and consciousness the letters of the blessed Unique Name [YHVH] . . . [and] each letter should be infinitely large in his [inner] eyes . . . [and] your mind's eye will enter them and the consciousness of your heart will be with Ein Sof [the infinite] united all in one vision and consciousness."

Meditation on No-Thing: Ayin Meditation

Ayin (nothingness) is fundamental to Kabbalistic understanding. However, there is an element of paradox involved in discussing it. Ayin can only be pointed to, but can never be truly spoken of. Once we begin to use words, we lose connection with Ayin, because Ayin is beyond all duality. It is the ultimate oneness. The use of words implies duality. For this reason, Ayin isn't written about often. It is one of "the names" or words associated with the first Sefira, Keter, and it retains that sense of undifferentiated divinity despite the beginning of emanation (atzilut) that ultimately results in the emergence of the physical universe.

The Book of Job (28:12) contains the phrase conventionally translated as "Where can wisdom be found?" (*HaChokhmah MeAyin Timatzeh*). The Kabbalists completely reread this as (the Sefira) Chokhmah emanates from Ayin. But there is an additional understanding that true wisdom comes from nothingness, and ultimately (and paradoxically) only silence can capture and express that.

Meditation on Ayin occurs in a number of different ways. It can be achieved by an emptying of the mind, but is more commonly attained by slowing down all thinking during other forms of meditation and coming into a state of pure "being" rather than "doing." Ultimately all meditation seeks to achieve a state of pure "being" rather than "doing," but as long as the mind is focusing consciously even on some "object" of meditation, there is still a vestige of activity.

The great Hasidic master Levi Yitzkhak of Berditchev writes in his book *Kedushat Levi*, "there are those who worship the Blessed Creator with their mind, the human mind, and those who are able to gaze upon Ayin, as it were. This is impossible [to do] with the human [rational] mind." In order to achieve this state, the meditator must transcend the rational mind.

YHVH and Ayin Meditation

YHVH was understood as embodying all of the Sefirot within its four letters. Its first letter *Y* (yud) is the smallest letter in the alphabet and symbolizes the Sefira Chokhmah, which is actually the second Sefira. So where is the first Sefira, Keter, in the name? As mentioned in Chapter 6, the word *keter* literally means "crown," and the yud itself has a tip at the top, which is its "crown." This is the part that symbolizes Keter, which is also referred to as Ayin. When meditating upon the ineffable name (YHVH) you can come to Ayin meditation by focusing on this tip of the yud and making this your initial focus before eventually even leaving that behind.

Niggun and Meditation

One other method of entering Ayin meditation is through the silence after singing a niggun (often a wordless melody) for a long time. The niggun prepares the ground for Ayin meditation by totally absorbing your awareness in singing it over and over and over. When the niggun ends, you may enter the very full silence of Ayin.

Ayin meditation is difficult to sustain because of the mind's tendency to race, as the earlier quotation from Sefer Yetzirah suggests. With other forms of meditation, you bring your attention back to the focus of meditation; however, with Ayin meditation you try to bring your focus back to nothingness. For this reason, Ayin meditation is usually not recommended until you have considerable meditation experience.

Meditation (Hitbodedut) among Bratzlaver Hasidim

Although many Hasidic groups are very involved in contemplative prayer and chanting, the Hasidim of Rebbe Nachman of Bratzlav have a unique form of hitbodedut (or *hisbodedus*, as they would call it, using the Eastern European pronunciation of Hebrew). Rebbe Nachman's Hasidim have the custom, following the way of their rebbe, of finding a secluded spot, preferably in nature, and spending an hour there at dawn (and preferably at dusk as well), pouring out their hearts to the Master of the Universe.

Rebbe Nachman insisted that this form of hitbodedut should be done in the language in which one is most comfortable, even if that's not Hebrew. For most of his Hasidim this was, and remains, Yiddish. Rather than being a silent form of meditation, Bratzlaver hitbodedut may be done at the top of your lungs. Around dawn at the outskirts of Jerusalem you might hear Bratzlaver Hasidim shouting out their inner thoughts, pleas, and even arguments with their Creator. Sometimes they might just shout out *"Ribono Shel Olam"* (meaning, "master of the universe") over and over. It's a very cathartic and eccentric spiritual practice, but a fundamental part of Bratzlaver Hasidism.

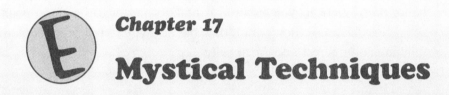

Chapter 17

Mystical Techniques

Mystical experience comes through different avenues and there are various traditional techniques Kabbalists use for attaining this experience of the Living God. For some it comes as an act of "grace," what the Zohar would call "arousal from above" (*itaruta d'l'ayla*). For others, it comes after much inner work. Even after much inner work, though, experiences may come unexpectedly, possibly as an outcome of all the effort or possibly as a moment of "grace."

Mystical Focus and Intention: Kavana

Kavana in its simplest form means performing an act with consciousness and intention. In the situation of a highly ritualized religious life like traditional Judaism, there is always the danger of actions becoming rote and automatic and ceasing to enhance a connection with God. On the other hand, prescribed activities can also make it easier to heighten your consciousness because they are predictable and you're not preoccupied with thinking about how to do the activity.

ALERT!

"Prayer without Kavana is like a body without a soul" (Isaac Abravanel, 1437–1508). Both spontaneous prayers and prayers read from a book can be said with great kavana. Prewritten prayers are difficult to say with kavana unless you know the words well and truly mean them.

Kavana and Mitzvot

When performing mitzvot, a basic goal is to try to remain as aware of the unifying purpose of the mitzvah as possible. A conscious attempt to keep a person focused on this was instituted in Tzfat, Israel, with specific kavanot said before doing a particular mitzvah. Many mitzvot are preceded by a blessing (*brakha*) that begins by focusing your attention on God and culminates with mentioning the particular mitzvah you are about to do. This can be used as a moment of meditation to enhance your kavana before doing the mitzvah.

Kabbalah had two general orientations toward kavana applied to mitzvot and to prayer. One was the "theurgic" potential of the act or prayer, meaning its ability to affect the upper worlds and then, as a consequence, have repercussions in this world. The other was the goal of uniting with the Eternal One by means of the prayer or mitzvah.

Ecstatic Kabbalists tend to see the goal of uniting with the Holy One as the ultimate purpose of all activity, whereas Theosophical Kabbalists tend to focus much more on attempting to bring more Shefa (divine energy) into the world. Of course, from the perspective of an Ecstatic Kabbalist, if you are able to unite with the Holy One, that itself brings more of God's Presence into the world.

Kavana and Prayer

The main arena for kavana is that of prayer. As opposed to the performance of a mitzvah, prayer is generally a sustained activity, something that you dwell on for a relatively long period of time. This makes it easier to put more of yourself into it and to intensify your kavana.

FACT

Midrash Tehillim (Midrash on the Psalms) from the tenth century says that Israel's prayers are not heard because of lack of knowledge of the pronunciation of YHVH. The biblical commentator Abraham Ibn Ezra called those who knew the secrets of the name *maskilim* (enlightened). Kabbalists came to be referred to by this term.

Psalms says: "YHVH is near to all those who call Him, to all those who call Him in Truth [Emet]" (145:18). Another term used for Kabbalah was *Derekh HaEmet* (the path of truth). Though Theosophical Kabbalists didn't try to pronounce the name, they believed they knew the secrets of it. It was this secret understanding of it that was part of their kavana during prayer.

According to the Zohar (vol. 2, 215b), prayer heals the body and soul of a person and makes her "whole" (*shalem*). This echoes the story of the four who entered Pardes, in which Rabbi Akiva entered in peace (*shalom*, which has the same root as shalem) and left in peace. The Zohar continues, saying that prayer affects four *tikkunim* (healings): Tikkun of yourself, Tikkun of this world, Tikkun of the upper world and the secret Tikkun of the Holy Name.

According to the Kabbalistic tradition, all kavana is ultimately for the purpose of attaining a state of devekut. A great level of kavana was even believed to be able to lead you to a state of *Gilui Eliahu* (revelation of secrets by Elijah the prophet).

Mystical Union with the Divine: Devekut

Devekut is generally considered the highest spiritual goal according to Kabbalah. The word itself can refer to a range of experiences, anywhere from keeping mentally focused on the Eternal One to total union with the Divine (*yikhud*). We find the verb form of the root (*dalet, bet, kuf*) in Genesis: "a man shall unite [*v'davak*] with his wife and they shall become one flesh" (2:24). Here, clearly the image is one of union. Ecstatic Kabbalists consistently used the term to refer to union with God, whereas Theosophical Kabbalists do not always.

There are a few passages in Deuteronomy that use the verb to refer to what our relationship to the Eternal One should be (Deuteronomy 4:4, 10:20, and 30:20, for example). These were very inspirational to Kabbalists and were quoted often. The verse of Deuteronomy 4:4 can be read in various ways. The standard translation is "You who cleave to YHVH your God are all alive today." Another way to understand it is "You who are in a state of Devekut with YHVH your God are truly and thoroughly alive right now." This verse is recited immediately before public reading of the Torah.

Ibn Ezra's commentary to Exodus 3:15 is a prekabbalistic passage on devekut: "If you become wise, the soul will stand in the secret of the angels and be able to receive great strength from the highest power.... Then it will be united with the glorious Name."

Abraham Ibn Ezra (1089–1164) was an important influence on Kabbalists. His commentaries, along with Rashi's and Nachmanides', are the most widely read. His philosophy and poetry were also channels through which he reached the mystics who came after him. His belief, for example, that through devekut with the universal soul, the individual soul could affect the world, had an impact on both Theosophical and Ecstatic Kabbalists.

Nachmanides on Devekut

As one of the earliest and most important Kabbalists, Nachmanides' words on devekut were fundamental. Nachmanides' influence came both through the disciples he raised, who themselves became significant voices, and the words he wrote.

In his comment on Deuteronomy 11:22, in which the verb form of devekut is used, Nachmanides writes, "you should remember God and His love always so that your awareness not separate from Him when you walk along the way, when you lie down, and when you wake up, to the point that your words with other people may be in your mouth and on your tongue, but your heart is in the Presence of God."

FACT

For Hasidim, Pirkei Avot 6:1 was inspirational: "All who engage in Torah for its own sake merit many things. . . . [the study of Torah for its own sake] dresses them in humility and awe . . . and reveals to them secrets of the Torah and they become like an overwhelming spring and an ever flowing river."

Devekut in Hasidism

Early Theosophical Kabbalah as it developed in Gerona focused on devekut as the center of spiritual quests. This was also true of Ecstatic Kabbalists throughout the centuries. Devekut resurfaced as primary once again in Hasidism in the eighteenth century. It became a more widespread goal as did the emphasis on kavana, meditation on the divine name, and spiritual ecstasy.

Levels of Devekut

There were Kabbalists who spoke of different levels of devekut. Isaac of Acco in his book *Me'irat Einayim* (The Illumination of the Eyes) wrote: "One who has merited the secret of being in a state of devekut will merit the secret of equanimity; and if one merits the secret of equanimity he will merit the secret of meditation [Hitbodedut]; and after meriting the secret of meditation, he will merit the Holy Spirit [*Ruakh HaKodesh*], and from this [level] to prophecy."

ALERT!

"To You, silence is praise" (Psalm 65:2). Though prayer (traditionally said out loud, however softly) is probably the most common path to devekut in Kabbalistic circles, meditation and silence are a powerful path to hearing "the subtle sound of silence" (I Kings 19:12).

In his book, Isaac of Acco describes different levels of devekut all stemming from the fundamental state of union with the Divine. This book had an impact in Tzfat and is quoted in the fourth and (until recently) unprinted chapter of Chaim Vital's *Sha'arei Kedushah* (The Gates on Holiness). Hasidim also have the sense of different levels of devekut, seeing it as the beginning of a certain quality of spirituality. In Hasidism, as with Isaac of Acco, the attainment of this state is not only for the spiritual elite, but instead should be a goal of the average person.

Ascent of the Soul

An important technique for acquiring mystical knowledge, solving difficulties, communing with souls of deceased Tzaddikim, and having visions is the ascent of the soul. This was a central method spoken of in Hekhalot and Merkavah mysticism and the technique continues to be mentioned in mystical writings at least into the nineteenth century.

Ascension of the soul was a process in which the mystic would be in a sleeplike state and have visions. There are descriptions by witnesses to these journeys written in the Middle Ages in which the body of the mystic appears inert for the duration of the ascension. When the journey is over the body comes back to normal life and, often, the person will describe the teachings and visions experienced during the soul's journey. Mystics were able to read about others' experiences of this because texts remained accessible throughout the many centuries.

A prime example of this is the account of the ascent of Rabbi Nekhunia ben HaKanah from the second century, in which his disciples were present in order to record the visions he described as he was ascending level after level.

Merkavah and Hekhalot manuscripts were preserved and copied by the Hasidei Ashkenaz (medieval German Pietists) who used various meditational techniques, including ascension, to achieve their mystical states. The works of the Hasidei Ashkenaz made their way to Provence and Spain and were read by the early Kabbalists influencing both the theosophical and ecstatic schools. The Zohar also recounts the experiences of the Hekhalot and describes each level and the visions beheld at each.

"Ben Zoma said: Who is wise? The one who learns from everyone. Who is powerful? The one who conquers his own impulse. Who is rich? The one who is happy with his lot. Who is honorable? The one who honors humanity" (Pirkei Avot 4:1).

Preparing for an Ascension of the Soul

An important account of the technique of ascension was written in Chaim Vital's *Sha'arei Kedushah* (The Gates of Holiness). He quotes the Zohar and Merkavah texts and includes the warnings they all mention in terms of the dangers inherent in the journey. Vital gives a fairly detailed account of the process and preparation for an ascent of the soul: "First, repent of all your sins both ritual and ethical; avoid idle conversation, pride, anger, and laziness. Cultivate humility; be happy in your lot."

Vital continues to explain the rituals necessary to prepare for ascension, writing that "at the time that you prepare yourself to be sanctified with the Holy Spirit, first purify your body with ritual immersion and clean clothing . . . [and] close your eyes, strip your thoughts of all matters of this world as though your soul has left you . . . [and] meditate upon the upper world and unite there with the root of your soul and with the Divine lights."

The Ba'al Shem Tov's Ascensions

The use of divine names was often a method of entering the state of the ascent of the soul. Probably the most famous description of this type of ascension is in the Ba'al Shem Tov's letter to his brother-in-law, Gershon of Kitiv.

The culmination of the account is when the Besht encounters the Messiah. He asks the Messiah when will he come. The answer he receives is "by this you will know: at the time when your teaching will be renowned and revealed in the world and your fountains will spread outward." This statement means that the Messiah will come when most people will be able to have these spiritual experiences.

FACT

In his letter to his brother-in-law, the Besht talks about how in every letter of the Hebrew alphabet there are worlds and souls and divinity, and when we pray and study we must attempt to unify them.

Rabbi Yitzkhak Safrin

In the middle of the nineteenth century, the Hasidic master Rabbi Yitzkhak Safrin writes about his ascensions of the soul. He also recounts the Besht's experiences and explains the story of the four who entered Pardes as an ascent of the soul. Most striking of all, he depicts Moses' ascent of Mount Sinai for forty days as the most masterful ascent of the soul.

Kabbalistic Color Visualizations

Among the techniques used by Kabbalists as part of their kavana is the visualization of colors. Kabbalists visualize the ineffable name, YHVH, using changing colors and vocalizations. Both the colors and the vocalizations (the vowels applied to the letters of the name) change according to the particular Sefira upon which the Kabbalist's kavana is focused. There is consistency throughout the centuries of the colors associated with each Sefira.

The color visualizations of the name were a form of kavana that Kabbalists used as part of the regular prayer service. Cordovero writes about it in *Pardes Rimonim* without going into much detail, as does Chaim Vital in the fourth and originally unpublished chapter of *Sha'arei Kedushah* (The Gates of Holiness).

A medieval manuscript reads: "When you . . . emit from your mouth a word indicating Keter you should have the Kavana and imagine the name YHVH between your eyes . . . white as snow and imagine the letters moving . . . and the entire secret is hinted at in the verse (Psalms 16:8) 'I place YHVH before me always.'"

Knowledge of the practice of color association with Sefirot and YHVH was limited to an enlightened few, and was mostly taught orally. Though it had been described in a few unprinted early manuscripts and written about vaguely in some later texts, it was usually accompanied by the mention of the necessity of receiving the teaching orally and only for those who could use it with appropriate reverence.

The color visualizations had two main functions: one was to transport the mystic to another plane of existence; the second was to connect to the divine realm and draw down Shefa (divine energy) to this plane of existence.

Weeping as a Mystical Technique

One of the less commonly known techniques of attaining mystical visions is that of weeping. It usually is part of a larger group of activities that express the attempt to achieve mystical insight and secrets. Descriptions about the practice of weeping appear in Hekhalot literature. There is also a Midrash about Rabbi Akiva not attaining the understanding of Torah that he longed for. He weeps intensely and subsequently sees clearly, reaching an entirely new level of understanding.

FACT

The meditational posture of Elijah the prophet (I Kings 18:42) was that of sitting with his head between his knees. This posture recurs throughout Jewish mystical history and literature from the days of the Merkavah mystics to the beginning of the modern era, often appearing in accounts of mystical weeping when seeking a vision.

Rabbi Shimon bar Yokhai, the central figure in the Zohar, is described as using the meditational posture of Elijah the prophet and weeping while attempting to encourage the revelation of some great mystical secret. It is not uncommon in the Zohar for decriptions of revelation to be accompanied by descriptions of weeping, but it is important to distinguish between weeping that is the result of an ecstatic experience and weeping that precedes an experience and is done in the hope of catalyzing knowledge of God.

Weeping is characteristic throughout religious life in mourning rituals as in the loss of a person close to you or as in the rituals accompanying the mourning for the destruction of the ancient Temple in Jerusalem. Two such occasions are *Tisha B'Av* (the ninth day of the Hebrew month of Av), the day the Jewish tradition says both Temples fell, and *Tikkun Khatzot* (the daily midnight ritual of mourning for the destruction of the Temple). Mystical weeping, however, falls outside the framework of ritual life.

Tears as a Catalyst

Weeping is often featured as a powerful force compelling internal change. In other words, tears express such an intense desire for something that it midwifes an intense change within an individual. In the passages of mystical texts that feature weeping as a technique, visual insight often results from the tears. These may be visions of the Merkavah, the divine throne, angels, or even the Shekhinah.

In the book *Shivkhei Ha'Ari* (Praises of the Ari) there is an interesting account concerning Rabbi Abraham HaLevi Berukhim, a disciple of Luria's. Luria told Abraham that he would die unless he went to the *Kotel* (the surviving outer wall of the Temple, usually called the "Western Wall" or the "Wailing Wall") and had a vision of the Shekhinah. Abraham went and wept considerably and did have a vision. When he returned to Tzfat, Luria remarked upon greeting him that he could see that he had experienced the Presence of the Shekhinah.

Yosef Karo, in his book *Maggid Meisharim*, which records teachings Karo received from his heavenly teacher (his Maggid), writes: "He further told me that if it is possible to shed tears during your prayer, at least on Mondays and Thursdays [when the Torah is read], it would be good and beautiful, and you would reach heights." Since Shabbat is a day of joy and pleasure, crying is inappropriate—it is for this reason that Karo's Maggid did not suggest weeping on days other than Monday and Thursday. Even the required rituals of mourning are suspended on Shabbat.

ALERT!

Job describes mystical weeping when interpreted from a Kabbalistic perspective: "All precious things his eye saw. From the crying of rivers he healed and brought forth light on that which is hidden" (28:10–11).

Mystical Weeping among Hasidim

The practice of mystical weeping continued in Hasidism. There's a famous saying by Rebbe Nachman of Bratzlav that "there's nothing as whole as a broken heart." Doing *teshuvah* (literally "returning" to God, but usually translated as "repentance") was a very important part of the Hasidic worldview. For some Hasidim, even a Tzaddik must always do teshuvah.

A passage by Elimelekh of Lyzhansk (1717–1787), a disciple of the Maggid of Mezeritch, explains the relationship between weeping and achieving a connection to the divine world. Elimelekh writes: "In every person there is a sublime Divine part even at the moment that he transgress, Heaven forbid. The Divine part of necessity must dress Itself in layers and layers in order to endure the great sorrow of the transgression and this is the secret of the exile of the Shekhinah. Afterwards when a person returns through Teshuvah and weeps over his sins, he is weeping over the exile of the Shekhinah and through this he breaks through the layers in which the Divine part is dressed and is revealed through his Tikkun." In other words, the power of weeping brings about the revelation of the Divine that is within us.

Asceticism: Separation from the Physical

Asceticism, that is depriving oneself of pleasure even to the point of suffering physically, is generally not part of the spiritual path in Judaism. In the Bible, a person who was an ascetic was called a nazir. Probably the most famous nazir in the Bible was Samson, who was dedicated from birth as a nazir. In his case, this distinction largely prohibited him from drinking wine and cutting his hair. In the era of the Talmud, an ascetic was called a *parush*, meaning "one who was separate" or "separated."

FACT

Hillel, who lived in the first century B.C.E., is quoted in Pirkei Avot: "Don't separate yourself from the community. . . . Don't say when I have leisure, I will study. Perhaps you will never have leisure. . . . The more Torah, the more life. The more Tzedakah [righteousness, charity], the more peace" (2:5–8).

The rabbis of the Talmudic period discouraged asceticism, considering it a sin of sorts to not enjoy the gift of life (within the boundaries of Torah, of course). Hillel, for example, considered it a religious obligation to bathe and to take care of your body. At the same time, asceticism was not uncommon during the period of the second Temple.

Asceticism to Philosophers and Kabbalists

Jewish philosophers of the medieval period largely accepted the Talmudic attitude of frowning upon asceticism. Maimonides, echoing Aristotle, advocated the "middle road" of moderation. Physical pleasures were seen as positive, but indulgence was severely criticized, as was materialism.

Kabbalists tended to have more ascetic tendencies than the philosophers. However, within the Jewish tradition it's a mitzvah to marry and have children, it's forbidden to fast on Shabbat or holidays, and a man is obligated to satisfy his wife sexually. Yom Kippur, the Day of Atonement, is a day of fasting, but the prophets made it clear that the only real purpose of fasting is to make you sensitive to the hungry so you'll feed them, and shelter the homeless, and clothe the naked. A reading from Isaiah to this effect has a prominent place in the Yom Kippur synagogue service.

Kabbalists and other mystics were concerned with the easy appeal of physical pleasures to the detriment of the spiritual. The eleventh-century mystical-ethical text *Khovot HaLevavot* (Duties of the Heart) by Bakhya Ibn Pakuda, and the son of Maimonides' (Abraham ben Moses ben Maimon's) Sufi-influenced Jewish mysticism—both expressed strong ascetic tendencies as a means to an end. The idea behind asceticism is to deny earthly delights as a stepping stone to greater spiritual growth.

The medieval German Hasidim were possibly the most ascetically inclined. Their idea of what it meant to be a Hasid was to deprive yourself of the pleasures of this world, to be in a state of *hishtavut* ("equanimity," serenity, and indifference to people's praise or insults), selflessness, and extreme altruism.

Ascetism: Sinful or Worthwhile?

While the Jewish tradition esteemed the intense spiritual devotion of ascetics, it felt it was a sin to deprive yourself of those things the Torah permitted. This division continued throughout the development of Kabbalah. Yosef Karo's Maggid encouraged his ascetic leanings and said he should "afflict his Nefesh [soul]," which probably meant fast, on Mondays and Thursdays and weep. The great Italian Kabbalist Moshe Chaim Luzzato, the

Ramkhal (1707–1746), wrote in his ethical book *Mesillat Yesharim* (The Path of the Upright) that "all that is unnecessary in this world, it is worthwhile withdrawing from, but all that is necessary . . . it is sinful to withdraw from."

FACT

The word *ascetic* comes from the Greek word "askesis." The ancient Greek term meant intense training or practice and applied to Greek warriors who underwent a severe physical regimen to be in optimal condition before battle. Ascetic now implies a person who renounces the pleasures of the world in the hopes of achieving a higher spiritual or intellectual state.

Eighteenth-century Hasidism, despite its emphasis on joy and celebrating life, still had its share of ascetics. Elimelekh of Lyzhansk saw it as a path for himself, but not for everyone, and considered asceticism as a corresponding idea to Luria's concept of "the breaking of the vessels," whose ultimate purpose is Tikkun (healing). Elimelekh said that while one Tzaddik brings about Tikkun through eating, another may bring it about through asceticism.

Chapter 18

Reincarnation in Kabbalah

Reincarnation is not a doctrine that people normally associate with Judaism. In fact, in mainstream Judaism there is barely a trace of it. Although the sages of the Talmud did not reference reincarnation, Philo of Alexandria (circa 20 B.C.E.–50 C.E.), an important Jewish philosopher with mystical tendencies, spoke of it and even believed in it. The Kabbalists, for the most part, saw it as real. At times, they wrote about it, while at other times it remained part of the oral transmission of esoteric secrets.

Is Reincarnation in the Bible?

There are no explicit expressions of reincarnation in the Bible. If you were to read it cover to cover, it is likely that nothing would particularly strike you as referring to a doctrine about reincarnation. However, those Kabbalists who believed in it found numerous biblical verses that they interpreted as proof texts for reincarnation in the Bible.

There are a number of different Hebrew terms for reincarnation. The most common is *gilgul,* the root of which means "revolving." Some related words are *gal*, which is "a wave"; *galgal*, which means "wheel"; and *gulgolet*, which is a skull or head. In English, other terms for reincarnation are "transmigration of souls" and "metempsychosis."

Kabbalists saw references to transmigration in the Bible both in verses that they read and in stories that they thought made more sense when considered in light of reincarnation. Kabbalists interpret Exodus 34:4, in which Moses fashions a second of set of tablets like the first, as an allusion to transmigration. They believe that in this story, a second physical form is provided for the timeless spirit of the Ten Commandments, and for that reason it represents an instance of reincarnation.

A few verses later, after a cloud descends on Mount Sinai and Moses is intimately in the Presence of God, the Bible states that YHVH "preserves loving-kindness for thousands [of generations] forgiving iniquity, transgression, and sin" (Exodus 34:7). Kabbalists often see transmigration of the soul as supporting the notion of reincarnation.

Some Kabbalists saw the possibility of 1,000 gilgulim (plural of gilgul), others saw 3 as the limit, which is a number mentioned in the continuation of the verse regarding the number of generations that may feel the effects of transgression.

Is Moses in Every Generation?

Another term used for the transmigration of souls in early Kabbalah is *ibbur*, which came to have a different, though related, meaning by the end of the thirteenth century. Deuteronomy 3:26 uses this root in a verb form regarding Moses. The root (spelled, *Ayin, bet, resh*) can mean a number of different things, and this verse is usually translated as God being angry with Moses because of the people's behavior. However, if the verb is translated as referring to "transmigrating" instead of "being angry" it may be read as "YHVH will cause me to transmigrate for your sake." In fact, some Kabbalists believed that the soul of Moses is reincarnated every generation to help the people endure their exile from the Holy Land.

A Matter of Interpretation

A verse from II Samuel reads: "[A]nd God doesn't take a Nefesh [soul/life], but devises means that none of us will be banished" (14:14). In addition to the previous example, Kabbalists also use this excerpt from the Bible as a proof text for the existence of transmigration. There are a number of similar verses in Ecclesiastes that Kabbalists perceive as proof as well.

It is easy to see how Kabbalists would read Ecclesiastes 1:9 as referring to transmigration: "That which was will be, that which was done is that which will be done, and there is nothing new under the sun."

Biblical stories that seem unrelated to the essential themes and narrative flow of the text are often interpreted by Kabbalists as teachings related to reincarnation. This is also the case when an inordinate amount of detail is given concerning what appears to be a minor point.

Transmigration (Gilgul) in Early Kabbalah

The doctrine of transmigration of souls appears in the very first Kabbalistic work, Sefer HaBahir, in the late 1100s. It is mentioned matter of factly, with no explanation or justification, as though its readers would understand. Because of this presumed familiarity with the subject, it is possible that reincarnation was a part of an oral tradition. The Bahir does not use the word gilgul or any other Hebrew term to refer to transmigration; it simply describes it and explains a verse from Ecclesiastes: "A generation passes and a generation comes" as "it had already come [before]" (1:4). The Bahir reads: "Why is it that there are wicked people who prosper and righteous who suffer? Because the Tzaddik [righteous] was wicked in the past and now he is being punished. And he is being punished because of the days of his youth? Didn't Rabbi Shimon [Baby-lonian Talmud, Tractate Shabbat 89b] say that no one is punished [by Heaven] under the age of 20? But this is not referring to his [current] life. I am speaking about what he already was in the past [meaning in a previous life]."

FACT

Rabbi Yitzkhak Sagi Nahor (Isaac the Blind), the greatest Kabbalist in Provence and teacher of the early Kabbalists in Gerona, was reputed to be able to sense "by feeling the air" if the person before him was a new soul or a transmigrated soul.

Gilgul and Jewish Philosophy

One of the striking elements of the Bahir's unapologetic presentation of transmigration of souls is the fact that in its historical context this was not an accepted Jewish idea.

Sa'adia Gaon, the first Jewish philosopher, dismissed the idea of reincarnation. In fact, the major Jewish philosophers for almost 300 years were all opposed to the idea of its existence. One important nonkabbalistic thinker who accepted reincarnation as a truth was Isaac Abravanel, but he lived in the fifteenth century. Given this historical context, it is hard to imagine that the author or authors of the Bahir were unfamiliar with this formidable opposition to transmigration. Yet, despite this opposition the Bahir clearly advocates the existence of the transmigration of souls.

Gilgul in Gerona

The Kabbalists in Gerona, including such major figures as Nachmanides, Rabbi Azriel, and Rabbi Ezra ben Solomon, all accepted transmigration but treated it as a great mystery. Nachmanides mentions it briefly when commenting on a verse from Genesis (38:11), which is concerned with Levirate marriage.

Sa'adia Gaon (890–942) was the leader of the Babylonian Jewish community, a major Jewish center. He was the first to translate the Bible into Arabic and to write a commentary on it, and he also wrote a commentary on Sefer Yetzirah. Most importantly, he was the first medieval Jewish philosopher. He attempted to reconcile Judaism, philosophy, and science.

Levirate marriage, in the Bible, occurs when a man dies childless; the brother of the deceased is obligated to marry his widow in order to produce offspring for the deceased brother. The early Kabbalists, including Nachmanides, saw this as related to reincarnation. He wrote: "This matter is one of the great secrets of the Torah. . . . [T]he ancient sages before the Torah knew that Levirate marriage was of great value. . . . They called it redemption. . . . And the Maskil [the enlightened, that is, the Kabbalist] will understand." The reason that Nachmanides refers to "the ancient sages before the Torah" is that this incident occurs many generations before Moses receives the Torah.

A number of Kabbalistic commentaries on the Torah address transmigration in their section on the particular portion that contains this account of Levirate marriage. Different Kabbalists saw reincarnation as a response to different issues, but solving the problem of childlessness was a major explanation early Kabbalists provided for the necessity of reincarnation.

ALERT!

Chaim Vital writes in *Sha'ar HaGilgulim* (The Gate of Transmigrations): "[K]now that whoever dies without children, the first incarnation is considered as though it didn't happen. If so, when he returns he must come with his Nefesh, Ruakh, and Neshama all together [three levels of the soul] . . . which only occurs if he's done good deeds and merits all three parts."

Though the major Kabbalists in Gerona all seem to accept the doctrine of transmigration of the soul, they do not write extensively about it. Their treatment of it as a great mystery that must primarily be taught orally means that we have little written evidence of their beliefs. Kabbalists in later centuries no longer expressed such hesitation in writing about gilgul.

Divine Justice, Compassion, and Reincarnation

In addition to amending childlessness, another major reason offered to explain the justification for *gilgul nefashot* (the transmigration of souls) is that of divine justice. There are stories in the Bible where injustice appears to occur. If God is loving, compassionate, just, and merciful, why do God's punishments sometimes seem excessive? This is essentially the same question as that regarding the righteous that suffer and the wicked that prosper. The Kabbalists identified certain characters in the Bible as reincarnations of others and through this process attempted to explain apparent injustice or find rectification of previous injustices.

In the story of Cain and Abel (Adam and Eve's first children) in the fourth chapter of Genesis, God accepts Abel's offering and rejects Cain's with no explanation and Cain subsequently kills Abel.

Some Kabbalists offer the explanation that Moses and Yitro ("Jethro" in English, who was Moses' father-in-law and a priest of Midian) were the reincarnations of Abel and Cain respectively. Jethro became Moses' advisor and, according to legend, a believer in the one true God. Here the problematic relationship in the Cain and Abel story is resolved through the connection between Moses and Jethro.

The entire Book of Job is the one biblical text that focuses on the issue of a righteous person who suffers terribly. Nachmanides, who wrote a complete commentary on Job, understood the book from the point of view of transmigration.

FACT

Some Kabbalists believed that the righteous only underwent transmigration if they had done a great sin. An example of this would be Joseph's ten brothers selling him into slavery (Genesis 37). According to one Kabbalist the ten were reincarnated as the ten martyrs, who were ten scholars (including Rabbi Akiva) martyred by the Romans early in the second century c.e.

The Kabbalists saw God as all-merciful and compassionate. Therefore, souls were given the chance to do *teshuvah* (repent and return to God and the proper path) through transmigrating into another body rather than enduring the pain of *gehinnom* (purgatory) in order to be purged of their transgressions.

How Many Reincarnations?

Kabbalists raised the question as to how many gilgulim a soul might undergo. Three gilgulim was a very common response, though there were some Kabbalists who thought 1,000 was possible. Which opinion one held depended on how one understood the purpose of transmigration.

If transmigration was seen as being a form of justice, then a soul might keep coming back until the transgressions it made were rectified. The soul of a wicked person might have three opportunities in which to rectify its mistakes. On the other hand, the soul of a Tzaddik might return 1,000 times in order to help the world.

The Soul of the Messiah

Another issue that arose with differing reactions was the question, "Are we all reincarnations?" In early Kabbalah, for example, Isaac the Blind was of the opinion that there were new souls and reincarnated souls and that he could distinguish between a new soul and an old soul by simply being in the presence of a person. There were those, however, who felt that all souls now are reincarnated and will remain so until the days of the Messiah.

Vital writes in *The Gate of Transmigrations:* "Moses' wife Tzipporah transmigrated into Devora [Deborah] the prophet. [When] Israel sang the 'Song on the Sea' Tzipporah wasn't there and was sorry. Through the merit of circumcising her son she was worthy of coming [back] as Devora to sing her song." *Devora* means "bee," among whom the female reigns as queen.

In a passage from Ezekiel, which was understood as referring to the Messianic era, God is quoted as saying: "I will put a new spirit/soul [Ruakh Khadashah] within you [or, in your midst]" (11:19). This was held as proof of the Messiah's soul being a new one. However, there were other Kabbalists who disagreed and felt that the soul of the Messiah exists in every generation and waits for the appropriate time to come. That soul, some Kabbalists believed, was the original pure soul of Adam. They explained that the three consonants of the name *Adam* show the lineage of that soul: Adam, (King) David, and Messiah. The Messiah traditionally was held to be a direct descendent of King David.

Reincarnation in Lurianic Kabbalah

As he did in many other areas of Kabbalistic thought, Isaac Luria introduced novel teachings into the discussion of reincarnation. He himself believed he could see the history of the souls of the people that he encountered. Based on this, he would tell his disciples who they had been, what transgressions they might have to do teshuvah and a Tikkun for, and offer them meditations to facilitate this.

Luria believed that every soul needed to study the entire Torah both in the conventional and mystical sense and fulfill all 613 Mitzvot. A soul would keep reincarnating until it had fulfilled this mission for which it had been brought into the physical realm in the first place.

Soul Sparks

Another novelty in Luria's understanding of gilgul was his notion of "sparks" in souls. He saw individual people as being the home to the spark of larger souls. In other words, the soul spark of more than one person can share the same root, but, nevertheless, each soul is unique. Therefore, the tikkunim that it could bring about in the cosmos and the upper worlds were directly related to the root of that person's particular soul spark.

ALERT!

Complicating matters further was the view that each person often had more than a mere nefesh, but also a ruakh level of soul and a neshama level of soul, too. Each of these had its root in a different part of the upper worlds. The Ari and his disciples believed that Luria could perceive all of this about a person.

Sparks of souls were part of larger soul "families" so to speak, and the other members of your soul's family could supplement your fulfillment of mitzvot and acts of Tikkun, thus shortening the number of gilgulim your soul had to undergo.

Which Soul Transmigrates?

Generally speaking, only the nefesh undergoes transmigration. For most Kabbalists, ruakh and neshama, both of which have higher roots, don't transgress. Therefore, for those who see transmigration as a form of punishment for an erring soul, the ruakh and neshama would not undergo transmigration.

Reincarnation and Mitzvot

There are two aspects connecting mitzvot and gilgul. Most Kabbalists believe a person's life of mitzvot and transgressions are the determining factors as to whether they will be reincarnated or not. There were also particular mitzvot that Kabbalists analyzed according to the doctrine of gilgul. The most common one was that of Levirate marriage, but there were others as well. According to the Jewish tradition, a person must be buried within twenty-four hours of death. This is usually seen as a sign of respecting the dead. In terms of gilgul, however, this becomes understood as an act facilitating the soul's transmigration.

FACT

The traditional Talmudic view was that people had 248 limbs and 365 sinews that correspond to the 248 positive and 365 negative mitzvot. Luria believed the soul had spiritual equivalents of these limbs and sinews. Only the mitzvah connected to a part of the soul animated and fulfilled that part. To be fully realized, a soul must fulfill all the mitzvot.

Can Souls Transmigrate Only into Humans?

Another controversy regarding transmigration was the question of whether or not a soul could only transmigrate into other humans. For some Kabbalists it was considered an insult to the human soul to consider its transmigration into nonhumans. Though everything has a soul, these Kabbalists saw the human soul as of a higher order. There were also those Kabbalists who believed that a soul, according to the severity of its trangression, could return in an animal or in another aspect of nature. For those who held this position, the very particular laws advocating kindness toward animals reinforce their opinion.

The Souls of Animals

There is a whole category of laws concerning the ritual slaughter of animals (*shekhitah*) that determines whether an animal is kosher and thus fit to be eaten. The conventional way of understanding these laws is to see them as aimed at preventing cruelty to animals. If you are going to eat meat, the laws of slaughter and *kashrut* (kosher) are meant to "humanize" the experience as much as possible. The slaughter is supposed to be swift and done with a particularly sharp knife in the vein that will kill the animal instantly. If the knife is not of the level of sharpness demanded, the slaughtering would not be kosher. Afterward, the animal must be covered with salt and soaked in water to drain the blood, for according to Leviticus, "the Nefesh [soul] of the flesh is in the blood" (17:11).

When considered in light of the idea of reincarnation even in animals, these very particular regulations can also be understood as out of kindness for the human soul that might possibly be in the animal's body. A related thought is that if we eat anything with the appropriate consciousness of the Divine we can raise up the spirit of what we have consumed and use the energy it gives us to do mitzvot.

All of the rules of ritual slaughter were also applied to sacrifices done during the time of the ancient Temples in Jerusalem.

Absorption of Another Soul: Ibbur

The word *ibbur* was originally used interchangeably with gilgul as a term for transmigration of the soul. Over time it came to have a separate, but related, meaning. Ibbur implies "transferring" and the word is also used to mean "conception." The same root is used for pregnancy, fetus, and related words.

As the meaning of ibbur separated from gilgul, it came to refer to a soul that inhabits another body for a limited period of time, as in a pregnancy, in contrast to a gilgul, in which a soul is in a new body for the life of that body. Usually there were two purposes that Kabbalists attributed to an ibbur temporarily entering a body. One was to fulfill some mitzvot or tasks that the soul had not completed in its previous lifetime. The other was to help a particular person to carry out a task for which this visiting soul was particularly known.

Though an ibbur is a temporary resident, the length of time the additional soul may inhabit another's body could last years. Primarily the ibbur was there for positive reasons, to bring strength, goodness, and aid in the performance of mitzvot.

In the book *Toldot Ha'Ari* (The Annals of the Ari), there's a story of a student entering the room where Luria sat with his disciples. The Ari arose, greeting him with sincere reverence. When asked why, Luria responded that the scholar embodied the soul of a tanna (a rabbi of the Mishna) known for performing a mitzvot of great compassion.

Dybbuk and Reincarnation

Over the course of time, Kabbalists also began to speak of an evil ibbur that was the soul of an evil person able to enter another's body because of some transgression the "host" person had done, often in secret. By the seventeenth century, the term *dybbuk* had surfaced to refer to an evil ibbur. The word dybbuk itself arose from Yiddish folk culture and was never used in Kabbalistic literature. In modern terminology we would probably diagnose a dybbuk as a case of psychosis, hysteria, or schizophrenia.

The word dybbuk comes from the same Hebrew root as the word *devekut*, implying another soul that is attached to the host's body. However, in this case the dybbuk is a very destructive force. Stories of dybbuks or dybbukim were not uncommon during the Second Temple and Talmudic periods, but they appear less frequently in the texts of the Middle Ages.

Exorcism of the dybbuk required someone with spiritual power and expertise in the area. In the 1700s a *ba'al shem* (literally a "master of the [divine] name") would often undertake this task. A ba'al shem, in exorcising the dybbuk, would try to free the soul from its attachment to the new body and find a way to give it spiritual resolution.

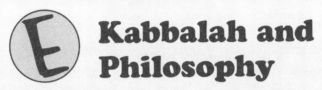

Chapter 19

Kabbalah and Philosophy

Kabbalah and Jewish philosophy reached the pinnacle of their impact during the Middle Ages. Many Kabbalists took an interest in philosophical questions. For some the interest occurred before their commitment to Kabbalah; for others it endured throughout their lives and contributed to their exploration of Kabbalah. In certain ways Kabbalah and philosophy addressed similar concerns, though they often came up with significantly different responses to the major religious questions that preoccupied them.

Maimonides and Esotericism

Maimonides is universally accepted as the most important and influential Jewish philosopher of the Middle Ages and probably of all time. For many he is the major figure of the Middle Ages in Judaism. He was the greatest Talmudic authority of his era in addition to being the premier philosopher. Maimonides achieved all this while making a living as a physician (ultimately becoming the physician to the sultan of Cairo, Egypt).

Maimonides evoked much controversy during his life. Some of his books, in fact, were burned. One of his two major works was the *Mishnah Torah*, which was an encyclopedic codification of Jewish Law that some people feared would replace the study of the Talmud. His other principle work was his philosophical magnum opus, the *Guide of the Perplexed*.

The Two Levels of the Guide

The *Guide* was a highly controversial book too, despite the fact that it had a strong esoteric level that was not easily accessible. There were two basic levels on which the text was written. One level was for the consumption of the general public, and the second, esoteric level, was written for a select few.

FACT

Maintaining the secrecy of certain doctrines of his was very important to Maimonides. Even though he did reveal some teachings in person, the students to whom he revealed them had to pledge to keep them secret. In fact, you can read in their writings testimony to this precondition.

Maimonides apparently believed that the deeper truths—that is, the esoteric truths—could not be understood by the masses and that if they were exposed to those ideas it would be bad for them. In other words, Maimonides felt that there were beliefs that were necessary for the successful functioning of society, and then there were the deeper truths that only the highly educated, philosophically inclined could grasp. Maimonides' belief parallels the Kabbalist's conviction, discussed in Chapter 1, that Kabbalistic ideas could be dangerous to the masses and therefore should only be taught to those ready to learn its secrets.

Encoded Teachings

The two levels on which the *Guide* is written are not obvious unless one reads it very carefully. The ideas that Maimonides does not want to reveal to the general public are spread throughout the chapters of the book. He doesn't write about these ideas systematically as he does with topics that are not part of his esoteric teachings. Someone who wants to figure out what he truly thinks about these issues has to piece together his ideas from all different sections of the large volume.

In addition, there are contradictions in the presentation of these ideas. The basic issues around which Maimonides' esotericism revolves are the question of the creation of the universe, *Ma'aseh Merkavah* (the Chariot of Ezekiel's vision), and the nature and eternality of the human soul. These are questions that Kabbalists also addressed with great interest.

European Jews and the Guide

As news spread that Maimonides had written this book in Arabic, European Jews in France and Northern Spain, who didn't speak the language, wanted a translation. The text was translated into Hebrew during Maimonides' lifetime. Two translations were undertaken simultaneously, one by Shmuel (Samuel) Ibn Tibbon, the other by Yehuda al-Kharizi. Ibn Tibbon's translation, done in southern France, ended up being the more popular of the two. It is a much more literal translation, but not nearly as well written.

Ibn Tibbon was in regular correspondence with Maimonides (who was already living in Egypt when he wrote the *Guide*), trying to clarify parts of the book that he didn't understand. In one letter that exists, Ibn Tibbon mentions contradictions in the book on topics that the Rambam (the acronym by which Maimonides is universally called in Hebrew) had dealt with in different sections. Some of these contradictions Ibn Tibbon was able to reconcile, but those concerning divine providence and the immortality of the soul he could not. He hoped Maimonides would provide solutions to these enigmas, but though Maimonides continued to correspond with him, he never clarified those elusive elements.

Maimonides said, "Anticipate charity by preventing poverty; assist the reduced fellow man, either by a considerable gift or a sum of money or by teaching him a trade or by putting him in the way of business so that he may earn an honest livelihood and not be forced to the dreadful alternative of holding out his hand for charity."

Commentaries to the Guide

A body of commentaries on the *Guide* eventually came into being. There were those who strongly opposed the book, others who were deeply in favor, and those who fell somewhere in between. Nachmanides was one who fell somewhere in between. Nachmanides, as a Talmudic giant, had a great appreciation of Maimonides' knowledge of Torah and Talmud, but as a Kabbalist, he disagreed strongly with Maimonides' apparent philosophical positions.

Among the commentators on the book there were those who saw it as part of a long line of esoteric works beginning with the Bible and continuing through rabbinic literature. These commentators felt that the *Guide*, as with the Bible and rabbinic works, could not be understood without a grasp of certain esoteric methods of composition. They saw Maimonides' contradictions in the text as intentionally placed there, much like the biblical inclusion of two Creation stories of Adam and Eve that seem to contradict each other.

These believers in the esoteric level of the Bible thought that this biblical feature is there to conceal the great mysteries in the Bible. Maimonides was likewise using what they considered the traditional esoteric literary devices of allusions and concealment of the deeper ideas that were not intended for the masses. These commentators also believed that Maimonides' concealments and contradictions corresponded to the very ones found in the Bible.

The contradictions (*s'tirot*) in the *Guide* were there to conceal the secrets (*s'tarim*); both words have the same apparent root.

Maimonides had tried to reconcile the Torah with philosophy and science as he knew it in his day. The philosophy was highly influenced by Aristotle, whom Maimonides studied through Arabic translations. Interestingly enough, Maimonides' son, Abraham ben Moshe ben Maimon, who was a great defender of his father in the controversy that surrounded him, became an important Jewish mystic in Egypt with much in common with Sufism (Muslim mysticism). Nothing in his mystical teachings seems to indicate any knowledge of Kabbalah.

FACT

The word *ben* in Hebrew means "son" or "child" of. The name of Maimonides' son Abraham, for example, Abraham ben Moshe ben Maimon, means "Abraham, son of Moshe son of Maimon."

The Rational, Irrational, and Nonrational

It is important to recognize the difference between rational, nonrational, and irrational thinking. Irrational thinking negates rational thinking, and nonrational thinking operates according to a different intelligence than logical, rational thought. The world of art and aesthetics, for example, requires nonrational intelligence to appreciate it fully; while much intelligence goes into the production of great works of art and literature, it has little to do with rational intelligence. Part of the difficulty of explaining the world of art and literature is that the verbal tools of explanation belong to the realm of linear thought in which the rational intelligence operates.

In contrast to this, the intelligence of art belongs to a realm of nonlinear, multitiered thought. Spiritual insights and sensibilities have a lot in common with aesthetic sensibilities. They both require a sensitivity to a dimension of reality that is very tangible to the person steeped in it, but difficult for someone on the outside of it to understand.

Philosophy and Torah

Philosophers see their objective as the pursuit of the truth through rational thought and inquiry. Even though Maimonides was deeply interested in, and influenced by, Aristotelian philosophy, he remained very committed to Torah and to halakhah (Jewish Law). Usually in cases of conflict between philosophy and Torah, Torah, which is seen as divine revelation, takes precedence. Because of the esoteric side of Maimonides' *Guide*, it is not completely clear what he ultimately thought about certain issues. It is unimaginable that he would ever publicly disagree with something in the Torah. Rather, he would explain that the literal reading is impossible because it contradicts logic and that the text is meant to be understood allegorically.

Kabbalah and Myth

The Kabbalists were also devoted adherents to Torah and mitzvot. It is important to note that their rereadings of the Bible were much more radical than those of Maimonides. Maimonides' rereadings of the Bible were very antianthropomorphic. Any physical imagery used in reference to God would be interpreted in a strictly allegorical manner. The Kabbalists, on the other hand, took some of the same imagery and reveled in it, all the while saying that if you believed it literally you were terribly wrong. In this way they were quite influenced by Maimonides' opposition to anthropomorphism.

The Kabbalists saw rationalism as essentially missing the power of the great mythic imagery of the Torah. Of course, this is not the sort of language they would have used to describe it. Myth was not a word in their vocabulary, but the visual imagery they used with relish touched a much more emotional, maybe pre-self-conscious part of people's spiritual lives.

Though myths are not historically factual and can contain quite fantastic elements, they contain a "truth" of a different order. They may touch an inner or emotional reality that history cannot, just as a dream's fantastic imagery, while containing components of reality, can depict an inner life that conventional "reality" cannot convey.

Kabbalah has two complementary components that are both very powerful. One is the understanding that all is God and that ultimately Ein Sof is all of reality. Along with the recognition that Ein Sof encompasses all is the conviction that not realizing this is to live in a state of illusion. This is a very important part of many Kabbalists' consciousness.

On the other hand, the revelation of the hidden, inaccessible Deity through the world of the Sefirot and ultimately through Creation is simultaneously, and paradoxically, also very real. This world is not an illusion; the illusion is mistaking what you see on the surface for the true reality, it is being unaware of the other central component. This understanding continuously displays itself in the consistent revelation of deep spiritual readings of biblical verses that on the surface sound very different.

FACT

In Pirkei Avot, Rabbi Khanina ben Dosa said: "All whose fear of sin precedes their wisdom, their wisdom will endure; and all whose wisdom precedes their fear of sin, their wisdom will not endure" (3:11), meaning moral behavior should be primary. Otherwise, you may reject an "inconvenient" insight because you would prefer to avoid it (instead of doing what's moral).

Different Approaches to Similar Questions

Prior to the Middle Ages, Jewish thought, with the exception of Philo of Alexandria, was not very philosophically oriented. The Bible and Talmud do not present a coherent theology or philosophy. There are many ethical, spiritual, and even philosophical ideas that are offered, but they are not argued in a systematic manner, as the Jews did not produce purely philosophical works the way the Greeks and the Romans did. The Talmud, though its reasoning processes are extremely rigorous and exhaustive, like the Bible does not take classical philosophical questions and argue them out. While these texts present amazing detail when addressing ethical or ritual practice, a philosophical insight in these circumstances would be more likely stated and not argued.

Medieval Jewish Philosophy

Medieval Jewish philosophy, on the other hand, under the inspiration of Islamic philosophy—which, in turn, was deeply influenced by ancient Greek philosophy—did begin to address philosophical and theological questions in a systematic manner. Major questions such as whether the universe is eternal or created, the existence and nature of God, and ethical questions about how we should live were all dealt with using logic accompanied by the statements and proof texts of Scripture.

Kabbalah, particularly Theosophical Kabbalah, responded to and reacted against this philosophical literature, particularly that of Maimonides. The power of Maimonides, despite the controversy surrounding him, cannot be underestimated. His knowledge of the classical sources was vast and authoritative and the force of his philosophical argumentation was truly formidable.

ALERT!

Despite using logic to attack religious questions, all the major Jewish medieval philosophers remained committed to the Jewish tradition in practice and belief, and generally attempted to explain, and not disprove, the truths of Judaism as they understood them in the context of philosophical presentations.

The Kabbalists were concerned with many of the very same questions that occupied the Jewish philosophers, such as the nature and existence of God, Creation, and ethics. However, their responses were radically different from those of the philosophers and, in fact, were much more consistent with the tenor of earlier Jewish literature such as the Bible, Talmud, and Midrashim.

Seeking a Spiritual Core

For Maimonides certain biblical ideas had to be explained and rationalized. To Maimonides, for example, the biblical sacrifices (*korbanot*) were a concession to the fact that the ancient Jews lived among idolaters who offered sacrifices to their gods. For the Kabbalists, the essence of a sacrifice was implicit in the word itself—*korban* (singular of korbanot), whose root (spelled, *kuf, resh, bet*) means "to bring close." So, the Kabbalists saw the entire process as bringing a person closer to the Divine and as having an effect even in the upper worlds. How could a Kabbalist say that the first person to recognize the one true God, Abraham, who also offered a sacrifice, was doing so because of the environmental influence of the pagans around him? For these reasons, to the Kabbalists, Maimonides' idea was indefensible.

Maimonides had a concept of devekut that was connected to his understanding of prophecy. He believed that someone who had mastered "metaphysics" could transcend his physical nature and be with God so thoroughly, like Moses (the ideal human), that he could even live without food or drink for forty days and nights (Exodus 34:28) and commune with God directly.

Maimonides also differed from the Kabbalists in that he saw the dietary laws of *kashrut* (the laws of what is kosher; that is, fit and proper to eat) as primarily concerned with health and secondarily concerned with moral development through attempting to consume meat while minimizing the pain toward the animal. The Kabbalists focused on following the rules of kashrut because they firmly believed the practice had an important effect on the soul of a person.

Influence of Kabbalah on Judaism

While Kabbalah's influence on Judaism was extensive, Jewish philosophy had a much weaker impact. A reason for this is that Kabbalah revitalized the spiritual underpinnings of the way Judaism is practiced on a daily basis, whereas Jewish philosophy's impact was largely intellectual.

Kabbalah did not, however, have much of an impact on halakhah (Jewish Law). In medieval times, the Zohar enjoyed some status in terms of halakhic decisions, but only if no other authoritative text was there to determine a decision. Lurianic Kabbalah, on the other hand, had a huge affect on many customs adapted by Jews, and Luria was even considered a halakhic authority. Despite Luria's influence on Jewish Law, the major areas in which Kabbalistic influence was felt were in the prayer life, ritual customs, and ethical perspectives of Jewish communities.

As Kabbalah gained in popularity, prayers entered the traditional *Siddur* (prayer book) that had previously not existed, such as the entire Friday night (Sabbath eve) service called *Kabbalat Shabbat* (the receiving of the Sabbath). Kabbalists also changed the way Jews celebrated the Sabbath by introducing the singing of Proverb 31 (called "A woman of valor"; *Eshet Khayil*) before the Friday night meal. This proverb was understood by Kabbalists not only as praise of one's wife, but as a poem about the Shekhinah.

FACT

Proverb 31 notes the characteristics of a noble wife: "She is clothed with strength and dignity. . . . She speaks with wisdom, and the Torah of loving kindness is on her tongue. . . . Her children arise and call her blessed, her husband also, and he praises her, 'Many women do noble things, but you surpass them all.'"

Hasidism also introduced customs such as forgiving anyone who may have hurt you either intentionally or unintentionally before you go to sleep at night. The Tu B'Shvat Seder, a festive meal on the fifteenth day of the Hebrew month of Shvat, the New Year for Trees, was instituted by Kabbalists in Tzfat and was largely modeled after the Passover Seder.

As you can see from the previous examples, Kabbalah has had a huge effect on the way Judaism is practiced over the centuries and in comparison, Jewish philosophy's impact on the practice of Judaism is minor. This is not to say that it is of negligible importance—that is certainly not the case. Its influence was essentially on the intellectual life of the community, and not on its religious lifestyle.

Kabbalah and Pantheism

It is slightly misleading to declare "the Kabbalah says" because there is often more than one opinion found in Kabbalistic literature, and this is certainly the case with regard to pantheism and panentheism. Pantheism is usually defined as meaning that the universe is equated with God. The term also has connotations implying that God is one with nature. Panentheism, on the other hand, means that instead of merely being identical with the universe, God also transcends the universe. Another view on God's relation to Creation and the universe is called theism, and believers in this are of the opinion that God is distinct and separate from Creation.

Panentheism and Ein Sof

In other words, in a panentheistic view, the question will come up as to whether it is Ein Sof's substance or essence that fills the Sefirot and the lower worlds, or is it only the power that emanates from the essence of Ein Sof that is manifested in them?

Many Kabbalists saw the human soul as "a part of God above" (Job 31:2). In terms of this, the same question arose. Is it the essence of God or the power that comes from the essence that's emanated? Rabbi Moshe Cordovero was a panentheist and very carefully presented his perspective, attempting to clarify its ramifications. The Ari, on the other hand, was more of a theist, seeing Ein Sof as distinctly separate from Creation.

Beliefs Affect Your Outcome

It is not always easy to discern what someone's perspective is because the person might use theistic language, but actually be a panentheist. Cordovero was the exception in trying to spell his views out very carefully. A panentheist and a theist may use the same phrase but intend significantly different meanings of it.

You may ask: how important are the distinctions argued about by panentheists and theists? Is arguing over this only splitting hairs? If it is purely a theoretical question, for some people it might be. For others, the different perspectives may affect their prayer and meditation life. If you perceive God as pervading your self and all that is around you, this can open you up to meditation that goes deep within yourself in order to find the less camouflaged divinity. This in turn can change the way you live your life and the way you look at the entire world around you.

Kabbalah and Ethics

At the same time that Kabbalists are very concerned with those mitzvot between humans and the omnipresent (*bein adam laMakom*), they are equally concerned with those between humans themselves (*bein adam lakhavero*). The latter is the Kabbalistic system of ethics, which is also made up by an entire body of Kabbalistic mussar (ethical) literature that began in Tzfat.

Among the most important books of this genre were *Reshit Chokhmah* (The Beginning of Wisdom"), by Elijah de Vidas, a disciple of Moshe Cordovero; *Shnei Lukhot HaBrit* (The Two Tablets of the Covenant), by Yishayahu (Isaiah) Horovitz; *Tomer Devorah* (The Palm Tree of Deborah), by Cordovero; and probably the most influential of all, *Mesillat Yesharim* (The Path of the Just) by Moshe Chaim Luzzato.

ALERT!

Deuteronomy says: "And now Yisra'el [Israel] what does YHVH your God ask from you, but to feel awe for YHVH your God, walk in all [God's] ways, and love [God] and worship YHVH your God with all your heart and with all your soul?" (10:12).

Even though the mitzvot between humans take precedent over those between humans and God, the awareness of God and awe and love of God should, on its own, catalyze a deep commitment to caring for other people. If your lifestyle is traditionally religious and your ethical behavior does not live up to those standards it is considered a "desecration of God's name" (*khilul hashem*). If, on the other hand, your ethical behavior is exemplary it is considered a "sanctification of God's name" (*kiddush hashem*).

There are countless Hasidic tales in which someone is in a deep state of devekut and somehow becomes aware of another person's pain or need and abandons his meditation to take care of the other person. The lesson to be taken from these tales and from the ethical Kabbalistic writings is that we are our brother's (and sister's) keeper, and must never fail to do justice to the bond between humans and with God.

Chapter 20

Kabbalah in the Twenty-first Century

There has been a steadily increasing interest in Kabbalah over the past forty years, and part of the reason for this surely stems from a greater awareness of the very fact of its existence. Another cause of Kabbalah's resurgence is the hunger of modern people, living in a society whose economic structure depends on so much being disposable, to nurture our souls and seek out something eternal yet grounded in history.

Rav Kook

Abraham Yitzkhak HaKohen Kook (1865–1935), better known as Rav (Rabbi) Kook, was one of the spiritual luminaries of the twentieth century and one of the last great creative spirits in the Kabbalistic tradition. He was born in Eastern Europe and received the customary yeshiva education consisting primarily of Talmud study, which he supplemented by studying the Bible, Hebrew language, general and Jewish philosophy, and Kabbalah.

Bridging the Secular-Religious Gap

Rav Kook was one of the only people in his era who tried to bridge the gap between the world of orthodox Judaism and the mostly socialist, very secular world of the Jewish community that was intent on rebuilding the Jewish homeland in Israel.

FACT

Members of the Jewish community that Rav Kook tried to unify with the world of orthodox Judaism were supporters of the Zionist movement, a largely secular movement that aimed to rebuild the original homeland of Jews in Israel.

Rav Kook was both a spiritual and a social pioneer, believing that a utopian society could be built in the land of Israel and seeing the often antireligious secularists as carrying on holy work by rebuilding the Jewish homeland. Rav Kook did not encourage religious Jews to withdraw from the world into a strict parochial society; instead, he attempted to work with all peoples, religious, antireligious, and secular, to create the conditions for a utopian/messianic era.

"The Lights of Holiness"

One of Rav Kook's greatest books is called *Orot HaKodesh* (The Lights of Holiness). It is constructed of numerous short entries that express his spiritual reflections. In an entry entitled "Divine Inspiration and the Intellect," he writes: "When a person accustoms himself to hearing the voice of God in everything . . . it's also revealed in the intellect. . . . Then the more a person contemplates and philosophizes, the more they increase the holiness of faith, devekut, and the awakening of Divine Inspiration." Rav Kook explains that the more a person intellectually explores his faith, the more attainable discovering a connection to God becomes.

Rav Kook said in *Orot HaKodesh* (The Lights of Holiness), "The inner science, which is the most inner of the innermost, is the science of the Holy which vivifies the light of life and isn't dependent on any other science. It is the sublime stream that emanates from Eden" (vol. 1, 63).

Kabbalah Without the Symbolism

Though Rav Kook was deeply inspired by Kabbalah, he didn't use its symbolic framework to convey his thoughts. In his attempt to combine the traditionally religious with the secular, Rav Kook spoke in a language that was still poetic, but more accessible to those who lacked the traditional background necessary to decipher Kabbalah's symbolic language.

The secular masses, who were not necessarily intellectuals, but rather laborers and kibbutz members, greatly appreciated Rav Kook and his support of the Zionist movement. The Kibbutz movement itself had created a secular form of mysticism that was termed by its main theorist, A. D. Gordon, "the religion of labor."

Contemporary Kabbalists

Today, there is a marked increase in the interest in Kabbalah that is visible in various segments of society; Kabbalistic ideas and symbolism have even surfaced in popular culture in the United States. Painters, poets, and other artists in Israel have either been inspired by Kabbalah or have used its symbols in their work. There has also been an increase in the study of Kabbalah in the orthodox and ultraorthodox communities, especially in Israel.

Newly Printed Texts

As evidence of this marked increase of interest in Kabbalistic ideas, books that were never before published, such as the works of Abraham Abulafia and the fourth part of Chaim Vital's *Gates of Holiness*, have recently found their way into print. Also in recent years, yeshivot (orthodox higher academies of Torah study), particularly in Israel, have been paying more attention to Kabbalah than they had in the past. Although most academics take a historical and nonorthodox approach to the texts, professors are taking great interest in exploring the ways that traditional, orthodox Kabbalists read and interpret historical Kabbalistic texts.

ALERT!

The study of mussar (ethical) literature as a spiritual path has also received more attention in recent years, perhaps as a result of the more widespread recognition that the mitzvot between one person and another are at least as important as those between a person and the omnipresent.

The Practice of Kabbalah

The interest in Kabbalah has grown along with a revival in Jewish meditation whose roots, as discussed in Chapter 16, are in the Kabbalistic tradition. Though Kabbalah has much in common with philosophy, keep in mind that it is not meant to be a purely philosophical system. Rather, it is meant to be a spiritual lifestyle that will make your relationship with God more meaningful and real.

Hasidism in the New Millennium

Hasidism has continued to flourish for three centuries now, though some of the practices of Hasidim have changed over the years. The first 50 to 100 years of Hasidism was the period of its greatest spiritual and literary creativity. It was during this time that Hasidism was established as the major spiritual force among Eastern European Jews. Though it is clear that Hasidism has become an eminently conservative force in the Jewish world, particularly today, it has nevertheless continued to be a vibrant presence in both Israel and the United States.

World War II destroyed most of the Hasidic world that existed during the 1940s because Hasidim had remained concentrated in Eastern Europe, where most of the atrocities of the Holocaust occurred. Some Hasidic dynasties managed to relocate in Israel and the United States, and since World War II they have re-created and rebuilt their lifestyle in different parts of the globe.

In Israel Hasidim have quite a bit of political power and the mostly secular population of Israel sees them as a very conservative social and political force. They tend to live among other Hasidic Jews, and have congregated largely in two ultraorthodox enclaves. One is Mea Shearim in Jerusalem and the other neighborhood is Bene Berak outside of Tel Aviv. In the last twenty-five years or so there has been a largely successful movement to increase Hasidic presence in Tzfat, in northern Israel.

The Chabad/Lubavitch Hasidic Dynasty

In the United States a number of Hasidic dynasties have re-established themselves. The most successful among them is the Lubavitch movement, also known as Chabad, an acronym of *chokhmah* (wisdom), *binah* (understanding), and *da'at* (knowledge). The Chabad movement gets its other name from Lubavitch, Russia, the town that served as the center of the movement for over a century.

Chabad grew enormously under the guidance of its seventh and last rebbe, Menachem Mendel Schneerson, who died in 1994 after leading the movement for over fifty years. One of the strengths of the movement comes from the fact that the rebbe put great emphasis on reaching out to the rest of the Jewish community, and as a result Chabad has been extremely receptive to non-Hasidim.

At the same time there's been a controversial element surrounding and splitting Chabad for approximately the last fifteen years. Rabbi Schneerson had a great deal of messianic fervor that fueled much of his outreach programs. He reached out to other types of Jews in the hope of raising their overall commitment to Torah and mitzvot.

ALERT!

Lubavitch, the name of the town in Russia where the Lubavitch/Chabad Hasidic movement originated and thrived for over 100 years, means "town of brotherly love" in Russian. This name is especially appropriate for the movement because of Rebbe Menachem Mendel Schneerson's emphasis on reaching out to the non-Hasidic community.

Chabad and Messianism

Many of Rebbe Schneerson's Hasidim believed he was the Messiah and expected him to usher in the messianic era. As he got sick in his last years, he was unable to respond to this faction of Chabad, which became increasingly vocal and whose belief in the rebbe as the Messiah wasn't even extinguished by his death.

The major leaders of Chabad are in the non-messianic camp but there is still a large grass-roots group that holds strongly to its belief in the rebbe as the Messiah, so there has been a very difficult split in the movement. Those in the non-messianic camp are worried that the effort of building Chabad's outreach to the nonaffiliated and nonorthodox will be wasted because the beliefs of the messianic faction will cause Chabad to lose credibility in the Jewish community.

There is a historical background to the Chabad group's belief in Rebbe Menachem Mendel Schneerson as the Messiah. There was a belief from the early days of Chabad (which was founded by Schneur Zalman of Lyady, who was a very young, but extremely impressive disciple of the Maggid of Mezeritch) that the seventh rebbe, who would be childless, would be the Messiah. Menachem Mendel Schneerson was the seventh Lubavitcher rebbe and was childless. Since Chabad, like almost all other Hasidic dynasties by the third generation after the Ba'al Shem Tov, passed its leadership on to a hereditary heir, the fact that the rebbe had no children created a crisis.

FACT

Menachem Mendel Schneerson exerted an enormous influence on the Jewish world and on Israeli politics, even though he had never visited the state of Israel. In fact, he almost never left Brooklyn, New York, except for his weekly visits to his father-in-law's (the sixth Lubavitcher rebbe) grave in Queens. His own grave, in the same cemetery, now attracts many visitors daily.

The Bratzlaver Hasidim

A somewhat similar situation occurred among the Bratzlaver Hasidim close to 200 years ago. Rebbe Nachman of Bratzlav, who died at the age of thirty-eight in 1810, had a son who died at a very young age, and therefore Nachman had no heir. Nachman himself, though he started his own branch of Hasidism that began with a small number of followers, was the great-grandson of the Besht. There was also a considerable amount of messianic fervor surrounding Rebbe Nachman, and after his death no one ever replaced him.

Though the Bratzlavers remained a small group for many years, they have attracted an increasingly large number of Hasidim and have inspired many outside the fold with Rebbe Nachman's teachings and tales. In addition, the Bratzlavers who are centered in Mea Shearim, Jerusalem, are very receptive to outsiders.

Rebbe Nachman's chair, which was smuggled out of Russia in pieces, sits in the center of the main Bratzlaver synagogue in Mea Shearim, Jerusalem. It sits empty like the Prophet Elijah's chair at a ritual circumcision and remains the one physical connection to the rebbe. Many Bratzlaver Hasidim make pilgrimages around Rosh Hashanah to Rebbe Nachman's grave in Uman in the Ukraine.

The openness of Lubavitch and Bratzlav to outsiders has also had a great impact on other groups interested in Kabbalah and Jewish mysticism. Though the Hasidic world has largely busied itself with survival and internal revival in contemporary days, it has inspired neo-Kabbalists and their fellow travelers to a huge extent.

Neo-Kabbalists and Neo-Hasidism

A combination of factors has created the phenomenon of what can be called neo-Kabbalah (new, or modified Kabbalah). Neo-Kabbalah is very influenced by the Jewish mysticism of the past two millennia, but it lacks the orthodox conviction that Kabbalah has always upheld. The phenomenon began coalescing around the late 1960s and early 1970s, primarily in the United States.

The influences upon this phenomenon come from a number of different directions. One influence was Martin Buber's (1878–1965) works on Hasidism.

FACT

Martin Buber was born in Vienna and was a well-known religious existentialist philosopher who translated the Bible into German. His best-known book is *I and Thou,* published in 1923. In 1904 he began studying Hasidism and translated many of its tales, which he felt were the heart of the movement. An active Zionist since 1898, he moved to Israel in 1938.

Buber made Hasidism accessible to the Western world. He wrote about it extensively and translated many Hasidic tales. His work was done in German, but eventually it was translated to other languages, including English, and had a significant impact on young Jews taking an interest in Jewish spirituality beginning in the '60s.

Abraham Joshua Heschel

An important thinker who affected young, spiritual seekers was Abraham Joshua Heschel (1907–1972). Heschel was a descendent on his father's side from the Maggid of Mezeritch and from his mother's side from Levi Yitzkhak of Berditchev. Another German-speaking Eastern European who narrowly escaped the Holocaust, he became one of the most influential Jewish philosophers of the twentieth century.

Though Heschel was very traditional, when he first came to the United States he taught at the Reform Hebrew Union College in Cincinnati and then at the Conservative Jewish Theological Seminary in New York City. His field was Hasidism, Kabbalah, Jewish philosophy, and ethics. Heschel was also very active in the civil rights movement in the '60s, marching arm in arm with the Reverend Martin Luther King, Jr., in Selma, Alabama. All of these components contributed to his impact on neo-Kabbalah.

Gershom Scholem

Another factor contributing to the rise in interest in the field was the academic research on Kabbalah that was primarily pioneered by Gershom Scholem (1897–1982). He immigrated to Jerusalem from Germany in 1923 and joined the Hebrew University first as a librarian, then as a faculty member, eventually establishing the Department of Kabbalah and Jewish Philosophy and becoming the first professor of Jewish mysticism at Hebrew University.

Scholem believed that prior attempts at studying Kabbalah from a scientific perspective were flawed because they treated Judaism as something static, whereas he believed Judaism to be a living, changing organism. Among his well-known works explaining his scientific approach to Kabbalah are *Major Trends in Jewish Mysticism* (1941) and *On the Kabbalah and Its Symbolism* (1965).

Scholem's encyclopedic knowledge of the field was based on unprecedented research that included thousands of manuscripts scattered in libraries around the world. His linguistic abilities, analytic powers, and exhaustive research enabled him to put the study of Kabbalah on the scholastic map. The fact that he wrote some of his major work in English in addition to Hebrew, German, and French, opened up the field of Kabbalah to a large public in the United States. Scholem also had quite a number of very capable disciples who have carried on his work around the world, but particularly in all the universities in Israel.

The Counterculture and the Chavurah Movement

The counterculture of the late '60s and early '70s in the United States had a spiritual component in it that led some people to the study of Indian religions and Zen Buddhism and sent others back to the mystical sources of Judaism. The fact that Buber's and Scholem's books had been published by this time and that Chabad and Bratzlaver Hasidism were accessible provided a place to begin for people who didn't necessarily have the Hebrew skills to go to original sources.

FACT

The chavurah movement grew mostly out of the branch of conservative Judaism led by people with an interest in Jewish mysticism and influenced by the counterculture of the '60s. A number of neo-Kabbalists were involved early in this movement, which also attempted to decentralize the synagogue service, emphasize lay leadership of services, and encourage communal study of Jewish sources.

Another reason that Kabbalah became increasingly known in the 1960s and 1970s in America was the beginning of the chavurah movement at the end of the 1960s in Boston and New York. A *chavurah* (which means "fellowship") is a group of people or families that study Torah communally, sharing aspects of Jewish life (deeper explorations of the Torah, celebrating holidays, etc.) outside of a synagogue for a more community-oriented type of religious study.

Rabbi Arthur Green, one of the major neo-Kabbalist thinkers and also an academic scholar of Kabbalah and Hasidism, was the founder of the first chavurah, *Chavurat Shalom* (The Fellowship of Peace), in 1968 in Boston.

By the time that the first chavurah was founded, Chabad's outreach program had already been in effect for nearly twenty years. Part of Menachem Mendel Schneerson's outreach attempt was to send representatives to college campuses to expose people to Chabad Hasidism and to mystical Judaism.

The first Chabad house of this kind was started in Berkeley, California. The two young rabbis sent there would both become central to neo-Kabbalah and neo-Hasidism. They were Rabbi Zalman Schachter (who later changed his name to Schachter-Shalomi) and Rabbi Shlomo Carlebach.

Reb Zalman and Reb Shlomo, as they are affectionately called, were both Eastern European refugees from the Holocaust who came to the States as teenagers. Both of them were able to bridge the gap between the world of authentic Hasidism and the counterculture of the '60s and '70s.

Shlomo Carlebach was a very talented songwriter and composed many melodies that eventually made their way into synagogues around the world. Some have become such standards that nowadays it's often not realized that he wrote them.

Egalitarianism

Another progressive step for Kabbalah and Hasidism evident in neo-Kabbalah and neo-Hasidism has been the increased influence of and openness to feminism and feminist voices in the Jewish tradition. The desire for an egalitarian Judaism has led to experiments in forging new communities and introducing new types of prayer services, modifying the language of traditional prayers to make them less male oriented, and ordaining female rabbis and cantors. All of these practices have contributed to the evolution of a more diverse theological and intellectual Jewish community.

Neo-Kabbalah and Jewish Meditation

The revived interest in Jewish meditation in recent years has led to the establishment of Jewish meditation centers, such as Chochmat HaLev in Berkeley, California, and Metivta in Los Angeles. These institutions are rooted in Kabbalah and Hasidism and are also part of the neo-Kabbalah movement with its emphasis on egalitarianism and connection with the authentic sources of the Jewish tradition.

The State of Research of Kabbalah

The academic study of Kabbalah has grown enormously since Gershom Scholem began the enterprise approximately eighty-five years ago. Despite the vast amount of research that Scholem did and that his disciples have continued to do, the field is still in its early stages.

Scholem focused his study on the origins of Kabbalah and its overall evolution. He also devoted much energy to the Zohar and the study of Sabbateanism, the messianic movement that began in the mid-seventeenth century around the figure of Shabbtai Tzvi. He laid the groundwork for virtually every area of Jewish mysticism and did in-depth studies in most areas.

The Generation after Scholem

A new generation has arisen that has begun to take issue with quite a number of Scholem's conclusions. Probably the most important of these scholars is Moshe Idel, who has done a prodigious amount of work on Ecstatic Kabbalah and particularly on Abraham Abulafia, subjects that Scholem took a great interest in, although he didn't write extensively about them. Idel also does overarching and in-depth work on a scale comparable to Scholem's. He's extremely prolific and much of his writing is available in English.

FACT

Opened in 1925, the Hebrew University of Jerusalem is one of the oldest and most prestigious institutions of higher learning in Israel and one of the nation's seven universities. Albert Einstein was a supporter of the Zionist's original idea to found an Israeli university, and he bequeathed all of his writings to the university.

Many people are currently working on studying the Zohar, but probably the main scholar in that field is Yehuda Liebes at Hebrew University. There are about fifteen to twenty professors in Israel alone, spread throughout its five universities with humanities faculty, who are doing significant research and writing studies on various Kabbalistic texts and subjects. Most of their work is in Hebrew and hasn't been translated, with the exception of the work of Yosef Dan, Rachel Elior, Moshe Hallamish, Yehuda Liebes, and Rifka Schatz-Uffenheimer.

Kabbalah Study in the United States

Academic research in Kabbalah is pursued in a number of universities in the United States such as at Brandeis University, where Rabbi Arthur Green teaches, Mount Holyoke College, where Lawrence Fine teaches, New York University, where Elliot Wolfson teaches, and University of Michigan, where Elliot Ginsburg teaches.

Kabbalah in Translation

There is not a lot of Kabbalistic work that has been translated into English. Paulist Press has published a number of volumes—for example, one of selections of pre-Zohar Kabbalistic texts, translated by Ronald Kiener; one of selections of the Zohar itself, translated by Daniel Matt; another of selections of works from sixteenth-century Tzfat (Safed), translated by Lawrence Fine; Chaim Vital's *Book of Visions*, translated by Morris Faierstein; and selections of the work of Rav Kook, edited by Ben Zion Bokser.

QUESTION?

If I don't believe in God, does it make any sense to study Kabbalah?
Very often what we think we believe or disbelieve depends on our definitions, preconceptions, and understanding. As the Hasidic Master Levi Yitzkhak of Berditchev said to a nonbeliever, "The God you don't believe in, I don't believe in either."

Eliahu Klein has translated some important work of Lurianic Kabbalah. Louis Jacobs has translated Moshe Cordovero's *The Palm Tree of Deborah* and two fascinating Hasidic texts: *Tract on Ecstasy*, by Dov Baer, the second Lubavitcher rebbe; and *Turn Aside from Evil and Do Good*, by Zevi Hirsch Eichenstein, the founder of the Zhidachover Hasidim (a not well-known but significant sect). All of these translations are accompanied by notes to clarify the works and make them more accessible.

Parts of the Zohar have been translated a number of times with varying results; however, there is currently a major project to translate the entire main body of the Zohar, and three out of a projected twelve volumes have already been published. It is the work of Daniel Matt, who is the premier translator of Kabbalistic works into the English language. In addition to the poetic, sensitive translation, it is accompanied by superb scholarly commentary.

Uses of Kabbalah

When Gershom Scholem was a very young man and began to take an interest in Kabbalah, he quickly realized that people who were considered "experts" did not have the knowledge he expected of them. He came to discover a wealth of literature that had not been studied for centuries and certain things that had been, but that he was convinced had been misunderstood.

There are those in the orthodox world who take issue with the academic approach to Kabbalah, thinking that, for example, believing the Zohar was not written by Shimon bar Yokhai is heresy and diminishes the authority of the work. Other students in the field would say that the words stand on their own and that if Moshe de Leon wrote them in the 1280s, they are no less true than they would be if bar Yokhai had written them more than 1,100 years before.

We live in a time when there is greater access to resources for the study of Kabbalah than ever before. There are many different approaches to it and numerous ways of studying it. You might want to sample different orientations and see which speaks to you the most. You might find that parts of one method feel right, but other parts don't. Possibly a combination of approaches will complement each other and satisfy your spiritual, emotional, and intellectual desires.

If we open ourselves up to its treasures, Kabbalah can be a powerful gateway to the inner riches we all possess and to the One that embraces and fills all.

Appendix A

Glossary of Terms

acronym: An acronym is made from taking the first letter of a few words and making a new word out of them (like NASA in English). Acronyms are very commonly used in Hebrew, especially with names of Rabbis, such as Ramban (for Rabbi Moshe ben Nachman) and Rashbi (Rabbi Shimon bar Yokhai). Since Hebrew is primarily written without vowels, only the consonants form the acronym.

Aggadot: Rabbinic legends that are found originally in both the Talmud and in Midrashic collections. (Singular: Aggadah.)

Ashkenazi: Adjective referring to Jews or Jewish culture of middle and eastern European origin. The Hebrew term for Germany in Medieval times was *Ashkenaz*.

atbash: An acronym for an interpretive method in which the first letter of the Hebrew alphabet (*aleph*) is substituted with the last (*tav*), the second (*bet*) with the second to last (*shin*), and so on. *Aleph*, *tav*, *bet*, *shin* spells "atbash." It's one of the thirty-two rabbinic methods of interpretation.

atzilut: Atzilut is the Hebrew world for "emanation." The root of atzilut is related to the word *etzel*. Etzel means "close to," implying "still connected to." Atzilut means that that which emanated from Ein Sof (the undifferentiated, unchanging Eternal One) always remains connected to It.

Ayin: Ayin means "nothing" or "nothingness." It can also be defined as "no-thingness," meaning a state in which there is no duality. The word *ein* in Ein Sof derives from the word *Ayin* and is spelled with the same letters.

commentary: Comments, annotations, or explanations of another work, often in essay form. Commentaries make up an essential part of the body of Kabbalistic texts. One of the most famous rabbis of all time, Rashi (Rabbi Shlomo Yitzkhaki), is only known for his commentaries on the Bible and Talmud. There are commentaries to all the major canonical texts and certain ones are virtually indispensable.

devekut: Often translated as "cleaving," the term has a range of meanings, including spiritual union with God.

d'rash: D'rash essentially means to investigate, to seek out, and to expound. In terms of reading the Torah, it is a teaching or application of the remez or pshat interpretation of the text.

dybbuk: Sometimes considered an evil ibbur, a dybbuk can also be a misplaced or lost soul seeking a body to escape a wandering existence that is the result of past wrongs it committed or an unnatural death.

Gemara: The bulk of the Talmud, the "oral Torah," sealed approximately between 400 and 500 C.E.

gematria: The numerical equivalent of Hebrew letters. Gematria is used to interpret the Torah, showing the relationship between different things or words based on a shared gematria. For example, one of the names of God shares the gematria of the Hebrew word for "nature," implying that this name of God refers to God's presence in nature.

genizah: A place to keep books that contain the name of God and are too old or unreadable to be used. These exist in traditional Jewish communities because of the Jewish law that writings containing the name of God cannot be destroyed.

gilgul: Reincarnation. Can be used to mean the person who is a reincarnation or to mean the occurrence of reincarnation or transmigration of a soul. (Plural: gilgulim.)

halakhah: Jewish Law. The root of the word means "to go" or "to walk," so halakhah implies "the path."

Hasidim: This term literally means "pious ones," and implies believers in Hasidism. (Singular: Hasid.)

Hasidism: A mystical movement begun in Poland and the Ukraine in the mid-1700s, founded by the Ba'al Shem Tov (1700–1760), also known as the Besht (an acronym for Ba'al Shem Tov).

hitbonenut: Coming from the word *Binah*, which means "understanding," hitbonenut means going inside oneself to achieve understanding. It is one of the Hebrew terms for meditation.

ibbur: A possession in which the spirit of a righteous person will inhabit the body of an individual in order to complete religious work or to finish something that person could not complete in life. This is generally a positive possession.

Kabbalah: From the Hebrew root that means "to receive," Kabbalah means received teachings. Kabbalah also denotes "tradition," meaning a body of knowledge and customs passed down from one generation to another. It can mean, more specifically, the *oral* transmission of tradition and knowledge containing the inner and secret mystical teachings of the Torah.

kavana: The focus, direction, and intention of your consciousness.

maggid: This term has numerous meanings, the most common of which is that of a traveling preacher. A maggid is also a heavenly messenger or teacher that visits someone to reveal secrets of Torah and often appears as a voice emerging from the person being visited by the maggid. (Plural: maggidim.)

Merkavah: A Hebrew word meaning "chariot." Merkavah mysticism is a form of early Jewish mysticism, the object of which was for practitioners to experience the divine revelation that occurred when Ezekiel beheld God's chariot (Ezekiel, Chapters 1–3).

Midrash: Homiletical interpretation of Scripture sometimes filling in narrative gaps in the text. There are two major types of Midrash: Midrash Halakhah, which is Midrash related to Jewish

Law, and "Midrash Aggadah," Midrash that usually served as commentary to biblical narratives.

Mishnah: The earlier, Hebrew component of the Talmud, written in almost outline form, "sealed" in approximately the year 200 C.E.

mitzvah: Literally, the word mitzvah is a commandment, but it has the connotation of "good deed." The Jewish tradition is constructed around 613 mitzvot. (Plural: mitzvot.)

nefesh: One of the Hebrew words for soul, less sublime than ruakh or neshama.

neshama: The eternal, higher soul.

nitzotzot: Divine sparks.

panentheism: The belief that instead of being identical to the universe, God also transcends the universe.

pantheism: The belief that the universe is identical with God. The term also has connotations implying that God is one with nature.

Pirkei Avot: A tractate of Mishnah that consists of moral sayings by the rabbis of the Talmudic era. Pirkei Avot literally means "Chapters of our Ancestors" (or "fathers").

pshat: The simple, literal meaning of the words in the Torah.

remez: Remez means "hint," but in medieval Hebrew came to stand for the allegorical reading of the Torah, which was the mainstay of Jewish philosophy.

Sefardi: Adjective referring to Jews and Jewish culture of Spanish, Middle Eastern, and North African origin. The medieval term for Spain is Sefarad, although sometimes it seems to refer to only a particular section of Spain.

sefer: The word for "book" in Hebrew.

Shabbat: The Day of Rest, understood by the Jewish tradition as referring to Saturday beginning at sunset of Friday and ending approximately twenty-five hours later when three stars are (or would be) visible in the Saturday night sky.

siddur: The Hebrew word for "prayer book," which comes from a root meaning "order."

sod: The secret meaning of the Torah. This is the level of reading Torah that Kabbalists focus their insights on.

Sufism: Islamic mysticism. (Sufi: an Islamic mystic.)

tabernacle: A portable sanctuary that Israelites used when they followed Moses out of Egypt. God gave Moses specific instructions regarding the construction of the tabernacle in Exodus (Chapter 25).

tallit: Pronounced *tallis* in Yiddish and in the Ashkenazic pronunciation of Hebrew, a tallit is a fringed prayer shawl, usually worn by men. The fringe serves as a reminder of of the 613 Mitzvot around which traditional Judaism is structured.

Talmud: Traditionally understood as "the oral Torah." The Talmud has two components: the Mishnah, written in Hebrew and sealed in 200 C.E., and the Gemara, sealed between 450 and 500 C.E.

and written primarily in Aramaic. There are two Talmuds, the Jerusalem Talmud (often called the Palestinian Talmud, in English) and the Babylonian Talmud.

theism: Another view on God's relation to Creation and the universe. Believers in this are of the opinion that God is distinct and separate from Creation.

Torah: This word has numerous meanings. Its root means "teaching." Torah can refer to the first five books of the Bible that are found in the Torah scroll. Torah can refer to the "written Torah" (the Bible) and the "oral Torah" (the Talmud). Torah can also refer to all religiously valid teaching.

Tzaddik: A righteous person. The Tzaddik is an ideal of human holiness. Tzaddik is also the term used to refer to the spiritual leader of a Hasidic sect.

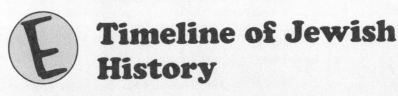

Appendix B

Timeline of Jewish History

The following timeline may serve as a brief overview of Jewish history. Many of the time periods, especially prior to the Common Era, are approximations. The dating system used differs somewhat from the traditional Jewish dating system for ancient history, and there may be discrepancies by as much as 150 years. However, this divergence disappears with the beginning of the Common Era.

Timeline of Events

2000–1700 B.C.E.	The Age of the Patriarchs—Abraham, Isaac, and Jacob.
1700–1300 B.C.E.	Israelites enter Egypt, are enslaved, and become populous.
1250 B.C.E.	Moses leads the Israelites out of Egypt.
1250–1200 B.C.E.	Israelite conquest of Canaan.
1020 B.C.E.	Saul is anointed the first king of Israel.
1000–961 B.C.E.	David reigns as the second king of Israel, with Jerusalem as his capital.
961–922 B.C.E.	Solomon rules as the third king of Israel and builds the First Temple.
922 B.C.E.	The Ten Northern Tribes secede and form the kingdom of Israel, leaving the kingdom of Judah.
726–722 B.C.E.	The northern kingdom of Israel is conquered by the Assyrians and the Ten Tribes are exiled into oblivion.
587–586 B.C.E.	The southern kingdom of Judah falls to the Babylonians; the First Temple is destroyed; much of the Jewish population is deported to Babylonia.
538 B.C.E.	Cyrus's edict permits the Jews to return to Judea.
515 B.C.E.	The Second Temple is completed in Jerusalem.
332 B.C.E.	Alexander the Great occupies Israel.
167–164 B.C.E.	Maccabean (Hasmonean) revolt against Antiochus IV. The Temple is seized and rededicated.
37 B.C.E. to 4 C.E.	Herod rules Judea with the support of Rome.
6 C.E.	Rome assumes direct rule over Judea.
66–72 C.E.	Jews revolt against Rome.
70 C.E.	Destruction of the Second Temple marks the beginning of the Diaspora.
73 C.E.	The fall of Masada.
132–135	Jewish revolt led by Bar Kokhba against Rome.
200	Compilation of Mishnah.
c. 390	Jerusalem (Palestinian) Talmud is completed.
c. 450–500	Babylonian Talmud is completed.
762	The Karaites break with Rabbinic Judaism.
1066	Jews settle in England.
1096	Crusaders massacre the Jews in the Rhineland.

1135–1204	The life of Moses Maimonides.
1144	Ritual murder charges at Norwich.
1146	Beginning of persecution of Jews in Muslim Spain.
1171	First Blood Libel charge brought in France.
1182–1198	Expulsion of Jews from France.
1240	Paris Disputation and burning of the Talmud.
1280–1290	Completion of the Zohar by Moshe de Leon.
1290	Expulsion of Jews from England.
1348–1349	Accused of causing the Black Death, many Jews are massacred in central Europe and France.
1394	Final expulsion of Jews from France.
1481	Spanish Inquisition begins.
1492	Jews expelled from Spain.
1497	Jews expelled from Portugal.
1516	First ghetto in Venice.
1564	Rabbi Josef Karo completes the Shulkhan Arukh.
1736–1760	Ba'al Shem Tov founds the Hasidic movement.
1770–1880	Haskalah movement.
1791	Emancipation of Jews in France.
1804	Tsar Alexander I establishes the Pale of Settlement.
1827	Tsar Nicholas I orders Jews to be conscripted in the army.
1830s	German Jews begin to immigrate to the United States.
1840s	Reform Movement begins in Germany.
1848	Full rights granted to German Jews.
1866	Emancipation of Swiss Jews.
1867	Final Emancipation of Jews of Austria-Hungary.
1870	Final Emancipation of Italian Jews.
1881–1882	Waves of pogroms begin in Russia.
1881–1924	Mass migration of Eastern European Jews to the United States.
1882–1903	First mass migration to Israel.
1894–1899	The Dreyfus Affair.

1897	Theodor Herzl convenes the First Zionist Congress in Basel, Switzerland.
1904–1914	Second mass migration to Israel.
1905	"The Protocols of the Elders of Zion" appears in print.
1917	Emancipation of the Jews in Russia.
1917	Lord Balfour writes the "Balfour Declaration"; Britain occupies Palestine.
1922	League of Nations establishes British mandate in Palestine.
1929	Arab riots in Jerusalem and throughout Palestine.
1929–1939	Almost 250,000 German and Austrian Jews arrive in Palestine.
1933	Hitler and Nazi Party come to power in Germany.
1935–1939	Anti-Jewish legislation enacted throughout many European countries.
1939	New White Paper severely limits Jewish immigration to Palestine.
1939–1945	Holocaust. Six million Jews die at the hands of the Nazis and their collaborators.
1947	United Nations General assembly votes in favor of the partition of Palestine.
1948	May 14, Declaration of Statehood by the State of Israel.
1948	Israel's War of Independence.
1952	Stalin orders the execution of Yiddish writers and poets in the USSR.
1956	The Sinai campaign.
1967	The Six-Day War.
1973	The Yom Kippur War.
1979	Signing of Israel-Egypt peace agreement.

Appendix C

Additional Resources

Dan, Joseph, ed. *The Heart and the Fountain: An Anthology of Jewish Mystical Experiences* (New York: Oxford University Press, 2002).

Dan, Joseph, ed., and Ronald C. Kiener, trans. *The Early Kabbalah* (New York: Paulist Press, 1986).

The Encyclopaedia Judaica (Jerusalem: Keter Publishing House, 1972).

Faierstein, Morris. *Jewish Mystical Autobiographies* (New York: Paulist Press, 1999).

Fine, Lawrence. *Physician of the Soul, Healer of the Cosmos: Isaac Luria and His Kabbalistic Fellowship* (Palo Alto, CA: Stanford University Press, 2003).

Fine, Lawrence, ed. and trans. *Safed Spirituality* (New York: Paulist Press, 1985).

Hallamish, Moshe. *An Introduction to the Kabbalah* (Albany, NY: State University of New York Press, 1999).

Idel, Moshe. *Kabbalah: New Perspectives* (New Haven: Yale University Press, 1988).

Idel, Moshe. *The Mystical Experience in Abraham Abulafia* (Albany, NY: State University of New York Press, 1988).

Idel, Moshe. *Hasidism: Between Ecstasy and Magic* (Albany, NY: State University of New York Press, 1995).

Jacobs, Louis. *Jewish Mystical Testimonies* (New York: Schocken, 1977).

Kaplan, Aryeh. *Meditation and Kabbalah* (York Beach, ME: Samuel Weiser, 1982).

Klein, Eliahu. *Kabbalah of Creation: Isaac Luria's Earlier Mysticism* (Northvale, NJ: Jason Aronson, 2000).

Matt, Daniel C. *The Essential Kabbalah* (San Francisco: Harper San Francisco, 1995).

Matt, Daniel C. *Zohar: The Book of Enlightenment* (New York: Paulist Press, 1983).

Matt, Daniel C. *The Zohar Pritzker Edition* (Palo Alto, CA: Stanford University Press, 2004–2006).

Scholem, Gershom. *Major Trends in Jewish Mysticism* (New York: Schocken Books, 1941).

Scholem, Gershom. *Kabbalah* (Jerusalem: Keter Press, 1974).

Scholem, Gershom. *On the Kabbalah and Its Symbolism* (New York: Schocken Books, 1965).

Scholem, Gershom. *Origins of the Kabbalah* (Philadelphia: Jewish Publication Society, 1987).

Wiesel, Elie. *Souls on Fire* (New York: Touchstone, 1972).

Books on Jewish Meditation and Kabbalah

Davis, Avram. *The Way of Flame* (San Francisco: Harper San Francisco, 1996).

Davis, Avram, ed. *Meditation from the Heart of Judaism* (Woodstock, VT: Jewish Lights Publishing, 1997).

Fink Gefen, Nan. *Discovering Jewish Meditation* (Woodstock, VT: Jewish Lights Publishing, 1999).

Verman, Mark. *The History and Varieties of Jewish Meditation* (Northvale, NJ: Jason Aronson, 1996).

Books of Neo-Kabbalah

Green, Arthur. *Seek My Face* (Woodstock, VT: Jewish Lights, 2003).

Green, Arthur. *Ehyeh: A Kabbalah for Tomorrow* (Woodstock, VT: Jewish Lights, 2003).

Matt, Daniel C. *God and the Big Bang* (Woodstock, VT: Jewish Lights, 1996).

Prager, Marcia. *The Path of Blessing* (Woodstock, VT: Jewish Lights, 1998).

Schachter-Shalomi, Zalman. *Paradigm Shift* (Northvale, NJ: Jason Aronson, 1993).

Schachter-Shalomi, Zalman. *Wrapped in a Holy Flame: Teachings and Tales of the Hasidic Masters* (San Francisco: Jossey-Bass, 2003).

Centers for the Study of Kabbalah and Jewish Meditation

Chochmat HaLev (Berkeley, California)

Elat Chayyim (Accord, New York)

Metivta (Los Angeles, California)

Index

THE EVERYTHING SERIES!

BUSINESS & PERSONAL FINANCE

Everything® Budgeting Book
Everything® Business Planning Book
Everything® Coaching and Mentoring Book
Everything® Fundraising Book
Everything® Get Out of Debt Book
Everything® Grant Writing Book
Everything® Home-Based Business Book, 2nd Ed.
Everything® Homebuying Book, 2nd Ed.
Everything® Homeselling Book, 2nd Ed.
Everything® Investing Book, 2nd Ed.
Everything® Landlording Book
Everything® Leadership Book
Everything® Managing People Book
Everything® Negotiating Book
Everything® Online Business Book
Everything® Personal Finance Book
Everything® Personal Finance in Your 20s and 30s Book
Everything® Project Management Book
Everything® Real Estate Investing Book
Everything® Robert's Rules Book, $7.95
Everything® Selling Book
Everything® Start Your Own Business Book
Everything® Wills & Estate Planning Book

COMPUTERS

Everything® Online Auctions Book
Everything® Blogging Book

COOKING

Everything® Barbecue Cookbook
Everything® Bartender's Book, $9.95
Everything® Chinese Cookbook
Everything® Cocktail Parties and Drinks Book
Everything® College Cookbook
Everything® Cookbook
Everything® Cooking for Two Cookbook
Everything® Diabetes Cookbook
Everything® Easy Gourmet Cookbook
Everything® Fondue Cookbook
Everything® Gluten-Free Cookbook
Everything® Glycemic Index Cookbook
Everything® Grilling Cookbook

Everything® Healthy Meals in Minutes Cookbook
Everything® Holiday Cookbook
Everything® Indian Cookbook
Everything® Italian Cookbook
Everything® Low-Carb Cookbook
Everything® Low-Fat High-Flavor Cookbook
Everything® Low-Salt Cookbook
Everything® Meals for a Month Cookbook
Everything® Mediterranean Cookbook
Everything® Mexican Cookbook
Everything® One-Pot Cookbook
Everything® Pasta Cookbook
Everything® Quick Meals Cookbook
Everything® Slow Cooker Cookbook
Everything® Slow Cooking for a Crowd Cookbook
Everything® Soup Cookbook
Everything® Tex-Mex Cookbook
Everything® Thai Cookbook
Everything® Vegetarian Cookbook
Everything® Wild Game Cookbook
Everything® Wine Book, 2nd Ed.

CRAFT SERIES

Everything® Crafts—Baby Scrapbooking
Everything® Crafts—Bead Your Own Jewelry
Everything® Crafts—Create Your Own Greeting Cards
Everything® Crafts—Easy Projects
Everything® Crafts—Polymer Clay for Beginners
Everything® Crafts—Rubber Stamping Made Easy
Everything® Crafts—Wedding Decorations and Keepsakes

HEALTH

Everything® Alzheimer's Book
Everything® Diabetes Book
Everything® Health Guide to Adult Bipolar Disorder
Everything® Health Guide to Controlling Anxiety
Everything® Health Guide to Fibromyalgia
Everything® Hypnosis Book

Everything® Low Cholesterol Book
Everything® Massage Book
Everything® Menopause Book
Everything® Nutrition Book
Everything® Reflexology Book
Everything® Stress Management Book

HISTORY

Everything® American Government Book
Everything® American History Book
Everything® Civil War Book
Everything® Irish History & Heritage Book
Everything® Middle East Book

GAMES

Everything® 15-Minute Sudoku Book, $9.95
Everything® 30-Minute Sudoku Book, $9.95
Everything® Blackjack Strategy Book
Everything® Brain Strain Book, $9.95
Everything® Bridge Book
Everything® Card Games Book
Everything® Card Tricks Book, $9.95
Everything® Casino Gambling Book, 2nd Ed.
Everything® Chess Basics Book
Everything® Craps Strategy Book
Everything® Crossword and Puzzle Book
Everything® Crossword Challenge Book
Everything® Cryptograms Book, $9.95
Everything® Easy Crosswords Book
Everything® Easy Kakuro Book, $9.95
Everything® Games Book, 2nd Ed.
Everything® Giant Sudoku Book, $9.95
Everything® Kakuro Challenge Book, $9.95
Everything® Large-Print Crosswords Book
Everything® Lateral Thinking Puzzles Book, $9.95
Everything® Pencil Puzzles Book, $9.95
Everything® Poker Strategy Book
Everything® Pool & Billiards Book
Everything® Test Your IQ Book, $9.95
Everything® Texas Hold 'Em Book, $9.95
Everything® Travel Crosswords Book, $9.95
Everything® Word Games Challenge Book
Everything® Word Search Book

Bolded titles are new additions to the series.
All Everything® books are priced at $12.95 or $14.95, unless otherwise stated. Prices subject to change without notice.